LEADERS, LEADERSHIP, AND U.S. POLICY IN LATIN AMERICA

LEADERS, LEADERSHIP, AND U.S. POLICY IN LATIN AMERICA

Michael J. Kryzanek

Westview Press
BOULDER • SAN FRANCISCO • OXFORD

F
1418
K77
1992

Copyright © 1992 by Westview Press, Inc.

Published in 1992 in the United States of America by Westview Press, Inc., 5500 Central Avenue, Boulder, Colorado 80301-2847, and in the United Kingdom by Westview Press, 36 Lonsdale Road, Summertown, Oxford OX2 7EW

Library of Congress Cataloging-in-Publication Data
Kryzanek, Michael J.
   Leaders, leadership, and U.S. policy in Latin America / Michael J. Kryzanek.
      p.   cm.
   Includes bibliographical references and index.
   ISBN 0-8133-7950-4
   1. Latin America—Foreign relations—United States.   2. United States—Foreign relations—Latin America.   3. United States—Foreign relations—1989-   .   4. Political leadership—Latin America—History—20th century.   5. Political leadership—United States—History—20th century.   I. Title.   II. Title: Leaders, leadership, and US policy in Latin America.
F1418.K77   1992
327.7308—dc20

91-38296
CIP

Printed and bound in the United States of America

The paper used in this publication meets the requirements of the American National Standard for Permanence of Paper for Printed Library Materials Z39.48-1984.

10   9   8   7   6   5   4   3   2   1

For my father,
EDWARD J. KRYZANEK

CONTENTS

PREFACE

From the North American perspective the Latin American leader has always been an intriguing if not exasperating individual. Although the image of the Latin leader has often remained mired in a cartoonish mold or become the stuff of tabloids, anyone who has spent time in the region or examined the politics of the various countries knows that the presidents, the generals, and the comman-dantes are critical to an understanding of how politics is conducted. But making the transition from surface description to comprehensive analysis in a book-length study is not an easy process. Explaining the range of political leaders, their governing style, and their in-volvement in the current movement for change in Latin America can be a seemingly endless labyrinth as one road of investigation leads to new questions and new unknowns. The challenge becomes trying to organize what is known about Latin American leaders and transforming that data into an understandable picture that not only explains what is common, but also what is unique and changing.

The task, however, becomes even more complicated when the linkage is made between Latin American leaders and U.S. foreign policy. Latin American leaders and their brand of leadership cannot be fully understood until the role that the United States plays in influencing the course of political and economic development in the countries of the region is described. U.S.-Latin American relations have evolved in the 1990s to a critical interaction between a new array of democratic leaders and a hegemonic power anxious to form a new "special relationship." In order to appreciate this evolving foreign policy dynamic, it is essential to join the discussion of Latin American leaders and leadership with the changing nature of U.S. involvement in the hemisphere.

It is my hope that *Leaders, Leadership, and U.S. Policy in Latin America* will serve to provide a broader understanding of the men and women who are so central to the politics and future direction of Latin America. The book is designed to offer the reader historical development, in-depth analysis of the three primary leadership models at work in Latin America today, discussion of the impact of contemporary problems—drugs, debt, and intervention—on leaders, and concluding sections on the future of Latin American leaders and the relationship of these leaders to the United States. Taken as a whole, *Leaders, Leadership, and U.S. Policy in Latin America* is an examination of the region from the view of those individuals responsible for order, modernization, and change.

Writing a book with the twin objectives of explaining Latin American leaders and showing the impact that U.S. policy has on their governing style and their policy prescriptions has in my case been made significantly easier as a result of considerable assistance and support. I would like to thank Boston University's Center for International Relations and its director, Hermann Eilts, for their support and encouragement while I was a visiting scholar. I also want to express my heartfelt thanks to David Scott Palmer of the center for his friendship and insight into Latin American politics. This book would not be in the form it is today without his suggestions and criticism. I also want to express my ongoing gratitude to Howard Wiarda of the University of Massachusetts–Amherst, who made numerous helpful comments on the manuscript. As in my earlier writings, there is much in my thinking that has been influenced by the ideas and observations of Howard Wiarda. Finally, I want to express my thanks to the other members of the Political Science Department at Bridgewater State College—Shaheen Mozaffar, Dave Sudhalter, Polly Harrington, and Guy Clifford—for their professional inspiration and collegial support.

As with any project, the author owes the greatest debt of gratitude to his family. In this case my wife, Carol, and my daughters, Laura, Kathy, and Ann, always have been cheering me on and expressing pride in my work. Needless to say, I could not have completed this project without them. But perhaps what pushed me forward the most was the memory of my father, Edward Kryzanek, who passed away at about the time that I was beginning this project. To him I lovingly dedicate this book.

Michael J. Kryzanek

INTRODUCTION

Previously, during the occupation of the marines, he would shut himself up in his office to decide the destiny of the nation . . . but when they left him alone with his nation and his power again he did not poison his blood again with the sluggishness of written law, but governed orally and physically at every moment and everywhere with a flinty parsimony but also with a diligence inconceivable at his age.

—Gabriel García Márquez
The Autumn of the Patriarch

Latin American politics has often been described as unstable, unpredictable, and subject to frequent radical shifts in governing regimes and political ideology. The image that many North Americans have of the political process in those nations to their south is one of great internal discord as competing elites and disenchanted masses create a tangled web of tension and immobility. If there is any unifying thread in this tangled web, it has been the prominence of political leaders who from their positions atop the governing systems must deal with the uncertainty and the conflict that are commonplace in the countries of the region.

Latin American leaders are critical for defining the unique character of politics as it is practiced in this region.[1] The way in which leaders operate and the governing systems that they have built or remodeled to fit their needs tell much about what Latin American politics is and wants to become.[2] In a part of the world where politics seems always to be in a state of flux and where governing institutions are often incapable of addressing crucial national issues, it is the leader who has become the focus of attention and the chief architect of public policy.[3]

The key position occupied by the political leader in Latin America has strong historical roots. There is a rich legacy of powerful men placing their mark on the land and on the people. The conquistadors (Hernán Cortés and Francisco Pizarro), the liberators (Simon Bolívar and José San Martín), the rugged caudillos (Juan Manuel de Rosas and Antonio López Santa Ana), the dictators (Anastasio Somoza and Rafael Trujillo), the liberal reformers (Rómulo Betancourt and Don Pepe Figueres), and the revolutionaries (Fidel Castro and Daniel Ortega) have all shaped the destiny of their respective countries and indeed of the hemisphere. These leaders and those like them have influenced not just the character of political life but also cultural patterns, intellectual movements, social relations, and, most importantly, economic directions. Moreover, in some countries, leaders such as Trujillo in the Dominican Republic, Somoza in Nicaragua, and François Duvalier in Haiti have so dominated national life that the countries they led were each transformed into a kind of personal fiefdom that existed for the personal pleasure and benefit of one man and his family.

The importance of leaders to Latin America is most in evidence when major shifts occur in the political structure and social organization of the region. Leaders, sensing the winds of change, have often charted new policy directions that quickly evolved into hemispheric trends. The political reform campaigns of Ippólito Yrigoyen in Argentina and José Báttle y Ordóñez in Uruguay ignited a push for greater democratization in Latin America at the turn of the century.[4] The modernizing programs of leaders such as Porfirio Díaz of Mexico and Domingo Sarmiento of Argentina set the stage for the heightened involvement of foreign interests in the development process.[5] The dramatic victory of Fidel Castro and Che Guevara in Cuba in 1959 electrified the continent and established revolution as a critical ingredient in the politics of Latin America.[6]

The impact that leaders have on the process of change in their countries and in the region reveals the extent to which the Latin American system allows individuals to place their mark on the political landscape. Largely free of competing or restraining institutions, bolstered by a citizenry that accepts aggressive, charismatic rule, and faced with endless policy dilemmas that cry out for action, political leaders have emerged as the key players in the vast mosaic of power contenders that make up the Latin American governing scene.[7] Yet despite these favorable political conditions that allow for greater leverage on the part of leaders, the Latin America of the 1990s is quickly evolving a governing climate in which expectations for change are high and tolerance for failure is low. For example, the future of democracy in the region will be affected by the popular response to policies that aim for a more efficient, less corrupt, and less dependent state. Latin American leaders will be judged in terms of whether they can balance managerial skills with social conscience while at the same time fending off threats from the revolutionary left and the the military right.

Although the study of leaders is essential if we are to understand the unifying role played by these individuals in Latin America, it is also important to examine leaders in terms of the ways in which they lead, their modes of operation, and their leadership styles. Latin American history is replete with the names of great and not-so-great leaders, and this history reveals stories of a very identifiable brand of leadership exercised by a full compliment of conquistadors and caudillos, reformers and revolutionaries.[8]

When examining the legacy of Latin American leadership, one is immediately struck by the presence of extremes and excesses. In Latin America one can find some of the world's most complete dictatorships; presidents holding national power five, six, seven times, or presidents winning elective office but never permitted to wield power; mind-boggling examples of venality, waste, and corruption; and far too many instances of heinous crimes that have transformed petty tyrants into strange legends of repressive rule. Unfortunately, one can get bogged down in the curious minutiae of Latin American leadership traits and neglect to examine a style of leadership that is apart from what we often hear or have come to accept as reality.

Latin American leadership, with its roots in Spanish corporatism and authoritarianism, accents paternalistic relations, familial networking, personalism and patronage, and the importance of balancing or co-opting competing interests.[9] Unlike traditional Western leadership models, which place emphasis on rationality, impersonality, specialization, merit, and institutional decisionmaking, Latin American leaders evidence an operating style based on friendships, personal interaction, subtle manipulation, and, when necessary, brute force. In recent years Latin American leaders have increasingly embraced leadership models that accent more rigid ideological modes of operation or seek to emulate the style of the technocratic managers found in the industrial world. But often beneath the ideological or technocratic veneer, Latin American leaders exhibit traits that place them in a clearly identifiable mold, one that separates them from their counterparts in Europe and North America.

The Latin American leadership style may face ridicule by those who see it as an impediment to efficiency and modernization, yet it is a natural outgrowth of the political scene. With uncertainty and unrest the watchwords of Latin American politics, leaders have devised modes of operation that strengthen their position and extend their survival. To name a relative to a key government position (especially in the military, to which Fidel Castro and Daniel Ortega have appointed their brothers) can assure that threats to the office of the president will be held to a minimum. To travel around the country and personally hand out land titles, housing deeds, or simply money (as Joaquín Balaguer of the Dominican Republic has done successfully for years) will create a special bond with the people and make it less difficult to marshal a popular opposition campaign. To ignore corruption and patronage in state enterprises or the military (as most Latin American presidents have done) is simply one way of buying the loyalty of those individuals who helped you get into office or have the power to strip you of that office.

Taken together, Latin American leaders and their unique brand of leadership have had a profound impact on the course of political development. We in Western democracies are forced to divide our attention among chief executives, legislatures, courts, bureaucracies, special interests, local governing bodies, and the media. Politics and governance in Latin America causes fewer distractions. All the actors and institutions mentioned are present in the Latin American political arena, but their importance and power relative to the chief executive is significantly reduced. In some Latin American countries the only power relationship that matters is the interaction between the president and the generals; in others presidents so control the key governing institutions that their performance is all that matters. As Latin American politics continues to move along the paths of democratization and privatization, undoubtedly simplistic relationships and extreme centralization of policymaking will be transformed. But no matter what stage of political and institutional development Latin American countries are in, leaders will have to be examined as central to the governing process and as key players in the drive for modernization.

One important variable that needs to be added to the discussion on Latin American leaders and leadership is the impact that relations with the United States have on who is in power, who stays in power, and how those in power perform their governing functions. Those familiar with Latin America know that what happens internally in a particular country cannot be easily separated from the interests of the United States. Although most Latin American leaders are not puppets of the United States or helpless pawns in U.S. geopolitical strategies, the heads of state in this region must constantly be mindful that Washington policymakers not only closely monitor internal affairs but are ready to influence events and personalities if our interests are being threatened.

The legacy of U.S. relations with Latin American nations easily supports the view that leaders form the centerpiece of U.S. foreign policy formulation and implementation. From the perspective of U.S. presidents, it is essential for our national security and for the continued advancement of our economic interests that leaders in Latin America remain friendly and cooperative and develop policies that do not create instability or endanger existing business arrangements.[10] The United States remains committed to a wide range of governing values and principles and abides by the fundamental tenets of international law; however, it often sees Latin America and Latin American politics in the more basic relationship of leaders and political power. As a result, at important periods in the history of Latin American states when change was imminent and the future direction of the region was being contested, the United States has been concerned more with the victor in an election rather than the election, the survivor in the coup rather than the coup, and the commandante of the revolution rather than the revolution.

The preoccupation of U.S. policymakers with Latin American leaders has led to numerous episodes in which this country became actively involved in trying to shape the political landscape in the region by controlling the process of leadership selection or transition. The United States plotted to effect the downfall of leaders like Jácobo Arbenz in Guatemala, Rafael Trujillo in the Dominican Republic, and Salvador Allende in Chile; it developed vigorous destabilization campaigns to weaken Castro in Cuba and Ortega in Nicaragua; it placed enormous pressure on dictators like Manuel Noriega in Panama and "Bebe Doc" Duvalier in Haiti to relinquish power and it gave extensive moral and financial support to democratic leaders like José Napoleón Duarte and Alfredo Cristiani in El Salvador, Violeta Chamorro in Nicaragua, and Guillermo Endara in Panama in their battle to establish and maintain popular governance. The strategy often followed by U.S. presidents was that if we could get the right person in office or help to drive the wrong one out, then our objectives could be more easily achieved and U.S.-Latin American relations would prosper. As Woodrow Wilson once said, "I am going to teach the South American Republics to elect good men."[11]

Although the United States has influenced Latin American leaders over the years and shaped their policy positions, one cannot ignore the fact that Latin American leaders have often fought the pressure and the meddling from Washington. Latin American leaders have worked with varying degrees of success to exert greater control over their relationship with the United States and when possible to establish increasing levels of independence. From the days when Latin American leaders were referred to as "our SOB," the relationship between the United States and the leaders of the region has matured to the point where policymakers face presidents who regularly criticize U.S. actions, refuse to cooperate with U.S. initiatives, and make decisions that not only displease us but compromise our interests. The days of intimidation and forced cooperation have been replaced by independence, noncompliance, and greater self-assurance.[12]

The Latin American leaders have moved boldly to challenge the dominance of the United States. Trade, aid, and investment ties to Western Europe, the Pacific Basin, and in some cases the Soviet bloc; the formation of regional organizations to enhance inter-American relations; the passage of laws limiting the extent of foreign economic control; and greater unity in openly criticizing U.S. policies are but some of the ways in which Latin American leaders have begun to assert their independence in light of perceived U.S. weakness or inattention.

By the onset of the Reagan administration Latin American leaders were aggressively pursuing policies that opposed stated U.S. objectives. The Latin Americans condemned U.S. support of Great Britain during the Falklands/Malvinas war and wondered out loud what meaning the Rio Treaty had in terms of protecting the hemisphere from foreign intervention. Central American leaders brushed aside Reagan administration caveats about negotiating a settlement of the contra war in Nicaragua and fashioned the Central American peace accord, which has become a model of peaceful solution of regional disputes. A cross-section of Latin American leaders from Alan García of Peru to Carlos Andrés Pérez of Venezuela have criticized the United States for its intransigence in solving the burgeoning debt problem and have forced the U.S. banking community to seek new and more equitable solutions by simply not paying interest payments or by refusing to comply with International Monetary Fund recommendations for fiscal reform.

With the onset of the Bush administration the trend toward outspoken independence continued. President George Bush faced Latin American leaders such as Carlos Salinas of Mexico, Cesar Gaviria of Colombia, Patricio Alywin of Chile, and Fernando Collor of Brazil, who were openly critical of U.S. policies on trade, aid, debt, and drugs. If there was surprise during the Reagan administration over the new approach of the Latin American leaders, the Bush presidency confirmed that the United States faces not only a changed Latin America but a changed Latin American leader.

But with renewed confidence comes greater challenges and heightened demands. The result is that the contemporary Latin American leader must possess special talents in order to survive in the contentious arena of politics. Latin American leaders must be adroit balancers and shrewd managers of personnel; they must be capable of controlling the contending social forces while building policy coalitions that solve problems; and perhaps most of all they must be willing to function in a political climate where there is often little time and little patience for leaders trying to transform a country.

Few Latin American leaders have been able to match these job requirements or perform the herculean task of governing societies torn by political, social, and economic discord. Some have tried to solve the leadership dilemma through centralized control and force or by relying on charismatic or ideological appeals. But even these attempts eventually encounter the realities of maintaining political power in a rapidly changing society. What all Latin American leaders have come to recognize is that they are products of their environment—they function within a unique sociopolitical and regional system that colors their behavior and affects their performance. Therefore, in order to understand Latin American leaders it is essential to explore the current conditions, both internal and external, that shape the character of leadership in this part of the world.

To accomplish this task I have sought to mix historical analysis with contemporary evaluation of Latin American leaders and their relations with the United States. This study begins with two chapters that lay the foundation for the study of Latin American leaders and leadership. As will be shown, Latin American leaders have often responded to events and pressures that surround them by expressing governing traits designed to provide a cushion against the harsh realities of politics. Throughout Latin American history, from the early days of conquest, leaders in this region have shifted with the political and economic winds, many times to survive but also because conditions merited a new leadership model. Moreover, the ever-present power and interests of the United States forced Latin American leaders to reevaluate themselves and come up with new job descriptions. The initial chapters thus chronicle the early formation of leadership types in Latin America and link those types to the manner in which leaders responded to the pressures coming from Washington policymakers.

With this historical foundation in place the study moves into the heart of Latin American leadership analysis. The contemporary political scene in Latin America is best organized around three major leadership models—the military general in transition, the democratic politician, and the revolutionary ideologue. Because in today's Latin America the democratic politician is the focus of attention and analysis, the return to the barracks by the generals has been one of the more overlooked transitions in contemporary Latin American history. Military leaders in the region find themselves fighting to maintain their status, their influence, and their perquisites in democratic governing systems that appear to be strengthening. Nevertheless, the current transition in the roles of the generals from supreme power-holders, to players outside the governing circle is one that many democratic politicians look at with great unease. But if the generals are moving through untested waters, so are the democratic politicians, who now must deal with the problems left over from the era of authoritarian rule. Although the major challenge in studying the democratic politician is to bring some order to the long list of civilian presidents who have risen to power since the early 1980s, the primary emphasis of the analysis will be to determine how these young and often inexperienced leaders deal with the enormous pressures of running governments and managing societies that are in the midst of critical transitions. If democracy is to become the accepted form of government in Latin America in the 1990s, then it will be the civilian politicians who must bear the heavy responsibility of ensuring that this process of political change succeeds.

Finally, Latin American leadership continues to have representation from the Marxist left. The revolutionary guerrilla, the Communist organizer, the nationalist caudillo remain part of the Latin American leadership landscape. Despite the fall of communism in Eastern Europe and the transformation of socialist doctrine, Latin America remains a region where the leftist leader still commands attention and respect. In fact, leftist leaders have shown a greater resiliency in this period of Communist fallout than many expected, suggesting that the defensive posture may be but a brief downturn as rebel leaders wait to capitalize on the errors and failures of democratic politicians.

All these leadership models are not only in various stages of consolidation, transition, and reevaluation, they are also being shaped by the signals, pressures, and threats they receive from the United States. As a result of the continuing role of the United States in Latin America's internal politics, all three models of leadership will be explored not merely in terms of their operational dynamics but also in terms of their responses to the policy positions and initiatives that emanate from Washington. In each chapter the analysis of the leadership model is joined with a discussion of the way in which the United States seeks to direct the course of politics in Latin America by influencing leaders and defining proper leadership. Examining leaders in Latin America is not only a matter of explaining current models but also of analyzing the challenges faced by the heads of governments. After a description of the character and mode of operation of the Latin American authoritarians, democrats, and revolutionaries, this study then moves on to a discussion of the problems leaders must deal with in order to meet their responsibilities as governors and perhaps, more importantly, as politicians anxious to survive.

The third section of this book presents three issue areas where Latin American leaders are regularly tested and where they must make decisions crucial to the life of their country. The first area to be studied is the way Latin American leaders have met the threat of drug cultivation and drug smuggling. In the Latin America of the 1990s no problem challenges the legitimacy and effectiveness of Latin American leaders as does the trafficking in illegal drugs. Drug lords have formed organizations with enormous power to intimidate government and in some cases challenge governing authority. In a number of countries, from Colombia to Peru to Bolivia to Panama, Latin American leaders are coping with the threat to their constitutional authority. Because this challenge has the prospect of weakening democracy and tearing societies apart, the manner in which leaders face this threat will be critical to their ability to survive and prosper.

Also of importance to Latin American leaders are the twin issues of debt and development. Latin America remains mired in skyrocketing debt obligations at a time when there are heightened demands for social reform and economic justice. After a dismal development record in the 1980s, Latin American presidents are struggling with paying huge interest payments to foreign banks and dealing with widespread discontent brought on by austerity programs and delayed action on critical projects beneficial to those mired in poverty. The problems faced by Latin American leaders has become even more complex because of their decision to embrace private-sector market techniques and jettison the bloated state enterprises that have served as the backbone of their economies since the 1950s. This change is not as dramatic as the drug challenge, but Latin American leaders nevertheless recognize that the future of their countries and their governments is at stake.

Because Latin America is so closely intertwined with the United States, Latin American leaders must accept the reality of intervention whether military, diplomatic, economic, or cultural. Latin American leaders long ago learned to accept the involvement of the United States in their internal affairs. In the modern era the situation has not changed markedly; recent U.S. presidents have invaded Grenada and Panama, used sanctions against Cuba and Nicaragua, placed enormous pressure on drug-producing countries such as Colombia and Peru, and propped up Central American governments with substantial aid. If the challenges faced by the Latin American leaders of today are to be fully appreciated, then it is essential that a section of this study be devoted to examining how presidents in this region react to the interventionist proclivities of the United States. It is a reality of hemispheric power politics that Latin American leaders must be capable of balancing their need for maintaining independence with the security concerns of the United States.

The concluding sections of the book are analyses of Latin American leaders from the perspective of what constitutes effective leadership and how the United States can contribute to strengthening effective leaders. Latin American leaders will be examined to determine the qualities of leadership that are necessary for success and survival in the highly charged political climate of the 1990s. Closely tied to this analysis will be a discussion of the role the United States must play in the future development of capable and stable democratic leadership in the region. The final chapter addresses the challenges faced by the United States as it seeks to form a new relationship with the region. What the United States does in terms of nurturing "good" leaders will be a critical ingredient in the long-range stability and development of the hemisphere.

By thus examining Latin American leaders from a historical perspective, by describing the current state of leadership models and challenges, and by positing some concluding judgments about the essential internal and external requisites for success, this study is an attempt to bring into sharper focus a part of Latin American politics that is oftentimes neglected. Strangely, the neglect is not so much because leaders and leadership are unimportant but rather because the influence of leaders and leadership is so pervasive in Latin America. This book is thus an attempt to create new approaches to understanding the place of leaders and leadership at the core of Latin American politics.

NOTES

1. Although the study of Latin American leaders has been primarily focused on biographies of individual leaders, there are a few works that seek to provide a more comprehensive and analytical approach. See Ernest A. Duff, *Leaders and Party in Latin America* (Boulder, CO: Westview

Press, 1985) and David Foster, ed., *Latin American Government Leaders* (Tempe: Center for Latin American Studies, Arizona State, 1975).

2. See, for example, the interviews conducted by Paul H. Boeker in his recent work, *Lost Illusions: Latin America's Struggle for Democracy as Revealed by Its Leaders* (La Jolla, CA: Institute for the Americas, Merkes Weiner Publishing, 1990).

3. One of the early and influential articles on the role of leaders in the process of change in Latin America is Robert Scott, "Political Elites and Political Modernization: The Crisis of Transition," in Seymour Martin Lipset and Aldo Solari, eds., *Elites in Latin America* (New York: Oxford University Press, 1967), pp. 117–143.

4. See Harold Davis, *Latin American Leaders* (New York: Cooper Square Publishers, 1968).

5. A helpful guide to the historical modernization of Latin America can be found in Edward J. Williams and Freeman Wright, Jr., *Latin American Politics: A Developmental Approach* (Palo Alto, CA: Mayfield, 1975), pp. 45–91.

6. One of the better personal profiles of Castro is Tad Szulc, *Fidel: A Critical Portrait* (New York: Morrow, 1986).

7. Charles Anderson posited the power-contenders theory of Latin American politics, a theory that has become a key analytical foundation for studying the region and the dynamics of political power. Charles Anderson, *Politics and Economic Change in Latin America* (New York: Van Nostrand Reinhold, 1967), pp. 87–114.

8. Harold Davis, *Revolutionaries, Traditionalists, and Dictators* (New York: Cooper Square Publishers, 1973).

9. Howard J. Wiarda and Harvey F. Kline, *Latin American Politics and Development*, 3d ed. (Boulder, CO: Westview Press, 1990), pp. 15–18.

10. Robert Pastor writes on the issue of national security and its impact on Latin American and U.S. interests in the hemisphere in Richard J. Bloomfield and Gregory F. Treverton, eds., *Alternative to Intervention: A New U.S. Latin American Security Relationship* (Boulder, CO: Lynne Rienner Publishers, 1990), pp. 57–79.

11. R. S. Baker, *Woodrow Wilson: Life and Letters*, vol. 4 (Garden City, N.Y.: n.p., 1931), p. 289.

12. See Michael Manley, "Southern Needs" *Foreign Policy* 80 (Fall, 1990): 40–51.

1

LEADERS AND
LEADERSHIP TYPES IN
LATIN AMERICAN HISTORY

I do not know why but the people bring me all their problems, how to build a house, who to marry, how to settle a family dispute, and what seeds to plant.

—José Antonío Páez, Venezuelan caudillo,
in a letter to Simon Bolívar

Since the early days of independence, the Latin American leader has been viewed as someone who not only heads the government but whose presence is so dominant that he is often seen as the essence of the country. He represents power in its most complete sense—as the capability to control or influence all aspects of national life. The Latin American leaders' responsibilities go well beyond governing. The people of this region have come to identify leadership in terms of hands-on involvement in the everyday problems of the nation and expect their leaders to bring order and a modicum of consensus to governing systems often torn asunder by political and social divisions. As a result, the Latin American political leader can be defined not only in Western terms as a stimulator of social change, a manager of economic prosperity, and a developer of policy prescriptions but also in uniquely Latin terms as problem solver extraordinaire, political godfather to a family of bureaucrats and party officials, and a kind of governing "glue" that holds the country together.[1] This is indeed a heavy burden to carry, but it is one that Latin Americans seem comfortable with and one that Latin American leaders have accepted as the norm.

13

If we are to begin to understand these special individuals and appreciate the unique manner in which they lead, it is essential to return to the roots of Latin American leadership and trace the development of the political leader. From its base in the Spanish system of governance and social organization to its modern-day manifestations, Latin American leadership has evolved as Latin America has evolved. Although the fundamental nature of Latin American leadership has remained whole over the years, the job description of these leaders has changed significantly. New leadership types have come to the fore with new functions and new agendas. These leadership types have not only defined an age but, true to the Latin American tradition, have been personally responsible for taking their respective countries and indeed the region toward new levels of development.

THE CONQUISTADORS AND THE VICEROYS

Latin America's first leaders were the men who followed the discoverers to the New World. Smitten with the prospect of acquiring land and riches, these soldiers of fortune saw the New World as an opportunity to move quickly up the social scale and establish a position of power that would have to be recognized in Madrid and indeed throughout Europe. It is important to stress the fact that these first leaders in Latin America were called conquistadors or conquerers because their mission and their mode of operation were to dominate and control the indigenous population in the name of Spain. These men were not terribly complex individuals who were sensitive to the ramifications of their campaigns against the Indian population, the reckless pursuit of wealth, or the terrible manner in which they administered the lands under their domain. Their official charge was a very simple one—to ensure that the wealth of the New World became the wealth of Spain. They did initiate very visible attempts to Christianize the Indian population (often with disastrous results) and to build an institutional infrastructure similar to what was found in Europe, but these efforts were clearly not the major thrust of the colonization. Gold and silver transported to Spain and land acquisition in the New World were the goals of the conquistadors and their extended families.[2]

The names of the conquistadors have become etched firmly in the history of this region. Hernán Cortés in Mexico, Francisco Pizarro in Peru, Pedro de Alvarado in Guatemala, Diego de Almagro in Chile are but some of the major figures who came to the New World in the Sixteenth century in search of fame, wealth, and power. With large armies, cannon and musket, and horses to speed their conquest, Cortés and the other conquistadors overran the Indian population, destroying their cities and their way of life. Once the Indians had been tamed and their ranks decimated with disease, the conquistadors began dividing up the land and developing the means through which the wealth of the region could be extracted and transported out. Indians were rounded up into what were termed *repartimentos*, or slave encampments, and new cities were built to house the victors and their growing complement of soldiers of fortune. In a relatively short period of time (Mexico was conquered by 1521, Peru by 1535) the New World had been transformed from an unspoiled and highly sophisticated Indian civilization to a vanquished continent organized for the purpose of enrichment and status.[3]

The impact that the conquistadors had on the formation of Latin America is significant and the basis for extensive scholarly discussion. The emphasis that the conquistadors placed on destroying the Indian culture, extracting and transporting the wealth to Spain, and acquiring land as a form of status enhancement is often viewed as retarding the development of the region, particularly the development of democratic institutions. As José Moréno states, "[the] peculiarities of the Spanish character inherited from the conquistadors have affected the development of democracy in Latin America. The deeply rooted values and attitudes—the need for personal dominance and freedom from spiritual bondage to other men, the respect for individuals who can assert their authority over others, and the inability to identify with external goals to which others may also identify—are conducive neither to the development of democracy nor to economic progress."[4]

The fact that the New World's first leaders were often social outcasts turned soldiers of fortune affected the way government and governing principles developed. Public administration in the New World quickly became a family affair as sons, brothers, and cousins of the conquistadors divvied up the wealth and parceled out the land. Little attention was placed on using the governing administration to control the excesses of its leaders or to plan adequately for the future. Politics became a complex game of intrigue and shifting alliances tied closely to wealth and status. Although by the mid-1500s Spain sent capable viceroys like Antonio de Mendoza to Mexico to rein in the excesses of the conquistadors, a rudimentary but definable leadership model had already taken shape.

Once Spain reasserted its authority and began bringing some administrative order to the New World with the establishment of a series of viceroyalties and regional units called *audiencias*, the leadership model that developed around the conquistadors was linked with a more formal, corporative model that stressed rigid hierarchy, clearly defined sectors of influence, and control centralized in the monarch. At the local level, however, in the thousands of municipalities (*cabildos*) and landed estates (haciendas), the importance of familial networks, the dominance of the patron, and the reliance on paternalistic methods for solving problems became the established code of leadership. A liberal tradition that accented individual rights, group participation in government, and a more routinized form of handling disputes never became a part of everyday life in the Latin America of the seventeenth and eighteenth centuries. The authoritarian mode of operation used by the patrons was enhanced by the viceroyalty system, which demanded allegiance to a labyrinth of legal and commercial requirements and frowned upon challenges to authority.[5]

By the end of the eighteenth century it was obvious that the residents of the New World, the *criollos*, were comfortable with the local model of leadership but tiring of the restrictions and arrogance that emanated from Madrid and the offices of the various viceroys. Despite some enlighted leadership by the Bourbon kings, especially Carlos III, the viceroyalty system and the control from Spain that it represented became a point of contention in Latin America.[6] The *criollos* were looking for new leaders and new leadership strategies to respond to the inequities of Spanish rule. With the onset of the nineteenth century new leaders did emerge and brought with them a different vision of the future.

THE LIBERATORS

In a manner similar to the movement for independence in the United States, the people of Latin America revolted against Spanish domination and established independent republics. The War of Independence in the thirteen colonies, however, was a fairly compact struggle in terms of geography and time and benefited from a unified cause and a clearly defined military leadership. The Wars of Liberation in Latin America were fought over the length and breadth of the continent, consumed huge blocks of time, and were led by a variety of leaders whose only link was the importance of driving Spain out. Because the movement for independence in Latin America developed out of a culture and political environment quite different from that in North America, it should be of no surprise that the men who fashioned the liberation would reflect the values, the prejudices, and the leadership style that was now deeply embedded in the sociopolitical system.

The great liberators of Latin America—Simon Bolívar in the Andes, José de San Martín in Argentina, Bernardo O'Higgins in Chile, Fathers Hidalgo and Morelos in Mexico, and Toussaint Louverture in Haiti—were men conscious of the way in which the world was changing. Monarchies were falling, ordinary citizens were leading political uprisings, democratic constitutions were being fashioned, and grandiose promises were being made about establishing basic human rights.[7] The liberators of Latin America were not mere soldiers with a particular mission to accomplish but rather political visionaries whose dream of Latin America after the Spanish were defeated was as expansive as that of Washington, Franklin, and Madison. But what these leaders quickly came to realize after the battles were over was that the transformation of Latin America into a region that began to approximate the United States was fraught with enormous obstacles.

Although men like Bolívar and San Martín were brilliant military tacticians, they became frustrated political leaders in the postindependence period. Regional disputes, recalcitrant local leaders, and general unwillingness to move away from the Spanish social and political system made attempts at unification and democratization impossible. Bolívar made impassioned speeches about the importance of following the models of government found in the United States and Europe, but few listened. The power of the local patron, the gulf between church and state, city and countryside, and the deeply entrenched authoritarian tradition destroyed Bolívar's dream of a United States of Latin America.[8]

The liberators were unable to sustain their influence as their counterparts did in the United States. Bolívar died of tuberculosis in 1830 as he was trying to leave a South America that he described as "ungovernable"; San Martín left Buenos Aires for England in 1824 in disgust over the petty feuding among elites and never returned to strife-torn Argentina; Hidalgo and Morelos died at the hands of the Spanish and left Mexican independence to Augustin Iturbide, a visionless aristocrat; O'Higgins was forced out of Chile by an ungrateful citizenry and died in neighboring Peru in 1842; and Toussaint Louverture was captured by Emperor Napoleon's men and thrown into prison where he died in 1803. In country after country the charismatic and heroic liberators gave way to local leaders whose chief concern was consolidating their power and protecting their fiefdoms from attack.[9]

The failure of the liberators to move beyond achieving independence to the formation of unified republics with progressive governing systems should not diminish the impact that these individuals have had on future Latin American leaders. Bolívar, for example, remains not only the great liberator of Latin America but a symbol of democratic governance and social reform. The fact that Latin America turned its back to the grand designs of Bolívar in the name of regionalism and personalistic power does not lessen his accomplishments. In fact, generation after generation of Latin American leaders continue to quote his words and pledge to implement his ideas. One of Bolívar's quotes often used by contemporay Latin American leaders centers around his fear of dictatorial rule: "The exercise of power by the same individual has often been the end of democratic government. Frequent elections are essential in popular governments; for nothing is more perilous than to allow power to remain in the hands of the same man."[10]

As we shall see in the next section these words of Bolívar went unheeded by those who followed him. The noble dream of Simon Bolívar crumbled under the weight of self-interest and power politics. At the close of his liberating campaigns Bolívar revealed his concern for the future of the Americas when he said, "There is no good faith in America, not among the nations of America. Treaties are scraps of paper; constitutions, printed matter; elections, battles; freedom, anarchy; and life a torment."[11]

THE CAUDILLOS

With the death of Bolívar and the departure of San Martín, Latin America was left in the hands of local and regional leaders whose primary interest was in maintaining their control over the land and the wealth that it contained. Many of these leaders were rough-hewn men with little education and meager interest in moving their country forward. In almost every Latin American republic, national leadership was taken up by what has come to be called the caudillo, or the man on horseback. The Latin American caudillo quickly spawned a brand of leadership that was at the center of politics in this region for over fifty years.[12]

In many respects the caudillos filled the void left by the Spanish crown. With Bolívar's dream of constitutional democracy unable to penetrate the political culture of the newly independent colonies, the caudillos moved in to establish their authority and to reformulate the boundaries of Latin America from viceroyalties and *audiencias* to independent nation states. Leaders like Juan Manuel de Rosas in Argentina, Antonio López Santa Ana in Mexico, Pedro Santana in the Dominican Republic, José Antonio Páez in Venezuela, and Francisco Solano López in Paraguay grabbed the reins of power after the Spanish left and ruled their country with a mixture of personalism, paternalism, and brutal repression. Some caudillos such as Gabriel García Moréño of Ecuador were religious fanatics who sought to refashion the country into a theocracy; others such as José Mariano Melgarejo of Bolivia were simply cruel and vengeful dictators concerned only with personal enrichment. If there is any link among these caudillos it is that they represented a leadership type that accented centralized control. Although the caudillos often permitted political party organizations and other intermediary institutions to form, it was clear that these organizations and institutions would not be permitted to function independent of the supreme leader or to challenge his authority.[13]

While in power the caudillos faced an endless stream of internal and external problems: conflicts between urban and rural interests, questions over the proper role of the Catholic church, border skirmishes, foreign indebtedness, and the constant malaise of unstable and incompetent leadership. The fact that many caudillos were unschooled in the practice of governance and ill prepared to deal with ever-expanding public policy issues left the Latin American republics at a distinct disadvantage and easy prey for new caudillos who could marshal the men and the guns to take over power. As one study of Latin American instability states: "Historians have grown haggard in the task of counting up all the insurgencies and civil war to which the 'Age of Caudillos' gave rise. Venezuela, for example, had suffered 52 important revolts by 1912. Bolivia had more than 60 revolutions by 1898 and had assassinated six presidents."[14]

The "age of caudillos" became a period when Latin America sank deep into the morass of local impoverishment and international dependency. The hacienda rather than the capital city became the center of power; economic activity settled into predictable patterns as many countries developed one staple crop as the source of foreign currency; and reliance on external markets and capital from European banks created grossly uneven trade patterns and debt-ridden treasuries. Overseeing this distinctly Latin American predicament were the caudillos, who in most instances were either incapable of building governments and fostering policies that dealt with the economic morass or were not in power long enough to address the problems.

In evaluating a particular era in a country or region one is reluctant to point to a specific factor that was critical in shaping political, economic, and social life. But in Latin America in the period after the wars of independence it is clear that the poor caliber of leadership, the climate of instability, and the narrow public policy objectives of those in power were directly responsible for retarding the growth of this region and for further deepening the governing malaise. During this period Latin America was most closely identified with the men who moved in and out of office and did little while in office to advance the interests of their country. As Edwin Fagg states about the Latin American caudillos: "That they were sometimes colorful and attractive as personalities does not diminish the harm they did. The riotous character of public life discouraged the penetration of Latin America by educators, immigrants, investors, traders and experts. . . . For a generation or two after independence Latin America in general lost ground."[15]

Fortunately for Latin America, the reign of the caudillos would come to an end and new leadership would seek to attain the goals enunciated by Simon Bolívar. But the leadership model the caudillos established with its emphasis on charisma and authoritarianism would not be easily removed from the Latin American leadership agenda. Raw power and personal gain had become permanent characteristics of Latin American leadership. Their reappearance could be expected.

REFORMERS AND MODERNIZERS

For most of the time after the caudillos, Latin American independence leaders seemed capable of controlling the direction of national life in their respective countries. But as Latin America neared the end of the nineteenth century, it was no longer possible to hold back the economic and social changes that were transforming the countries of this region. The arrival of European immigrants, the demand for those inventions and institutions that would speed modernization, and the emerging voice of the working and middle class placed enormous pressure on governing regimes and led to the elevation of a new breed of leader who pledged to bring his country into the twentieth century.

The period of time from approximately the 1870s to the onset of the Great Depression of the 1930s saw the ascendancy of a group of leaders who can be categorized as either reformers or modernizers or both. These leaders recognized that Latin America had indeed fallen behind in its internal development and needed to bring the modern world to the hemisphere. This era became the age of railroad construction and industrialization, education and democratization, foreign investment and trade diversification. Latin America was alive with change as political leaders, either responding to popular pressure or seeking to push their nations forward, initiated programs and promulgated laws that brought this region out of the lethargy and backwardness of the postindependence period.[16]

The age of reform and modernization gave Latin America some of its most distinguished political leaders. In Argentina, Domingo Sarmiento was credited with developing the nation's public education system and initiating a massive infrastructure program. In Chile, José Balmaceda linked economic modernization with extensive reform of the electoral and constitutional systems. In Uruguay, José Báttle y Ordóñez unified his country, tamed foreign interests, and instituted a social welfare system that became a model for the rest of Latin America.

Although most of the reformers and modernizers mixed political and economic change, some of these leaders will be remembered for their skill at organizing and mobilizing the emerging social forces in their countries. Benito Juarez in Mexico is recognized as the father of the country not only because of his successful war against the French interlopers who controlled the country in the 1860s but because he worked tirelessly as president to represent the interests of the Indian population. President Ippólito Yrigoyen in Argentina came to symbolize the demands of the restive working classes in Argentina when he assumed national leadership in 1916. Yrigoyen pushed for progressive social legislation like the minimum wage and also was responsible for organizing the working classes into the powerful Radical party.[17]

Not all these leaders were champions of the emerging social forces in Latin America. In Mexico, Porfirio Díaz assumed power soon after the administration of Juarez and became what can be called a "modernizing tyrant." Díaz and his associates, the cientificos, were apostles of the positivist school of thought, which accented unending material progress. Together these men transformed Mexico by opening up the country to foreign investment and foreign control while paying little attention to social reforms or democratization. Díaz brought railroads, telephones, roads, and new industries to Mexico but at the same time sowed the seeds of rebellion by closing his regime off from the people.[18]

Some countries like Bolivia, Paraguay, Ecuador, Peru, and Venezuela had few visionary leaders and as a result saw their countries fall further behind in the march toward modernization. In fact the Southern Cone countries of Chile, Argentina, Uruguay, and also Brazil under the enlightened leadership of King Pedro II (who some have called the most admired individual of his time in Latin America) made significant modernizing strides that quickly separated them from their Andean neighbors. The Southern Cone countries began to resemble European nations in that they developed sound education and social welfare systems, moved forward to diversify their economic base, and formed strong trade and cultural ties to countries like Spain, Portugal, Italy, and Great Britain.

Most observers of this era in Latin American development praise the reformers and modernizers as responsible for pushing and pulling their nations forward, but there are those who question the models used in reform and modernization. Many of these leaders became strong advocates of philosophies and governing systems that had no basis in Hispanic culture. European positivism and liberalism, the constitutional frameworks of the United States and France, and the material values of capitalist societies became the standards for change in Latin America. Latin American leaders often grafted a philosophy or governing framework onto their existing societies, believing it would enhance the country's march toward modernization. But although this grafting did accomplish much in terms of progressive change, it was always a tenuous bonding that conflicted with the corporatist and conservative nature of Hispanic society.[19]

What the reformers and modernizers did for Latin America was thus not only usher the region into the twentieth century but lay the groundwork for an eventual contest between the Western liberal model of development with its roots in Europe and North America and the Hispanic system with its roots deep in the culture of Latin American society. The social and political forces unleashed by the reformers and modernizers could never be quashed, but that did not mean that the advocates of a more controlled society would not seek to limit change or return to the days when powerful men ruled Latin America unencumbered by constitutions, election laws, social welfare programs, and progressive modernization policies.

THE AUTHORITARIANS

From the onset of the Great Depression until the late 1950s and the early 1960s Latin America experienced the rise of a new wave of authoritarian leadership. Reacting to the dislocations created by the rise of working-class politics, the increased calls for liberal democracy, and the failures of civilian politicians to control the unrest that accompanied social change, Latin America returned to its roots as strongman rule became the norm. But the kind of authoritarianism that spread throughout the region during this period was different from the unsophisticated and retrogressive rule of the nineteenth-century caudillos. Although some of these authoritarians behaved in ways that were reminiscent of the early caudillos, most leaders "improved" upon the methods of control used by their predecessors and developed models of governance that allowed them to deal with the emerging social forces and policy dilemmas that faced Latin American society.[20]

In some countries authoritarian rule was maintained at a rather simple level. The regimes of Trujillo in the Dominican Republic, Somoza in Nicaragua, Duvalier in Haiti, Jorge Ubico in Guatemala, and Fulgencio Batista in Cuba mixed harsh repression with economic control to create family-run countries that brought enormous wealth to those within the clan network. The longevity of these leaders was often the result of astutely balancing modernization schemes, close ties to the United States, support from business elites, and simple fear. Although these modernized caudillos have helped to maintain the stereotype of the bemedaled Latin American dictator enriching himself at the expense of a terrified population, it is important to remember that these leaders could not have stayed in power (for upward of thirty years in some cases) without being shrewd manipulators of the citizenry and effective managers of prosperity for those elites who mattered.[21]

The likes of Trujillo and Somoza stand out as the most objectionable examples of authoritarian rule. The regimes of leaders like Juan Peron in Argentina, Getulio Vargas in Brazil, Gustavo Rojas Pinilla in Colombia, and Marcos Pérez Jímenez in Venezuela set the tone for governance in Latin America during this era. Although clearly in the authoritarian mold, these leaders have been defined most appropriately as populists who used the changing pattern of social relations in the region to enhance their power and to redefine the role of the state. Peron and Vargas in particular have been examined as the prototypes of this populist authoritarian. Both men developed their power base in the military but rose to national leadership because they went outside of the military and tapped into the vast army of disenchanted workers who were ready to mobilize behind someone promising them a better life.[22]

Under these populist authoritarians, countries like Argentina and Brazil changed significantly. The role of the state expanded dramatically in both the areas of social welfare and economic development. Nationalizations created huge state sectors, expanded social welfare commitments, and ballooned the government deficit, and new groups such as labor unions and workers' parties emerged as agents of support for the leadership. A kind of democratic structure could be found in these countries in terms of elections and political party formation, but there was no mistaking the fact that these were authoritarian regimes that did not hesitate to crack down on dissident voices and monitor all social movements.

For a time Peron, Vargas, and the others enjoyed immense popularity. But after the bills for the programs came due and key elites both in and out of the military began to tire of the shift in social and political power, the populist authoritarians went the way of other dictators. Military coups or conservative political groups put an end to the spending and the mobilization of what the Argentines called the *descamisados*—the shirtless ones. Peron was deposed, Vargas committed suicide, Rojas was pushed out of office in favor of the Conservative-Liberal experiment in controlled democracy, and Pérez Jímenez fled to Europe as moderate democrats took the reins of government.[23]

One unusual variant of the authoritarian populists in Latin America is the manner in which the governing party in Mexico, the Partido Revolucionario Institucional (PRI), controlled the political system. The leadership style of the PRI can best be described as political bossism. Rather than rely on personalism, charisma, and overt force, the PRI developed its power on a base of patronage and machine politics. Despite the fact that Mexico had its popular leaders like Lázaro Cárdenas, the strength of the PRI was in its ability to bring the various sectors of the nation together into a huge political organization. Labor unions, agricultural workers, and professional associations were linked closely to the party hierarchy with the promise of jobs, promotions, and access.[24] Again, there were visible signs of a liberal-like political environment, but at the same time these signs were accompanied by regular use of force, intimidation, and fraud. Just as individual authoritarians practiced *continuismo*, the Mexican PRI practiced a unique form of institutional *continuismo* that has lasted into the 1990s.[25]

As Latin America headed into the 1960s and the heady days of the Alliance for Progress, the evolution of authoritarianism had been to some countries both an economic boon and a sad legacy of terror. One point was very clear: These authoritarians represented the resiliency of military rule in Latin America and the ability of this class of leaders to adapt to the changing character of regional life. As John Johnson states, "The substitution of technically trained managers of violence for the heroic leaders of the past has had much to do with the growth of the new military."[26] The professionalization and modernization of the military in Latin America had by the 1960s created a sense of confidence and obligation. Latin America would not see the old-line caudillos again or the family-based dictators, but the rule of leaders like Peron, Vargas, Rojas, and Pérez showed that the generals could lead their nations toward modernity and would not hesitate to do so when the opportunity presented itself.

THE DEMOCRATS

The political tug-of-war in Latin America between the tradition of authoritarian rule and the dream of democratic government was never so pronounced as during the period of President John F. Kennedy's Alliance for Progress. After decades of harsh military rule throughout the hemisphere, Latin America began dismantling authoritarian regimes and replaced them with governments headed by civilian politicians committed to free and open elections, social reform, human rights, and the rule of law. Encouraged by a U.S. presidential administration anxious to divorce itself from any affiliation with dictatorships and spurred on by the competition from revolutionary Marxists, a new generation of leaders rose to power pledged to establish constitutional democracy.[27]

Some of the democratic leaders during this era were exiled as opposition politicians who had led the fight to unseat dictatorial rule. Juan Bosch in the Dominican Republic, Victor Raúl Haya de la Torre in Peru, Victor Paz Estensorro in Bolivia, and Rómulo Betancourt in Venezuela experienced the frustration and danger of challenging entrenched authoritarian regimes but prevailed to see the political movements they founded either gain power or radically change the configuration of power in their respective countries. Rómulo Betancourt, for example, became the modern-day successor to Simon Bolívar after his Acción Democrática (AD) party led the successful revolt against the dictator Pérez Jímenez and started Venezuela on the road to stable democratic rule.[28] For others, like Haya de la Torre, whose writings on social democratic reform energized this new generation of leaders, fighting the Peruvian oligarchy would lead only to fraudulent elections and dashed hopes of leading the country into the age of democracy.[29]

Although the main current of leadership thought in Latin America during this era was liberal and reformist, civilian politicians were not all of the same mold. Eduardo Frei in Chile rose to power in 1964 representing the Christian Democratic party and a Christian Democratic philosophy that sought to act as an alternative to capitalism and communism.[30] In Colombia in 1957 ex-presidents Lleras Camargo of the Liberal party and Laureano Gómez of the Conservative party founded the so-called Civil Front, which in effect stopped La Violencia by creating a "controlled democracy" built on the principles of alternating power between the two principal parties in the country.[31] In Puerto Rico Luis Muñoz Marín developed a close relationship with the United States based on the principle of economic cooperation.[32] And in Brazil João Goulart fashioned a clearly leftist government that pledged to reorder national priorities and give a voice to the nation's masses.[33]

Although from diverse backgrounds and ideologies, these democratic leaders were often the products of political party organizations. Latin America during the late 1950s and 1960s was the center of democratic party activity. Civilian politicians recognized that if they were to challenge the strength of the powerful conservative elites in their countries, they would have to build equally powerful organizations committed to democratic reform and constitutional stability.[34] In some instances Latin American political parties were modeled after European social democratic organizations; in other cases the APRA (Alianza Popular Revolucionaria Américana) movement of reform and nationalism articulated by Peru's Haya de la Torre became the standard. What united these political parties was their desire to ensure that civilian democratic leaders would be able to mobilize the middle-class professionals, the urban workers, the students, and the rural campesinos at election time and when the opponents of democratic governance threatened to intervene.

Despite the fact that this era of Latin American democratic leadership and reform received great attention and fanfare, especially in the United States, it was essentially an unfortunate "bridge" between two quite different authoritarian periods. What started out as a democratic revolution quickly became what Robert Wesson calls, "the disastrous decade for democracy" as civilian politicians were replaced by new generals or leaders who followed the dictates of the conservative elites.[35] Only in a few countries—Costa Rica under the

adept leadership of Don Pepe Figueres and Venezuela with its oil
and strong two-party politics—did democracy survive.

Those who observed this brief democratic interlude attribute
the decline of civilian leadership to a number of sources. With the
assassination of President Kennedy and the onset of the Vietnam
War, the Alliance for Progress program came to a halt and with it
the millions of dollars that were helping the civilian leaders address
the myriad of social ills facing their countries.[36] Also some of the
democratic leaders were inexperienced in governance and intransigent
in their dealings with powerful elites. Bosch in the Dominican
Republic and Goalart in Brazil are perhaps good examples of democratic leaders who hurt their own cause and helped trigger a military
response.[37]

But at the heart of the problems facing democratic leadership
during this period was that Latin American society did not seem
ready for the openness, the uncertainty, and the change that accompanied democracy. What democratic leaders needed more than
U.S. aid assistance and governing skills was a societal consensus that
the road to national development was best built on elections, land
reform, social welfare legislation, and mobilization of the masses. As
Charles Ameringer states,

> The generation of Betancourt, Figueres and Muñoz Marín ultimately
> broke the power of the dictators, not merely by overcoming them
> physically but by helping to create the atmosphere which made them
> absolute. However, because of the length and difficulty of the struggle,
> this generation of leaders was unable to seize the opportunity which
> their opposition had made. The tragedy of their victory was that it
> took so long to achieve, that they had expended so much of their
> energy in the struggle and that the delay had created new problems
> for which their solutions seemed inadequate.[38]

Though many democratic leaders failed in their mission to reconstruct
Latin American society and created enormous disillusionment among
those who saw this era as the final breakthrough for popular rule,
the process of democratization had begun in earnest, a process that
would continue despite the overwhelming power of the military.

THE REVOLUTIONARIES

Although the history of political leadership in Latin America has been based on a contest between authoritarianism and democracy, it is impossible to ignore the role that revolution and revolutionary leadership have played in the development of this region. The struggle to radically restructure the social, economic, and political foundations of Latin America may seem to be a rather recent trend considering the enormous influence of the Cuban and Nicaraguan guerrilla wars, but the revolutionary tradition can trace its roots to the Indian mining and land-ownership strikes against the Spanish in Mexico and the slave revolts in French-controlled Haiti.[39] Although these incidents of revolutionary action were largely without any ideological base or programmatic framework, they nevertheless revealed the early discontent present among various segments of Latin American society and the willingness of those segments to forcefully register their opposition to the status quo.

The age of the caudillos effectively silenced much of the discontent among the Latin American masses, but the broadening of inequities between the elites and the urban and rural classes and the refusal of conservative leaders to initiate reforms that would address the needs of the poor gave impetus to those who saw the importance of taking radical action. The first real sign that revolution was an integral part of the Latin American political configuration came again from Mexico. The Mexican revolution not only brought forth a spirit of widespread institutional and structural change but gave Latin America its first revolutionary leaders and heroes. Emiliano Zapata with his demand for land reform in the South and Pancho Villa with his strange mix of rugged populism and nationalistic bravado in the North are now permanently enshrined in the pantheon of heroes who fought for social justice and economic independence.[40]

The importance of the Mexican revolution spread beyond the mythology surrounding the exploits of Zapata and Villa as more mainstream leaders such as Venustiano Carranza and Álvaro Obregon promoted the 1917 constitution, which articulated a broad list of radical changes in the areas of working conditions, unionization, and church-state relations. Later on Lázaro Cárdenas enforced the more controversial articles of the constitution dealing with the protection of the nation's resources by taking on the U.S. oil companies.

Through the efforts of these leaders, the Mexican revolution became one of the important turning points in Latin American history and the Mexican constitution a model for the establishment of governing principles that create a fairer and more sovereign nation.

The intervention of the United States in Latin America also contributed to the development of revolutionary leadership. The involvement of U.S. military and civilian personnel in Nicaragua from the Wilson administration through the presidency of Herbert Hoover led to the formation of guerrilla groups bent on challenging the presence of U.S. soldiers. The most famous of these guerrillas was Augusto Sandino, who successfully fought the marine contingents only to be assassinated by the U.S.-trained constabulary headed by Anastasio Somoza.[41] The inability of Sandino to translate his guerrilla victories into permanent control of the Nicaraguan government did not diminish his influence. Sandino's opposition to U.S. meddling in Nicaraguan politics and his death at the hands of a U.S.-supported tyrant transformed this revolutionary leader into a symbol of defiance that is at the core of the modern-day Sandinista movement.

Revolutionary cowboys like Zapata and Villa and guerrilla ranchers like Sandino may have possessed the leadership skills necessary to head small armies and engage in hit-and-run attacks, but they never were able to control national power or fashion policy in their mold. It would take someone like Fidel Castro to move beyond revolutionary war to revolutionary government. Like his predecessors, Castro fought against the inequities of Cuban life and the cruel dictatorship of U.S.-supported Fulgencio Batista. Castro, however, was more than a revolutionary warrior; he was a committed Marxist with a clear view of how to defeat the enemy and lead the country away from what he saw as capitalist injustice and U.S. imperialism.[42]

Castro and his Argentine associate, Ernesto "Che" Guevara, skillfully moved from their base in the Sierra Madre and constructed a popular guerrilla organization that eventually drove Batista from power. The victory of Fidel Castro sent shockwaves throughout Latin America and Washington as it became clear that the Cuban leader was intent on leading his country along a revolutionary path, a path that embraced Marxist principles and Soviet friendship. Latin American revolution had truly arrived, and revolutionary leadership attained a kind of respectability that worried reform democrats and struck fear into the generals.

The impact of Castro's revolution on Cuba and other revolutionary situations in the region was enormously significant. His fanatical commitment to Marxism affected all segments of Cuban life from land to housing to education to relations with the United States. In a short period of time Cuba was transformed into a classic Communist state with Castro as the sole definer of Marxist orthodoxy.[43] Because of Castro's success at challenging the dominance of the United States, revolution quickly spread throughout the hemisphere in the 1960s and the names of revolutionary leaders were heard more frequently. Che Guevara left Cuba (after a leadership squabble with Castro) and ended up in Bolivia, where he led a failed revolution attempt and was killed. Catholic priest Camilo Torres took up the gun and organized guerrilla fighters in Colombia, signaling the growing radicalization of religious leaders. In Venezuela Douglas Bravo, supported by arms from Castro, sought to destroy the emerging democratic government of President Raúl Leoni and in Guatemala César Montes and Yon Sosa struggled to bring an end to years of authoritarian rule.[44] Although much of the revolutionary activity was concentrated in the rural areas, urban guerrillas also formed during this time. The ERP (Ejercito Revolucionario Popular) in Argentina and the Tupamaros in Uruguay became prototypes of effective use of urban terror to intimidate authoritarian regimes.[45]

Revolutionary leaders were no more able than reform democrats to sustain themselves in the face of renewed interest by the military in governing Latin American nations and counterrevolutionary programs introduced by the United States. By the late 1960s Fidel Castro stood alone as the symbol of revolution in Latin America. Guerrilla activity continued in Guatemala, Colombia, and Peru, and in Chile in 1970 Salvador Allende became an elected version of Castro as he assumed the presidency. But the mix of excitement and fear engendered by the revolutionaries was soon replaced by the harsh reality of rule by the generals, who in most cases gained support from the middle class by promising to put an end to the violence and the doctrinaire threats of the leftists.

The failure of revolution and revolutionary leadership to spread its influence beyond Cuba and Fidel Castro during this period should not be interpreted as another example of a tangential political trend in the region. Rather the victory of Castro and the support he received throughout the hemisphere, particularly with the leftist guerrillas in Central America, clearly established revolution and revolutionary leadership as integral parts of a new Latin American political system. The social and economic forces that gave birth to guerrilla warfare and revolutionary government were still present in Latin America and would once again challenge the reform-minded policies of civilian politicians and the authoritarian regimes of the military.

BUILDING ON THE PAST

Political scientist Charles Anderson once described Latin America as a "living museum" because it revealed a propensity to hold on to its past traditions and institutions while adding on new traditions and institutions.[46] Examining Latin American leaders and leadership in many ways reinforces Anderson's perception of how this region operates and changes. The leaders and leadership types discussed previously exhibit both a sense of modernity and unbreakable ties to the past. It is true that the historical movement from the conquistadors to the revolutionaries is an evolutionary one in which Latin American leaders responded to the challenges they faced with new techinques and new definitions of their mission. But it is also true that each leadership type mirrored the past and was limited in the ability to completely break from the political and cultural mold that was formed at the time the Spanish introduced their system to the New World.

The roles played by Cortés and Bolívar have been especially important in the development of a unique brand of Latin American leadership. The bold and ruthless conquistador dedicated to controlling the Indian population and dominating the land joins the visionary and reform-minded liberator to create the underlying tension between authoritarianism and democracy that drives the political life of this region. Although it is risky to engage in a kind of reductionist argument and elevate leaders and leadership to the level of principal definers of Latin American development, at the same time, however, it is impossible to ignore the impact that leaders like Cortés and Bolívar and the leadership types they represented had on a culture steeped in personalism, individualism, and hero-worship.

Latin America's beginning as a region where leaders sought to dominate and exploit and its later liberation by leaders who vainly fought to bring European-style democracy made a lasting political imprint. By the time each of the Latin American nations were formed they were torn between the need for order and centralization of power that existed in the preindependence era and the desire to break from the past and establish governments based on liberal principles. The fact that the conquistadorial system and the aristocratic nature of the viceroyalties had the benefit of three hundred years of political control contributed to the inability of the liberators to turn Latin America away from its corporatist roots and embrace Western democratic models.

The leaders and leadership types that governed Latin America during the national period merely added to the conquistador and liberator models. The caudillos and the dictators continued the authoritarian tradition established by Cortés, as these leaders also sought to dominate and exploit. The modernizers and the democrats tried to implement the vision of Bolívar by moving Latin America forward and introducing governing principles and practices that accented openness and fairness. The fact that the caudillos and dictators remained in power much longer than the modernizers and democrats further reinforces the influence that the conquistadorial model has had on political leadership in Latin America. The authoritarian tradition is clearly the norm in Latin America and the authoritarian leader the representative of that norm.

The discussion of authoritarians and democrats can lead to a natural question: How do we deal with the presence of revolution and revolutionary leadership in Latin America? The answer to that question may be found by recognizing that revolution comes from the Latin *revolver*, to return to. Revolution and revolutionary leadership are also part of the "living museum" of Latin America because their roots can be found at the time of the conquistadors and the liberators. The conquest of the New World was a profoundly revolutionary event because the conquistadors sought to wipe away the Indian culture and replace it with a Spanish-Christian culture. The liberation of Latin America was revolutionary in that the object of the wars was to break away from Spain and to replace the Spanish system with one that more ably fit the times and the needs of the *criollos*.

As Latin America evolved, however, revolution and revolutionary leadership, unlike the authoritarian and democratic traditions, remained dormant. But because Latin America is a "living museum," revolution would once again become part of the political landscape. The resurgence of revolution was made possible because leaders like Zapata, Sandino, and Castro brought to their countries the realization that there are alternative roads to development and that revolution is not an alien process but rather a return to the roots of Latin American history.

The influence of leaders on Latin American politics cannot easily be measured. Authoritarians, democrats, and revolutionaries have all made contributions to Latin American development but have also been responsible for retarding modernization. Although there is a bias in Western countries in favor of democratic development, Latin America has also advanced under authoritarian and revolutionary regimes. Democratic leadership is often preferred because of its openness and respect for procedure, but authoritarianism with its penchant for stability and revolution and with its emphasis on mass mobilization and income redistribution can also be seen as shaping Latin American development. What brings these disparate leadership types together, however, is that they are part of a distinct Latin American political tradition, a tradition that relies heavily on cues from the past while continuing to evolve and modernize.

NOTES

1. James MacGregor Burns in *Leadership* presents his views on the many roles of leadership from both the Western and the non-Western perspective (New York: Harper and Row, 1978), pp. 444–462.

2. See, for example, Kirkpatrick Sale's critical assessment of Christopher Columbus and the early explorers and conquerors. Kirkpatrick Sale, *The Conquest of Paradise: Christopher Columbus and the Columbian Legacy* (New York: Knopf, 1990).

3. See F. A. Kirkpatrick, *The Spanish Conquistadores* (Cleveland: Meridian Books, World Publishing, 1967).

4. As quoted in Elisea Vivas, "The Spanish Heritage," *American Sociological Review* 10 (1945):184.

5. See Richard M. Morse, "Toward a Theory of Spanish American Government," *Journal of the History of Ideas* 15 (1964):71–93.

6. Ronald C. Newton, "On 'Functional Groups,' 'Fragmentation,' and 'Pluralism' in Spanish American Society," *Hispanic American Historical Review* 1 (February 1970):1-29.

7. Victor Alba answers the question, "How Did Latin America Emerge?" in Victor Alba, *The Latin Americans* (New York: Praeger, 1969), pp. 48-103.

8. Gabriel García Márquez has written a controversial novel that breaks down the grand myths that have surrounded Bolívar since the days of independence. See *The General and His Labyrinth* (New York: Knopf, 1990).

9. See William Spence Robertson, *The Rise of South America As Told in the Lives of Their Liberators* (New York: Free Press, 1946).

10. Hubert Herring, *A History of Latin America*, 3d ed. (New York: Knopf, 1968), p. 264.

11 Ibid., p. 286.

12. Richard Morse, "Political Theory and the Caudillo," in Hugh Hamill Jr., ed., *Dictatorship in Spanish America* (New York: Knopf, 1965), pp. 52-68.

13. See Kalman Silvert, "Leadership Formation and Modernization in Latin America," in Kalman Silvert, *Essays in Understanding Latin America* (Philadelphia: Institute for the Study of Human Issues, 1977), p. 25. See Also Jacques Lambert, *Latin America: Social Structure and Political Institutions* (Berkeley: University of California Press, 1967), pp. 149-166.

14. See "A Historical Survey of Politics and Techniques of Insurgency Conflict in Post-1900 Latin America" (Washington, D.C.: Atlantic Research Corporation, Georgetown Research Project, 1964), pp. 11-111.

15. Edwin Fagg, *Latin America: A General History*, 2d ed. (New York: Macmillan, 1969), p. 262.

16. For a discussion of the impact of this era of reform, see Simon G. Harrison, *Utopia in Uruguay, Chapters in the Economic History of Uruguay* (New York: Oxford University Press, 1938).

17. David Rock, *Argentina, 1516-1982* (Berkeley: University of California Press, 1985), pp. 162-213.

18. See Edwin Lieuwen, *Mexican Militarism* (Albuquerque: University of New Mexico Press, 1968), pp. 1-5.

19. Glen Dealy, "The Tradition of Monistic Democracy in Latin America," in Howard J. Wiarda, ed., *Latin America: The Distinct Tradition* (Amherst: University of Massachusetts Press, 1974), pp. 71-103.

20. For a good overview of this period, see Edwin Lieuwen, *Generals vs. Presidents: Neo-Militarism in Latin America* (New York: Praeger, 1964).

21. Robert Alexander, "Caudillos, Coronels and Political Bossism in Latin America," in Thomas V. DiBacco, ed., *Presidential Power in Latin American Politics* (New York: Praeger, 1977), pp. 7–18.

22. See Robert Crassweller, *Peron: The Enigma of Argentina* (New York: W. W. Norton, 1987) and John W. F. Dulles, *Vargas of Brazil* (Austin: University of Texas Press, 1967).

23. Tad Szulc, "Types and Significance of Recent Latin American Dictators," in Robert Tomasek, ed., *Latin American Politics* (Garden City, NJ: Doubleday, 1969), pp. 41–55.

24. Robert Scott, *Mexican Government in Transition* (Urbana: University of Illinois Press, 1959), pp. 162–176.

25. See Peter H. Smith, *Labyrinths of Power: Political Recruitment in Twentieth Century Mexico* (Princeton, NJ: Princeton University Press, 1979) and Daniel C. Levy and Gabriel Szekely, *Mexico: Paradoxes of Stability and Change* (Boulder, CO: Westview Press, 1987). See also Roderic A. Camp, *The Making of Government, Political Leaders in Modern Mexico* (Tucson: University of Arizona Press, 1984).

26. John Johnson, *The Military and Society in Latin America* (Stanford, CA: Stanford University Press, 1966), p. 102.

27. See William L. Furlong, "Democratic Political Development and the Alliance for Progress," in Howard J. Wiarda, ed., *The Continuing Struggle for Democracy in Latin America* (Boulder, CO: Westview Press, 1980), pp. 167–184.

28. See Charles Ameringer, *The Democratic Left in Exile* (Miami, FL: University of Miami Press, 1974).

29. Harry Kantor, *Patterns of Politics and Political Systems in Latin America* (Chicago: Rand McNally, 1969), pp. 470–478.

30. See Federico Gil and Charles Parrish, *The Chilean Presidential Election of September 4, 1964* (Washington, DC: Institute for the Comparative Study of Political Systems, 1965).

31. See Robert H. Dix, *Colombia: The Political Dimensions of Change* (New Haven, CT: Yale University Press, 1967).

32. See Henry Wells, *The Modernization of Puerto Rico* (Cambridge, MA: Harvard University Press, 1969).

33. Wayne A. Selcher, "Contradictions, Dilemmas and Actors in Brazil's *Abertura* 1979–1985," in Wayne A Selcher, ed., *Political Liberation in Brazil* (Boulder, CO: Westview Press, 1986), pp. 55–96.

34. See Michael J. Kryzanek, "Political Parties, Opposition Politics and Democracy in Latin America," in Wiarda, *The Continuing Struggle,* pp. 127–145.

35. Robert Wesson, *Democracy in Latin America: Promise and Problems* (Stanford, CA: Hoover Institution Press; New York: Preager, 1982) p. 20.

36. Lee C. Fennel, "Leadership and the Failure of Democracy," in Wiarda, *The Continuing Struggle*, pp. 201–214.

37. Jerome Levinson and Juan de Onis, *The Alliance That Lost Its Way* (Chicago: Quadrangle Books, 1972), pp. 85–86, 88–91.

38. Ameringer, *The Democratic Left in Exile*, pp. 298–299.

39. Richard M. Morse, "The Heritage of Latin America," in Wiarda, *Latin America: The Distinct Tradition*, pp. 25–69.

40. James D. Cockroft, *Neighbors in Turmoil: Latin America* (New York: Harper and Row, 1989), pp. 83–86.

41. See Richard Millett, *Guardians of the Dynasty* (Maryknoll, NY: Orbis Press, 1977).

42. See Jaime Suchlicki, *Cuba: From Colombus to Castro* 2d ed., rev. (Washington, DC: Pergammon Brassey's, 1986).

43. See Herbert Matthews, *Revolution in Cuba* (New York: Charles Scribner, 1975).

44. See Richard Gott, *Guerrilla Movements in Latin America* (Garden City, NJ: Doubleday, 1971).

45. See James Kohl and John Litt, *Urban Guerrilla Warfare* (Cambridge, MA: MIT Press, 1974).

46. Charles Anderson, *Politics and Economic Change in Latin America* (New York: Van Nostrand, 1968), p. 104.

2

LATIN AMERICAN LEADERSHIP AND U.S. POLICY: THE PURSUIT OF INTERESTS

Why did you not start press campaigns against Somoza, why did you not invade Venezuela when Pérez Jímenez was in power, why did you support Trujillo for 30 years, why have you not declared yourselves against Stroessner? What do you want us to think when you have supported and still support regimes of corruption and crime?
— Carlos Fuentes

The interaction between Latin American leaders and the United States has often been disappointing. The vast gulf that separates the North Americans from the Latin Americans is reflected in the ways leaders from both sides of the border express the frustrations of dealing with their counterparts. Latin American leaders bemoan the fact that the North Americans do not understand them and fail to provide them with the kind of support that will strengthen their political positions. U.S. officials from presidents to ambassadors to members of Congress seem regularly distressed that their relations with Latin American leaders are tense and filled with an undercurrent of animosity. The Latin American leaders accuse us of arrogance and insensitivity; we respond in kind by pointing to the corruption and malfeasance that stunts economic growth in the region. Although both these perceptions have some foundation, they nevertheless do little to bridge the gap between two neighbors.[1]

A key reason for the division between Latin American leaders and the United States is that Washington policymakers have traditionally expected heads of governments in the hemisphere to advance our interests. The use of friendly leaders to achieve foreign policy objectives is certainly not a new strategy, but in Latin America it has become one of the principal bedrocks of our involvement. This reliance on Latin American leaders as "advance men" of U.S. foreign policy paving the way for our interests has led to some unfortunate results. U.S. presidents, for example, have developed unrealistic expectations about what Latin American leaders are capable of achieving while in office and are exasperated when our policies fail to turn out properly.[2] Moreover, the United States has not fully appreciated the internal political dangers that face Latin American leaders who attempt to balance U.S. interests with their own national interests. U.S. policymakers often forget that Latin American leaders regularly risk public censure for even appearing subservient to U.S. interests.

Not surprisingly, when our interests were threatened and a particular leader was willing to protect those interests, the United States could be counted on to heap praise and economic assistance on a head of state we previously ignored or quietly berated.[3] But take away the threat to our interests and the United States often slipped into the pattern of treating Latin American leaders as petulant schoolchildren whose friendship had to be maintained despite the fact that their behavior annoyed us.[4] In too few instances was the relationship between the United States and a Latin American leader based on respect and admiration and a desire to work cooperatively from a basis of equality.

This natural antipathy between the Latin American leaders and the United States hides the fact that both sides need each other. Latin American leaders have come to depend on the United States to bolster their sagging economies, to support their claims of legitimacy, to limit the potential of their adversaries, to help them remain in power, and on occasion to provide them with a safe haven should they be unceremoniously thrown out of power. For its part the United States has shown that the implementation of its foreign policy in the Western Hemisphere is dependent on leaders who are willing to cooperate with Washington and take public policy positions that protect our vital interests.

Because this conflict between what Latin American leaders want and need and what the United States wants and needs is at the core of the relationship, it is necessary to expand upon the theme of how national interests and government leadership intersect. Thus in this chapter I concentrate on defining what U.S. objectives have been in Latin America over time and then explore how the attainment of those objectives has led to the development of a range of relationships and support systems with leaders in the region.

PROTECTING OUR "SOFT UNDERBELLY"

Ever since the announcement of the Monroe Doctrine in 1823 the United States has made clear its concern over the encroachment of foreign powers in what we considered our sphere of interest. Despite the fact that the Monroe Doctrine was for its first seventy-five years either unenforceable or ignored by other powers operating in the hemisphere, the principle that the United States was willing to protect the region closest to its borders from external threats became the foundation of our relationship with Latin America. Latin American countries welcomed the doctrine as a sign of mutual cooperation in the defense of the hemisphere. But from the perspective of the United States, protecting the region from foreign powers was an insurance policy against any direct threats to our security.[5]

With the onset of the twentieth century and the development of the United States as a world power, presidents became more concerned about foreign encroachment in the hemisphere. The Caribbean and Central America were transformed into strategic outposts for the United States as presidents from Theodore Roosevelt through Woodrow Wilson worried that this so-called soft underbelly could pose a danger to our dominance in the region.[6] Throughout this period the United States relied heavily on Latin American leaders to ensure that its efforts at protecting the hemisphere from external threats were supported and that individual countries cooperated in the fight against foreign intervention. The United States not only fostered the ascension to power of leaders who agreed with our objectives in the region but sought to remove or weaken those leaders who openly developed ties with foreign powers we felt were a danger to U.S. preeminence in the hemisphere. Theodore Roosevelt strong-armed the naming of Frenchman Philippe Bunau-Varilla as Panamanian ambassador to the United States in order to guarantee Colombian compliance on the Panama Canal Treaty; U.S. presidents during the so-called Dollar Diplomacy era frequently sought to influence leadership transition in the Dominican Republic, Nicaragua, and Haiti as a way of ensuring that foreign debts were paid and that foreign economic influences would not overshadow those of the United States; and Calvin Coolidge justified the deployment of marines in Nicaragua in 1927 in support of Conservative leader Adolfo Díaz as necessary to protect the isthmus from what he termed foreign (German) infiltration.[7]

The practice of U.S. presidents intervening in the leadership selection and transition process in Latin America in order to ensure our security interests became most pronounced after World War II when the fear of Communist expansionism consumed Washington. The United States praised Latin American leaders who were "bulwarks against communism" and cemented the relationship with generous foreign assistance programs, favorable trade deals, and always plenty of military aid. Trujillo in the Dominican Republic, Somoza in Nicaragua, Carlos Castillo Armas in Guatemala, Batista in Cuba, Pérez Jímenez in Venezuela, and Duvalier in Haiti were actively courted by the United States despite the fact that these leaders had little base of popular support and maintained themselves in power through cruel repression and widescale corruption.[8] Trujillo, for example, was praised on the floor of Congress as "on the side of God and Christianity"; Pérez Jímenez was given the Order of Merit by a grateful President Eisenhower.[9] These tyrants recognized early on that regular pronouncements castigating communism along with vigorous pursuit of alleged leftists would ensure that the U.S. aid, trade, and investment pipeline remained open. Leaders like Trujillo and Somoza became masters of playing the "anti-Communist game" and reaping the rewards from an appreciative United States.

When Latin American leaders followed paths that were deemed dangerous to hemispheric security, the United States did not hesitate to develop strategies to replace them. The covert operation in Guatemala to unseat the leftist government of Jácobo Arbenz in 1954 became an early model of CIA destabilization. The covert support of the counterrevolutionary army of Colonel Carlos Castillo Armas (trained in Somoza's Nicaragua) revealed the extent to which the United States would go to bring down governments that sought to change the existing power balance in the region.[10]

The preoccupation with national security and Latin American leaders who threatened that security reached its zenith with the arrival of Fidel Castro on the scene. The plans to remove Castro and put an end to his alliance with the Soviets are now legendary, from the failed Bay of Pigs invasion to the outrageous clandestine efforts to assassinate the Cuban leader. Removing Castro became akin to an obsession for the United States, especially as a result of the Cuban missile crisis and the prospect of a Soviet challenge to our security a mere one hundred miles from Florida. Castro, however, proved to be a wily adversary as he was able to solidify his position in power and continue to annoy U.S. political leaders with his blatant support for Marxist revolution.[11]

The failure of the anti-Castro campaign did not stop U.S. presidents from connecting the pursuit of national security with the development of close ties to Latin American leaders. As revolution spread throughout the hemisphere and Soviet influence increased, the United States entered a new era of support for military governments and tacit acceptance of their programs to stem the tide of left-wing politics. Although presidents Richard Nixon, Gerald Ford, and Ronald Reagan were far more conscious of the negative image that dictatorships engender, they nevertheless worked closely with the generals in countries like Argentina, Brazil, and Chile and promised that "quiet diplomacy" would smooth out the harsh edges of authoritarian rule.[12]

Ronald Reagan took the traditional U.S. concern with linking Latin American leaders with our security interests further than ever before with his order to invade Grenada to put an end to the leftist New Jewel Movement and his relentless efforts to make the Nicaraguan Sandinistas and their leader Daniel Ortega (in the words of Reagan) "say uncle." Reagan's destabilization campaign against Ortega and the Sandinistas made it clear that the United States saw the Nicaraguan revolution as a direct threat to the security of the United States. The president on a number of occasions suggested that allowing the revolution in Central America to continue would eventually create a series of falling dominoes ending on our southern border with Mexico.[13]

Throughout its relationship with the Latin American republics, the United States has linked its pursuit of national security with support for authoritarian leaders. Despite the criticism that accompanied these alliances, the United States has infrequently looked to democratic leaders in order to protect our "soft underbelly." Democratic leaders were often viewed as too weak and too willing to compromise in the face of social pressures for radical change. Protecting our southern border thus was placed in the hands of petty dictators, political schemers, and the more modern generals. These supporters of U.S. security interests were in many ways successful in maintaining U.S. control in the hemisphere, but the manner in which they ruled and the dependent ties they established with the United States sowed the seeds of revolution and Marxist influence.

EXPANDING OUR ECONOMIC HORIZONS

The protection of our borders and the retention of our supremacy in the hemisphere are primarily defensive in nature, but the United States has also pursued policies that sought to expand our influence and enhance our power. Since the early days of U.S. relations with Latin America, presidents and foreign policy officials have recognized the vast commercial potential of the region. Staple agricultural products, essential mineral deposits, and vast business opportunities made Latin America a vital segment of U.S. corporate profit strategy. The term *sphere of influence* took on real meaning when it was used to describe the importance of Latin America to our national interests. As political scientist Edward Williams states, "the entire history of inter-American relations is explained by the desire of the United States to protect and expand its economic interest in Latin America."[14]

Building an economic bridge to Latin America was made possible because the United States worked aggressively to ensure that political leaders in the region would be receptive to our commerical interests. U.S. ambassadors and special emmisaries were sent to Latin America with the expressed mission to develop friendly ties with heads of state no matter how far they may have strayed from our vision of good government or how weak their administrative skills may have been. As one observer of the relationship between foreign business interests and Latin American leaders states, "Affairs are expedited if you deal with one man. You don't have to wait until things are approved by a congress. To a foreign country operating in Latin

America it is of primary importance to have a stable government."[15] The United States learned this basic rule of Latin American politics well and proceeded to seek out leaders who could provide stability and "expedite" deals.

In many instances Latin American leaders, desperate for capital, expertise, and all that was modern, welcomed the U.S. government and the businesspeople who followed. But although U.S. business brought modernity to Latin America in exchange for access to the vast resources and potential of the region, too often the presence of U.S. business interests led to greater indebtedness, mismanagement, and dependence. Many Latin American countries quickly developed into societies where foreign businesses became enormously influential in terms of providing jobs, foreign currency, and infrastructure. Latin American leaders found themselves forced to balance internal political interests with the new external interests. For those leaders who could not balance these interests, the prospects of being replaced by nationalists, revolutionaries, or those who merely wanted access to the benefits of foreign business deals became all too real.

The examples of Latin American leaders cooperating with U.S. business interests and thereby advancing U.S. political interests are many. The Mexican dictator Porfirio Díaz based his modernizing program on close ties with the capitalist barons of his era. Rockefeller oil, Hearst cattle and land, and Guggenheim mineral interests spread throughout Mexico during Díaz's regime. After years of instability in Mexico and numerous border skirmishes, the United States valued the order imposed by Díaz and his willingness to allow U.S. businesses to control vital Mexican land and resources.[16]

In the post–World War II period the relationship between Cuba's Fulgencio Batista and U.S. sugar, tourist, and gambling interests was the foundation of close ties between these two countries. Batista became the model of leadership dependency in Latin America as he frequently bowed to pressure from the Eisenhower administration and from organized crime figures with business ventures in Cuba. In neighboring Puerto Rico the relationship between leaders and U.S. economic interests took a different turn as that island's most recognized political figure, Luis Muñoz Marín, instituted a series of programs designed to encourage U.S. factories to come to the commonwealth and invest in manufacturing. The 1947 Puerto Rican Industrial Incentives Act allowed U.S. industries to receive exemptions from taxes for extended periods of time. Muñoz Marín was hailed in the United States for his economic programs and for recognizing the importance of promoting private-sector growth strategies.[17]

The rise of Castro's revolution and the growing nationalistic spirit in Latin America put a damper on regional leaders' desire to openly cooperate with the United States or appear to advance U.S. interests. Nevertheless, the United States still had friends in the hemisphere and cultivated those friendships. After the 1965 revolution in the Dominican Republic the United States showered President Joaquín Balaguer with over $400 million in economic aid. In return Balaguer instituted policies that brought U.S. sugar and manufacturing interests to the country. The Central American countries, particularly Somoza's Nicaragua, continued to trade almost exclusively with the United States and allowed major banana, cocoa, cotton, and sugar interests to play a key role in their economies. And in Brazil the generals who stripped João Goulart of power relied heavily on U.S. capital and technology in order to advance their push for industrialization and modernization.

As Latin American leaders faced greater pressures for lessening the reliance on U.S. trade and investment, there were more instances of reaction to the U.S. business presence in the hemisphere. Lázaro Cárdenas of Mexico was the first Latin American leader to challenge the economic power of the United States when he nationalized the Rockefeller oil interests in 1936. Despite the protestations of the oil companies over proper compensation for their property, the Roosevelt administration was determined to solve the dispute and show Latin America that indeed the United States was a good neighbor. Cárdenas's eventual victory in the nationalization controversy earned him the respect of his people and set the stage for future battles over national rights to natural resources.[18]

Other successful nationalizations of U.S. business interests were the Peruvian takeover of the International Petroleum Company (IPC) oil interests in 1969 and the Venezuelan oil nationalization in 1976. Peruvian president Fernando Belaúnde faced intense pressure from the Nixon administration including the invoking of the Hickenlooper amendment, which denied aid to those countries nationalizing U.S. property. Belaúnde was eventually pushed out of power in favor of the military, and the Nixon administration was criticized for weakening the political base of a recognized democratic leader by withholding aid. Nevertheless, the United States continued the economic boycott until the dispute was settled in 1972 when the military successors to Belaúnde signed an agreement with the IPC.[19] In Venezuela, however, President Andrés Pérez presided over the transfer of the $5 billion oil industry to the nation without incident and set the stage for a period of economic expansion and modernization that moved Venezuela to the frontlines of Latin American development.

The ability of Latin American leaders to successfully negotiate with the United States over property rights and compensation has had its limitations. Arbenz's land-reform program in Guatemala brought out United Fruit and the CIA, Castro's expropriation of nearly $2 billion in U.S. business paved the way for the Bay of Pigs, and Salvador Allende's nationalization of U.S. copper interests brought on aid, loan, and trade cutbacks from the Nixon administration. Challenging the business interests of the United States has often meant that Latin American leaders were put at risk and that the viability of their economies was threatened by a full range of trade, aid, loan, and investment weapons.

One of the ironies of U.S. economic expansion in Latin America is that after all that effort to ensure a receptive climate for our business interests, this country is slowly but surely redefining its commercial presence in the hemisphere. Long-standing trade patterns are being adjusted, investment is moving elsewhere, aid commitments have been sharply reduced, and new economic powers are entering the region. The United States continues to be the foremost economic power in Latin America, but our presence in the region is being downgraded and constantly reevaluated.[20] Moreover, the Latin Americans are demanding that the United States conduct its business from within a new set of guidelines and with new watchwords. *Joint venture* and *trade access* have now become the key phrases of economic relations between the United States and the Latin American nation-states.

The Latin American leaders of today recognize the changing business relationship and also the tentativeness of the U.S. position in the region. As a result these leaders have become bolder in their demands, more outspoken in their criticism, and more stubborn in their negotiations. Pérez of Venezuela has led the fight to create a debt moratorium and Salinas of Mexico has fought vigorously to develop better trade and debt arrangements with the Bush administration. In many ways the development of a stronger Latin American leader can be traced to the changed economic relationship with the United States. As this country has weakened in terms of its economic control in Latin America, the Latin American leaders have begun to assert themselves.

KEEPING "GOOD" LEADERS IN POWER

No foreign policy objective of the United States in Latin America has caused as much controversy as our constant concern that governments in the region remain stable. U.S. presidents and policymakers have been regularly castigated in Latin America for interfering in the internal affairs of neighboring countries in the name of political stability. What is more, the same Latin Americans are appalled that when the United States has interfered in the name of stability it has usually been to prop up a leader or a regime that is viewed as antithetical to the aspirations of the people and the region. Rather than accompany the forces of social and political change in Latin America, the United States is viewed as a stubborn proponent of the status quo and a bothersome meddler in the politics of leadership transition.[21]

Although the Latin Americans fume over our concern with leadership stability and our inability to accept the unpredictability of their political process, the United States has remained steadfast in its commitment to ensure that those nations in its sphere of influence do not sink into a pattern of coup d'états, assassinations, general strikes, palace revolts, and guerrilla warfare that disrupt the economy, endanger U.S. personnel and property, and create a climate of uncertainty. As a result the United States has often, in the words of Howard Wiarda, supported "whatever government friendly to our interests happened to be in power, while also keeping lines of communications open to the moderate opposition. Maintaining stability meant not necessarily defending the status quo but included supporting change and reform to head off the possibility of instability arising from popular dissatisfaction."[22]

To the United States "good" government in Latin America has never been defined in absolute terms as a reflection of the principles we view as essential. "Good" government and "good" leaders have rather been evaluated in a much broader context and according to a vastly different set of standards. These differing standards have led U.S. presidents like Franklin Roosevelt to exclaim that Anastasio Somoza was an S.O.B. but our S.O.B. and years later Jimmy Carter to write a complimentary letter to Somoza's son, Anastasio, Jr., praising his record on human rights in the face of massive opposition to his dictatorial rule.[23] Numerous other examples of U.S. support for leaders who headed unpopular or corrupt governments have fostered the image that the U.S. commitment to democratic governance, human rights, and the rule of law is so weak that it is easily compromised when faced with the prospect of political instability.

The fact that we have supported dictators like Somoza, Trujillo, and Batista and encouraged the generals in Argentina, Brazil, and Chile must be balanced with the considerable efforts on the part of certain presidential administrations to bring what we viewed as "good" government and "good" leaders to the region. In some instances, as during the presidency of Woodrow Wilson, the United States took it upon itself to teach "good" government and to bring "good" leaders into power. We therefore intervened in the Dominican Republic, Cuba, Nicaragua, Haiti, and many of the other Central American republics to bring stability and institute political, governmental, and administrative reforms.[24]

Although it is easy to see this interference as the height of U.S. arrogance and designed to merely ensure an environment conducive to U.S. business interests, many of the military and civilian representatives sent to these countries to oversee the reforms were genuinely concerned about assisting the local leaders in achieving their goals of stability and democracy. The record of this interventionist era in terms of democratic reform and modernization is a matter of dispute, splitting the advocates of nationalistic self-determination and the supporters of North American development, but the final analysis may rest upon the fact that once the United States left these countries they quickly fell into a cycle of instability or were transformed into military dictatorships with tacit approval from Washington.[25]

The administration of John Kennedy and the introduction of his Alliance of Progress program may very well go down in the history of inter-American relations as the golden age of U.S. support for "good" government and "good" leaders. During this period the

United States took the lead in advocating government reform and
social change and worked to disassociate this country from its ties
to authoritarian regimes. Although in hindsight the push for reform
and change in Latin America by the Kennedy administration was
more a nervous reaction to the popularity and rhetoric of Fidel
Castro, it was nevertheless wholeheartedly supported by the people
and the leaders in the hemisphere. President Kennedy became a
revered hero in the region and the United States was viewed as
having turned the corner on its fixation with stability at any cost.

The brevity of the democratic reform era, the speed with which
Latin America returned to authoritarianism, and the willingness of
the United States to downplay its commitment to constitutional rule
and civilian leadership proved to many in the hemisphere that the
lure of stability over the uncertainty of change was too strong. The
seven-month rule of social democrat Juan Bosch in the Dominican
Republic in 1962 was used by critics of the United States as a vivid
example of our failure to support constitutionally elected civilian
politicians. Bosch's ascendancy to the presidency was heralded by
the Kennedy administration, but his ouster by the generals met with
only weak protests. State Department officials complained of Bosch's
leadership deficiencies and his leftist policies but failed to bemoan
the departure of a leader who represented what was supposed to be
a solid trend toward reform and change.[26]

U.S. concern for the advancement of governments and leaders
that mirrored what we viewed as "good" was generally absent during
the Vietnam War era and did not return until President Jimmy
Carter's presidency. Carter's commitment to establishing human rights
as a central part of U.S. foreign policy once again brought the issue
of stability versus change to the front burner of U.S.-Latin American
relations. The linking of U.S. economic assistance to improving
climates of human rights in Latin America bolstered the spirits of
democratic leaders and advocates of social reform who were targets
of military rule.[27]

Critics of the Carter policy complained that injecting human
rights into the foreign policy matrix antagonized allies in the region
and led authoritarian leaders to resist more vigorously attempts to
interfere in matters they considered internal. President Carter and
the advocates of human rights he appointed to key positions, such
as U.N. Secretary Andrew Young, responded to the criticism by

emphasizing that the United States had an obligation to ensure that governments in the hemisphere protected human life and did not penalize political and social leaders for advocating reform policies.[28] In the end the debate over human rights and the fate of repressive regimes was settled by the election of Ronald Reagan, who immediately made distinctions between Communist totalitarians and third world authoritarians and played down human-rights abuses such as the murder of four U.S. nuns in El Salvador.[29]

Although the administration of Ronald Reagan was primarily interested in facing up to Communist expansionism in the hemisphere and more willing to deal with repressive regimes through quiet diplomacy, it is important to stress that the United States during the 1980s came to the realization that support for democratic leaders and democratic practice was critical to the preservation of our security interests. Faced with the growing threat of Marxist revolution in Central America, the Reagan administration promoted a program of democratic development that had as its centerpiece the election of reform-minded civilian leaders. Hundreds of millions of dollars was spent in El Salvador, Honduras, and Guatemala to support democracy and democratic presidents and to show the region and the world that the United States now recognized the importance of democratic stability in the fight against leftist revolution. Many were skeptical of this newfound commitment to democratic stability of the Reagan administration, but Central American politicians were nonetheless grateful that the United States had finally decided to put as much money into propping up democrats as it had into propping up dictators.[30]

Involving a country with enormous resources and power in the internal affairs of its neighbors in order to advance a set of foreign policy objectives is always destined to create ill will. But from the Latin American perspective the history of U.S. efforts to achieve political stability in the region has suffered from an inability to deal with the "messiness" that accompanies social change. Much of the controversy surrounding our pursuit of political stability in the region could have been avoided if presidents and policymakers had a greater degree of confidence in the democratic process in Latin America and could not be intimidated by the conflict engendered by social change. As James Kurth pointedly states, "genuine political stability in Latin America . . . can only be achieved by governments that

enjoy popular support and that are moving toward broadly shared
political and economic development. . . . This will entail, from time
to time, some U.S. acceptance of short-term political instability in
order to achieve a greater long-term stability."[31]

WORKING TO DESTABILIZE "BAD" LEADERS

U.S. interests in Latin America have generally been based on
the premise that developing friendly relations with governments and
particularly leaders would ensure that our concerns over security,
economic opportunity, and stability were fulfilled. But as the socioeconomic climate in Latin America changed, especially after World
War II, and the twin specters of revolution and nationalism were
embraced throughout the hemisphere, the United States was forced
to deal with leaders and regimes that worked against our interests.
Faced with the prospect that Latin America might not remain solidly
in our sphere of influence, the United States had to adjust its strategy
to encompass the fact that there were, for want of a better word,
"bad" leaders in the region that had to be replaced or at least
weakened.

The campaigns waged by the United States against unfriendly
leaders varied widely depending on the perceived threat to U.S.
interests and the level of commitment by the president or the secretary
of state. The arrogance of President Theodore Roosevelt as he railed
against the Colombian leaders (calling them jackrabbits) for their
failure to approve his policies for the Panama Canal and the pious
protestations of Woodrow Wilson against the Mexican leader Vic-
toriano Huerta for buying arms from the Germans are often cited
as examples of U.S. officials' scant patience with Latin American
leaders who refused to cooperate or worked against our interests.
In both these incidents U.S. presidents acted to create the circumstances whereby anti-U.S. leaders were either pressured to assent to
our requests or forced to accept the consequences of our power.

The interventions of the United States during the Big Stick
and Dollar Diplomacy eras set the tone for future campaigns to rid
the hemisphere of "bad" leaders heading governments that challenged
the pursuit of U.S. political and economic objectives. But although
the United States built its reputation during the Roosevelt and

Wilson presidencies as willing to threaten or weaken leaders who worked against our interests, it was not until the cold war and the victory of Castro's revolution that Washington began to fashion aggressive policies designed to rid the region of leaders who adhered to ideologies or development schemes viewed as dangerous to hemispheric security and U.S. hegemony.

The terms *covert war, counterinsurgency,* and *destabilization* entered the lexicon of U.S.–Latin American relations as Washington began to develop strategies to deal with the rise of leaders and regimes that openly threatened U.S. economic and security interests. Social revolution was linked with Communist expansionism and Latin American leaders who advocated radical or even quickened change were viewed as working to undermine the so-called special relationship that had developed between North and South America.[32] Defining who was an acceptable leader in terms of U.S. interests and who was an undesirable became more difficult. The United States faced a leadership crisis in the hemisphere, as only the harsh generals seemed willing to hold views comparable to those of U.S. policymakers.

Because the process of building stable democratic leadership systems was painstakingly long and filled with frustrations and the alternative of working with revolutionary leaders simply out of the question, the United States chose to rely on CIA-funded clandestine operations, huge appropriations to bolster Latin American police forces and antiguerrilla military units, and elaborate schemes to wreck Latin American revolutions. Although the full range of government operations in revolutionary countries became targets of U.S. policy, Latin American revolutionary leaders received special attention. It was during this period that Thomas Mann, President Lyndon Johnson's assistant secretary for inter-American affairs, enunciated a new doctrine (often called the Mann Doctrine) that suggested that the United States would no longer oppose military coups and rightist dictatorships if those changes were the result of moves to unseat procommunist leaders.[33]

From this kind of mind-set the United States during the late 1960s and into the 1970s worked to remove revolutionary leaders from the Latin American political scene. The CIA operation to capture Che Guevarra in Bolivia, the expanded sabotage and assassination campaigns against Castro, the training and support given the government of Uruguay in its effort to stop the Tupamaro urban guerrillas, and the much-discussed programs of the Nixon administration to convince Chilean military leaders and opposition politicians to stage a coup against Marxist president Salvador Allende replaced democratic institution-building, economic development, and social reform as the core of U.S. policy in Latin America.[34] Fear of revolution and revolutionary leadership was so great that Presidents Johnson and Nixon received extensive support from Congress for their Latin American counterrevolutionary policies.

A counterrevolutionary policy so vigorously applied in a region where radical change and bold leadership were welcomed by the vast majority of the people was destined to create political problems for the United States. Although the United States got most of what it wanted in terms of dismantling revolutionary leadership in Latin America during the 1970s (all except that of the ever-cunning Fidel Castro), this country became so closely associated with supporting stability over change that it lost contact with a new generation of regional leaders. As Latin American society gradually emerged from years of bureaucratic-authoritarian rule, U.S. policymakers had to start from ground zero to develop ties with a new leadership corps. Moreover, the postauthoritarian civilian leaders were less receptive to U.S. overtures and suspicious of our promises of cooperation, remembering how this country failed to support liberal democrats and conspired against the revolutionaries.

Despite the reservations of some civilian leaders in Latin America, President Reagan was convinced of the need to send a clear signal to revolutionary governments. Reagan's invasion of Grenada, his policies toward the Sandinistas in Nicaragua, and his continued refusal to deal with Fidel Castro expanded the pressure on leftist governments. Although some may say that the Reagan years contributed to the intensification of revolutionary activity in Latin America, during Ronald Reagan's presidency the ability of revolutionary movements to score military successes was substantially weakened. U.S. military assistance and training programs served as modern containment strategies that eventually wore the left down and strengthened the resolve of civilian governments.

When George Bush took office in 1989 he benefited from the destabilizing campaigns of his predecessor and the growing legitimacy of democratic reform leadership in the region. Nevertheless, President

Bush also added a page to the history of U.S. attacks against "bad" Latin American leaders. The December 1989 invasion of Panama to remove General Manuel Noriega from power was clearly a personal response from the president of the United States to the blatant U.S.-bashing and drug-smuggling of the Panamanian dictator. Although the invasion achieved its short-term goals of removing Noriega and replacing him with an elected president, the weakness of the new government, the continuation of the drug network in the country, and the long, drawn-out effort to bring the Panamanian dictator to trial showed that going after "bad" leaders often brings limited change. But from the Bush administration's perspective, the invasion was defined as a "success" if for no other reason than that we got someone out of power who took joy in challenging our power.

THE MORE THINGS CHANGE . . .

U.S. interests in Latin America have been a model of consistency. Security, opportunity, and stability have become the watchwords used to define how we see the region and what kind of political environment we hope will develop there. The expectations that we have for Latin America have also been applied to the manner in which we gauge Latin American political leadership. U.S. presidents and foreign policy officials have over the years worked best with those Latin American leaders whose vision of what was good for their country coincided with our own. The pursuit of national interests by supporting leaders who share those interests can certainly be justified, but at the same time building relationships on the basis of goals that were often one-sided and viewed with suspicion and anger throughout the region can be seen as laying the groundwork for opposition and revolution. What had always been missing from U.S. relations with Latin America was a commitment to develop a mutuality of interests and a respect for Latin American leaders who pursue interests that do not mesh with our own.

During those eras in U.S.-Latin American relations when presidential administrations added new goals to the foreign policy agenda and made bold moves to support leaders who challenged the existing rules of hemispheric behavior, Latin America became invigorated with the prospect that Washington was finally attempting to base its regional policy on a mutuality of interests. The Latin Americans have consistently pushed for policies based on shared responsibilities, equitable agreements, and respect for national integrity. Unfortunately, those eras when the United States began to approach the Latin American vision of mutuality of interests (notably Kennedy's Alliance for Progress and Carter's human-rights commitment) were short-lived or were criticized as impractical and unwise.

The practice of the United States holding firm to the interests of security, opportunity, and stability has weathered the storm of criticism from Latin America, but that does not mean that the principle of mutuality of interests has retreated to the background or that this country has not been forced to accept some modifications in its definition of national interest. If change has come to the area of U.S. interests in Latin America, it is because leaders in the region have been determined to move Washington away from the reliance on old formulas. The Latin American leaders of today are demanding that the United States include them in the process of protecting the hemisphere and are aggressively advancing policies that address the issues of economic and financial inequality between North and South America. Most importantly, they are demanding that the United States respect their politics and avoid seeing radical change and social unrest as threats to "normalcy."[35]

Progress toward the creation of a mutuality of interests between the United States and Latin America is by no means complete. In fact, with every victory there has usually been an accompanying defeat. The United States will not move easily from being the dominant force in the region to becoming an equal partner willing to make concessions on interests that have been the bedrock of this relationship since the days of the Monroe Doctrine. But what may happen is that Latin American leaders, strengthened by their victories in starting the peace process in Central America, negotiating debt agreements, and developing more equitable trade arrangements, will continue to press the United States to expand its interest agenda once again. This time the Latin American leaders will demand that the United States hold to its commitments on human rights, democratization, social reform, and acceptance of change and not reject these goals in the name of security, opportunity, and stability.

NOTES

1. Carlos Rangel, in his book *The Latin Americans and Their Love-Hate Relationship With the United States* (New York: Harcourt, Brace, Jovanovich, 1977) expands upon the theme of tension between North and South America.

2. Some excellent anecdotal discussions of U.S. presidents and their outspoken views on Latin America can be found in George Black, *The Good Neighbor: How the United States Wrote the History of Central America and the Caribbean* (New York: Pantheon, 1989).

3. A good case study of such a relationship can be found in Pope Atkins and Larman Wilson, *The United States and the Trujillo Regime* (New Brunswick, NJ: Rutgers University Press, 1972).

4. Many analysts of U.S.-Latin American relations believe that the era of benign neglect began with the mission of Nelson Rockefeller to Latin America and the subsequent publishing of his findings, which deemphasized the large public role of the United States in the region. See *The Rockefeller Report on the Americas: The Official Report of a U.S. Presidential Mission for the Western Hemisphere* (Chicago: Quadrangle Books, 1969).

5. As the diplomatic historian Thomas Bailey states, "It is possible—though by no means probable—that there would be somewhat more European territory in the Americas today if the Monroe Doctrine, or some similar doctrine, had not been proclaimed. It became an increasingly potent stick behind the door." Thomas Bailey, *A Diplomatic History of the American People* (New York: Appleton-Century Crofts, 1964), p. 190.

6. Much of the strategic thinking concerning the Caribbean comes from Admiral Alfred Thayer Mahan. For a discussion of Mahan's writings on the Caribbean see G. Pope Atkins, *Latin America in the International Political System* (New York: Free Press, 1977), pp. 248-249.

7. See Hans Schmidt, *The United States Occupation of Haiti 1915-1934* (New Brunswick, NJ: Rutgers University Press, 1971), and Neill MacCauley, *The Sandino Affair* (Chicago: Quadrangle Books, 1967).

8. See Jan Knippers Black, *Sentinels of Empire: The United States and Latin American Militarism* (New York: Greenwood Press, 1986).

9. As quoted in Edward J. Williams, *The Political Themes of Inter-American Relations* (Belmont, CA: Duxbury Press, 1971), p. 102.

10. The most complete analysis of the U.S. role in the overthrow of the Arbenz government can be found in Stephen Schlesinger and Stephen Kinzer, *Bitter Fruit: The Untold Story of the American Coup in Guatemala* (New York: Doubleday, 1982).

11. Jorge Dominguez, in his book *To Make A World Safe for Revolution: Cuba's Foreign Policy* (Cambridge, MA: Harvard University Press, 1989) gives a balanced and thorough discussion of U.S. policy toward Castro from the missile crisis into the 1980s, pp. 34–60.

12. Michael J. Francis, "United States Policy Toward Latin America During the Kissinger Years," in John D. Martz, ed., *United States Policy in Latin America, A Quarter Century of Crisis and Change, 1961–1986* (Lincoln: University of Nebraska Press, 1988), pp. 28–60.

13. See, for example, President Reagan's address to a joint session of Congress on April 27, 1983. For the full text, see *State Department Bulletin*, June 1983.

14. Williams, *The Political Themes of Inter-American Relations*, p. 9.

15. Renato Poblete, S.J., "The Phenomenon of Dictatorship," in John J. Considine, *Social Revolution in the New Latin America* (South Bend, IN: Fide Press, 1965), p. 52.

16. See Stanley R. Ross, "The Peace of Porfirio," in Stanley R. Ross, ed., *Is the Mexican Revolution Dead?* (New York: Knopf, 1966), pp. 37–48.

17. Henry Wells, *The Modernization of Puerto Rico* (Cambridge, MA: Harvard University Press, 1969).

18. President Cárdenas praised the Roosevelt administration for its restraint and said that the U.S. action was, "a policy that is winning the affection of many peoples in the world." U.S. Department of State, Press Release 18 (April 2, 1938), pp. 435–436.

19. See Adalberto J. Pinelo, *The Multinational Corporation as a Force in Latin American Politics: A Case Study of the International Petroleum Company in Peru* (New York: Praeger, 1973).

20. See Abraham Lowenthal, "Rediscovering Latin America," *Foreign Affairs* (Fall 1990): 27–41.

21. For an example of such a critique see Sergio Bitar, "Economics and Security: Contradictions in U.S.-Latin American Relations," in Kevin J. Middlebrook and Carlos Rico, eds., *The United States and Latin America in the 1980's* (Pittsburgh, PA: University of Pittsburgh Press, 1986), pp. 591–614.

22. Howard J. Wiarda, "Updating U.S. Strategic Policy: Containment in the Caribbean Basin," in Howard J. Wiarda, *Finding Our Way: Toward Maturity in U.S.-Latin American Relations* (Washington, DC: American Enterprise Institute, 1987), p. 159.

23. For a more complete discussion of this controversial incident see Robert A. Pastor, *Condemned to Repetition: The United States and Nicaragua* (Princeton, NJ: Princeton University Press, 1987), pp. 67–71.

24. One of the best analyses of the impact of U.S. intervention in a Latin American country is Bruce Calder, *The Impact of Intervention: The*

Dominican Republic During the U.S. Occupation of 1916-1924 (Austin: The University of Texas Press, 1984).

25. Calder, however, concludes in his study of the U.S. intervention, "foreign intervention, as practiced by the United States in the Dominican Republic . . . was a policy neither wise nor just, a policy basically unproductive for all concerned." Calder, *The Impact of Intervention*, p. 252.

26. See John Bartlow Martin, *Overtaken By Events: The Dominican Crisis From the Fall of Trujillo to the Civil War* (Garden City, NJ: Doubleday, 1966), pp 547-590, for an insider's view of the U.S. experiment in bringing democracy to the Dominican Republic under Juan Bosch.

27. See Robert A. Pastor, "The Carter Administration and Latin America: A Test of Principle," in Martz, *United States Policy in Latin America*, pp. 61-97.

28. Sandra Vogelgesang, "What Price Principle? U.S. Policy on Human Rights," *Foreign Affairs* (July 1978): 819-841.

29. See, for example, "Communist Interference in El Salvador," U.S. State Department, Bureau of Public Affairs, no. 80, 1981.

30. See my discussion of the impact that El Salvador's President José Napoleón Duarte had on Congress as it debated aid appropriations for his country. Michael J. Kryzanek, *U.S. Latin American Relations*, 2d ed. (New York: Praeger, 1990), pp. 155-156.

31. As quoted in Richard Newfarmer, *From Gunboats to Diplomacy: New U.S. Policies For Latin America* (Baltimore, MD: Johns Hopkins University Press, 1984), p. 13.

32. For a critical view of U.S. counterrevolutionary strategy see Michael Klare and Peter Kornbluh, *Low Intensity Warfare: Counter-Insurgency, Pro-Insurgency and Anti-Terrorism in the Eighties* (New York: Pantheon, 1988).

33. Jerome Levinson and Juan de Onis discuss the Mann Doctrine in "Domininance and Fragmentation in U.S. Latin American Policy," in Julio Cotler and Richard Fagen, eds., *Latin America and the U.S.: The Changing Political Realities* (Stanford, CA: Stanford University Press, 1974), p. 88.

34. See Paul Sigmund, "Crisis Management: Chile and Marxism," in Martz, *United States Policy in Latin America*, pp. 157-174.

35. See Carlos Andrés Pérez, "OAS Opportunities," *Foreign Policy* 80 (Fall 1990): 53-55.

3

MILITARY LEADERSHIP
IN AN ERA OF DEMOCRACY

Not a leaf moves in this country if I am not moving it! I wish to make
this clear. All the economic plans, all the laws pass through the presidency,
because to govern, gentlemen, you have to stay on your toes.
                                            —General Augusto Pinochet

Much has been made of the transition to democracy in Latin
America—the staging of open and fair elections, the rise of civilian
rule, the return to constitutionalism, the reinvigoration of political
parties, and the general recognition that public policy should be
formulated from within the context of popular participation, set
procedures, and political compromise. But although democratic resurgence has occupied center stage in Latin America, there has been
another equally important transition taking place. After controlling
the reins of government power for upward of twenty years in some
countries, the generals have left office and moved back to the barracks.[1]
Authoritarian rule with its emphasis on order, discipline, loyalty,
and what some have described as antipolitics failed to sustain its
early popularity as a check against the Marxist left and as an efficient
system of national modernization.[2] Harsh rule, arbitrary decisionmaking, and failure to deal with the social tensions related to economic
restructuring created a groundswell of opposition to those military
leaders who were once hailed as the solution to the uncertainties
of development.[3]

It is natural, of course, to concentrate on this new democratic
phase in Latin American politics, especially because it appears that
the foundations for maintaining popular rule may be stronger and
more resilient than in the past. Yet the process of democratization

in Latin America should not blind us from examining the changes that have occurred in the ranks of the military. With the generals out of power and in retreat, the Latin American military establishment has been forced to redefine its role in the political system and its relationship to the new leaders that are now controlling the government. Military leaders must not only adjust to life outside the mainstream of national politics but articulate a new agenda of objectives and a new job description. Just as assuming governmental power often initiates a period of introspection and reassessment, so too does retirement from governmental power require self-renewal and a review of past practices.

Besides the transition from authoritarianism to democracy in Latin America, there is also a transition taking place in policymaking circles in the United States concerning how this country intends to work with military leaders and civilian governments with strong military influence. After developing close ties with military leaders during the Johnson, Nixon, and Ford administrations, the United States, for human-rights purposes during the Carter presidency and for both budgetary and democratic governance reasons during the Reagan and Bush presidencies, redirected its relationship toward authoritarian regimes.[4] By the end of the 1980s the United States was foursquare behind the democratic juggernaut and openly critical of military regimes

This shift away from moral and financial support of military leadership in Latin America not only helped strengthen fledgling democracies but contributed to a significant transformation within the officer corps. As has been the case with many governing trends in this region, military reform and redemocratization are the result of both internal changes and external pressures. It is this combination of domestic and foreign influences that holds the key to understanding the way in which military leaders view themselves and their place within the Latin American political arena.

THE LATIN AMERICAN MILITARY: TRANSFORMATION OR HOLDING ACTION

The Latin American military has long defended its role in politics and its responsibilities to the nation. Besides performing the traditional duty of protecting the state from external threats, military leaders have over the years added new duties related to the issues of internal security, economic development, and fiscal management. As a result of assuming these responsibilities, military leaders welcomed the description of their role as "guardians," "builders," "guarantors," and "stabilizers" and felt comfortable with the common interpretation of the armed forces as having a special mission in Latin American society.[5] As an Argentine colonel stated as early as 1926: "The real meaning of national defense is vast and complex; it can be defined by saying that it includes all those activities and security measures necessary to assure the tranquility, prosperity and independence of a nation, as well as rapid victory in case of conflict."[6]

In the modern era, the definition of military responsibility in Latin America has been linked to a number of leadership models designed to legitimate the role of the armed forces in national development. In the 1960s the Latin American military emulated the so-called Nasseristic model of political involvement as it undertook the task of nation-building, social reform, and economic modernization.[7] Later on in the 1970s the bureaucratic-authoritarian model reigned supreme with the military committed to state capitalism, stringent austerity programs, and expanded opportunities for a new entrepreneurial class.[8] The 1980s, however, ushered in a new era in which past models of military leadership were viewed as outdated and unworkable and military heads of state were roundly castigated for their failures and excesses.[9]

As a result, the economic "miracles" that the generals achieved in Brazil, Chile, and Argentina were recast as mere short-term successes, limited to a small segment of the population and maintained through the cruelest forms of control and repression. As countries like Brazil, Chile, and Argentina slipped further and further into recession and social polarization, the military leaders lost not only their power but their legitimacy as performing a special development role in Latin America. Political scientist Gary Wynia sums up the root causes of the decline of military rule when he states: "military authoritarian regimes have yet to create enduring solutions to the problems of political participation, communication between the government and its citizens and political succession. . . . [Military leaders] have a clearer idea of the kind of polity they oppose than what they hope to organize in its place."[10]

With the generals in retreat, their reputation tarnished, and the traditional models of legitimating their role in politics coming under increased scrutiny, the military is today faced with the task of forming a new image and developing a rationale for its continued involvement in the political process. This is an unpleasant task for many military leaders who have enjoyed unquestioned authority, but as civilian leaders settle more securely into their positions of power, a number of signs point to the beginning of a period of adjustment by the military to the power realities of modern-day Latin American politics.

In country after country, high-ranking military officers have turned their attention away from national political leadership and toward a concern with rehabilitating and advancing the institutional interests of the armed forces. Military leaders of the 1970s had come out of their closed societies to run government and administer public policy; the current officer corps is looking inward to protect their budgets, preserve their perquisites, and ensure that civilian presidents do not engage in campaigns to further tarnish their image and weaken their power.[11]

In Argentina the armed forces have shifted their energies from repressive campaigns designed to eradicate leftists to ensuring that newly empowered democratic governments do not extend the hand of justice beyond a limited ciricle of top military officers involved in the "dirty wars." The decision by President Carlos Menem in December 1990 to grant amnesty to former military presidents Jorge Videla and Roberto Viola underscored the success the military was having in reentering the mainstream of Argentine society.[12] In Chile the remnants of Pinochet's ruling military elite are scrambling to control the extent that redemocratization will touch the sinecures they developed during the post-Allende years. The exposure by the Chilean press of a massive bank scheme that resulted in huge losses to depositors has made the scrambling all that more difficult.[13] In Bolivia, Colombia, and Peru military officials are coming under heightened criticism as civiliam politicians and U.S. drug enforcement agents not only question their ability to defeat the private cocaine armies but their involvement in lucrative protection rackets that hinder the drug war. The trial in Miami in December 1990 of former Bolivian interior minister Luis Arce Gómez, dubbed the "minister of cocaine," further reinforced the perception that the Latin American militaries are a key stumbling block to the war on drugs.[14]

Even in countries with a strong military presence and weak civilian leadership such as El Salvador, Guatemala, and Honduras, the military is not immune to the changing nature of politics in this region. Increased retirement and reshuffling of key officers, internal and external pressures for professional reforms, and the uncertainties of funding the large military machine have had a marked effect on the power potential of the armed forces. As Aaron Segal correctly remarks about the travails of the Latin American military, "These are trying times for Latin American military officers and ordinary soldiers. Everywhere, their competence and even integrity is being questioned. At the same time, military budgets—in real terms—are being cut while much of their equipment is becoming obsolete."[15]

What has happened in the Latin America of resurgent democracy is that military leaders have been forced to function not only in a new political environment but required to play by a new set of rules and behavioral standards. The officer corps in many Latin American countries are now expected to be champions of constitutionalism, obedient servants of civilian politicians, unwavering supporters of popular rule, and responsible partners in the process of efficient governance. These new elements of the military job description also come at a time when resources are scarce and the influence of the armed forces on the budget process has been reduced. This combination has made the military into an institution that recognizes the necessity of working with the existing civilian leaders to limit the damage and preserve a measure of power and privilege.

The apparent transformation of military rule has not been smooth or uniform. Military leaders have only grudgingly accepted the new political values and expectations and in some countries have continued their outright control of national politics or dominance of civilian-led governments. In recent years we have seen the Ecuadorian military kidnap the democratically elected president, the Argentine military stage numerous minicoups, the Haitian generals maintain their tight grip on the populace, and the Castro regime continue to function as a military government in the guise of revolutionary fervor. Moreover, the military has gained in stature in countries like Peru where they have been called upon to fight the leftist Sendero Luminoso (Shining Path) movement and in Venezuela where the government of President Andrés Pérez ordered them to quell the 1988 urban riots.[16] Yet despite these pockets of blatant military intervention or renewed influence, the push for democracy has been so overwhelming and sustained in the region that the generals have been unable to reestablish their authoritarian philosophy or completely protect their power position. In contemporary Latin America it has become smart politics to be a democrat and leave one's authoritarian proclivities behind.

Yet the fact that incidents of military intervention and heightened influence are occurring in Latin America poses the question of whether military leadership is undergoing a transformation or more a holding action. The signs of democratization and professionalization within the Latin American military must be examined in the context of its long-standing beliefs in the value of societal stability, in anticommunism, and in protecting the nation from radical change. As has often been the case in Latin America, what lies on the surface of politics need not be taken as the true character or meaning of events. Latin America continues to be a region where the authoritarian tradition is firmly embedded in the political culture and the governing psyche. The continued control of the political process by key generals in countries like Guatemala, El Salvador, and Haiti and the possession of a kind of veto power over public policy that the military has in countries like Argentina, Chile, Bolivia, and Peru suggest that if a transformation of military leadership has indeed occurred in Latin America it may very well be temporary and reflect the view by the officer corps that there is a time to lead and a time to consolidate power.

What may be even more disturbing than the residual power of the military is the increased willingness of civilian leaders to call upon the military to maintain order as heightened social protest and leftist activity grips many Latin American countries. The military, without much effort on its part, is returning to the forefront of politics to fulfill its traditional role of "guardian" and "bulwark" and is in the process of validating the fears of many in Latin America that civilian democrats are incapable of maintaining order and normalcy. As James Petras and Morris Morley state:

[Liberal democratic regimes] have responded to the growing support for the parliamentary and guerrilla left, mass mobilization politics, and the rising levels of class struggle—precisely the outcomes the military's original decision to "return to the barracks" was intended to prevent—by making the kind of concessions that once again reposition the generals for direct intervention into the political arena.[17]

THE RELUCTANT MILITARY MANAGERS

The debate over whether the contemporary Latin American military is transformed or engaged in a holding action can best be analyzed if we add the title "managers" to the long list of job requirements that have developed over the years. The demise of military leadership and the strengthening of civilian democracy has turned the armed forces inward and forced them to emphasize institutional rather than political or personal objectives. Just like managers in any large bureaucracy, the officers of the Latin American military hierarchy have come to realize the importance of defining their power and success within the context of the political system. Rather than being separate from the system, the military has moved to a position within the system.

As good managers, military leaders have sought to become less visible and more interested in the mundane details of institutional organization and development. In Mexico, for example, the 145,000-member armed forces have continued to pledge their loyalty to the PRI-led governments but in return have elicited numerous benefits and few questions about the bloated officer corps. President Salinas, once in office, continued this tradition. According to George Grayson, "Salinas has cultivated friends at the Defense Ministry. As secretary of budget and planning, he regularly visited military installations, knitted close ties with senior officials and granted most requests for higher pay and new equipment."[18] Similar strategies have been followed in Argentina, Peru, and Brazil with great success as civilian presidents worked with the military hierarchy to modernize the armed forces, which in most cases meant significant pay increases and budgets that sustained only marginal decreases in the face of heavy austerity programs.

Perhaps most importantly, military officers in Latin America are acting like managers in that the principles of efficient administration, professionalization, and loyalty are being espoused with greater frequency. The generals are now quite conscious about how they present themselves and what public positions they take. Although one can question the honesty of their commitment to civilian rule and their willingness to transform the military institution into an efficient tool of national defense, the days of military bravado and claims of political responsibilities are slowly disappearing. Even in military-dominated El Salvador, a new corps of military leaders are savvy enough to know the benefits of mouthing the democratic line when U.S. aid cuts are threatened.[19]

But in order to avoid making the Latin American military establishment into something that it is not and being carried away with this theme of institutional and leadership transformation, it is important to describe the motives behind the rise of the new military manager and the ways in which military managers are pursuing their objectives. Although the officer corps in Latin America are taking on a new face and espousing values that suggest reform, they are at the same time engaged in activities that suggest a firm commitment to remain power contenders and to revitalize an institution that could again lead and govern.

The signs that the new military managers are following the road of both reform and revitalization can be found throughout Latin America. In Argentina, the military leader of the 1987 "Holy Week" and "Monte Caseros" coup attempts, Lt. Colonel Aldo Rico, along with his mentor, Col. Mohamed Ali Seineldin, who led the 1988 "Villa Martelli" mutiny, have been active, despite their forced retirement, in challenging the military policies of the government of President Carlos Menem. Despite frequent rebukes from the government, Rico and Seineldin continued to threaten a military revolt. In late 1990, on the eve of President Bush's arrival in Buenos Aires, units loyal to the two officers staged another unsuccessful minicoup that at least for the time weakened their base of support. It is interesting to note, however, that by late 1991 Lt. Colonel Rico had sought to reenter the mainstream of Argentine politics by running for the governorship of Buenos Aires Province. Rico placed a distant third in the balloting, but his Movement of National Dignity party gained three seats in the lower house of Congress.

The change of tactics by Rico may signal a new role for the military in Argentina. With President Carlos Menem changing defense ministers frequently (four times since 1989), cutting the budget for the armed forces dramatically, and pressing for the conviction of soldiers involved in the coup attempt in 1990, the ability of disgruntled rightist officers to challenge civilian politicians has diminished significantly.[20] Nevertheless, the fact that Argentina has faced four military uprisings since 1983 points clearly to the continued desire be some elements of the military hierarchy to influence politics and national development.

In Chile, General Augusto Pinochet may have lost out in his bid to stop the process of democracy, but he has ensured that the political system must recognize his potential for challenging the authority of elected leaders. Despite the victory of Patricio Alywin for the presidency in late 1989, Pinochet retains his position as army commander until 1998 along with the other heads of the armed forces. Furthermore, Pinochet, before leaving office, engaged in an appointment campaign designed to ensure that public officials loyal to him are situated in key administrative positions. A key Pinochet aide initiated a program to replace over three hundred mayors who wield substantial powers of patronage and spending. Also, Pinochet developed a controversial plan to encourage justices in the Chilean court system to retire early and allow the outgoing government to appoint judges who would most likely mirror the authoritarian values of the military government. Although the Alywin government pledged to fight Pinochet's attempts to maintain a conservative hold on the country, it was clear that the general and his military would remain an important force in Chilean politics.[21]

In Brazil the military has not as yet cast a shadow over the march to democracy. The military remained quiet during the campaign that eventually brought Fernando Collor to the presidency, perhaps because the charismatic moderate politician was seen early on as a national leader with conservative credentials. The tacit acceptance of Collor by the Brazilian military, however, should not be taken for granted. The Brazilian political system continues to be organized in ways that allow the military to maintain its power and its potential for future involvement in national governance. As Alfred Stepan suggests, the Brazilian military rather than civilian politicians remains in control of the defense ministry, the intelligence services, and the powerful National Security Council. Legislative control over military budget appropriations continues to be weak, and the ability of the new president to promote and replace key military leaders is as yet untested. Although some have suggested that the military fall from power was so great in Brazil that a resurgence in the near future is unlikely, the new democratic government will face a governing system that allows the military to remain powerful and out of civilian control.[22]

Perhaps nowhere in Latin America has the effort to transform military leaders into efficient managers of national defense been more pronounced than in Peru. In 1987 President Alan García signed into law a reorganization of the armed forces that combined the ministries of the army, navy, and air force into a single ministry. García claimed that the change would improve efficiency and lessen the competition for scarce budget resources, but the officer corps saw the law as an attack against their influence. The promulgation of the law touched off a mutiny among some units of the air force and created the atmosphere of a coup. García was able to convince loyal troops to protect civilian rule and retired the leader of the mutiny, Air Force Commander Luis Abram Cavallerino. The victory by García, however, was not complete because the move to force the military to become loyal managers subsided as the Shining Path revolutionaries intensified their activities. García subsequently increased military budgets, named an army general to the defense post, and relied more heavily on military advice in the rebel war. What had been a successful campaign to reform the military turned into a brief political diversion as domestic instability revitalized the military machine.[23]

García's successor, Alberto Fujimori, faces a much different problem in that he needs the military to fight the increasing terrorist threat from the leftist Shining Path rebels. The Peruvian military, however, appears to be incapable of controlling the terrorism because of frequent shake-ups of the high command and open challenges to the military establishment and has resorted to repression as a way of maintaining order. As a result, Fujimori has begun to look to U.S. military trainers rather than the Peruvian military as the source of reform and efficiency.

The above litany of examples highlighting the conflicts over the managerial role being assumed by the Latin American military establishment suggests that the transformation of the officer corps into nonpolitical professionals committed only to the defense of the country is at best incomplete and at worst a cosmetic attempt to mask their craving for power and leadership. What has changed within the leadership hierarchy of the Latin American military, however, is leaders' understanding of the social forces that drive a country toward democratic rule and the near impossibility of gov-erning a nation in the grip of debt and recession. In many respects the Latin American military leaders have become more mature and sophisticated in their approach to domestic politics. They recognize that discipline, order, and force are not the only antidotes to social change and economic instability. Although most officers likely cringe at the leadership of the civilians who head Latin American govern-ments today, they nonetheless realize that replacing those civilians would do little to solve the vast array of maladies facing the region. In many respects the Latin American military suffers from what used to be termed the "Gorbachev syndrome"—why push a civilian leader out of power if the result is a nation in the throes of economic and social collapse?

The new military managers thus wait and hold on to what they have, confident that deteriorating social, economic, and political conditions will expand their influence and heighten their status. They may be managers rather than political leaders, but beneath the veneer of administrative professionalism there continues to reside the traditional views about the special mission of the military. French social scientist Alain Roque sums up the current civil-military relationship when he states:

> There is no doubt that there is not today, nor has there been for several years, the political space either internally or internationally for a military offensive against the new democracies. However, the military are still there. They have repudiated none of their past actions and have in no way modified their values or their conduct.[24]

AMERICAN PRESIDENTS AND THE NEW MILITARY MANAGERS

The United States has for most of the twentieth century been faced with a dilemma in its relations with the Latin American states. Presidents and policymakers have shown a great uneasiness when faced with the prospect of supporting authoritarian leaders who are pledged to ensure stability and promote the security interests of the United States. Although many political leaders in this country never warmed to the idea of backing dictators in the name of geopolitics and unnamed vital interests, the United States was able to convince itself that the domestic politics of a neighboring country was none of our business, especially if that country opened up its borders to our trade and investment and mouthed the proper counterrevolutionary language.

But as the calls for democracy in Latin America became a tidal wave of protest, the United States was faced with a more complex dilemma—how to advance the process of democratization, depoliticize an aggressive military establishment, and still secure our vital interests in the hemisphere? The old credos used to endorse military rule would simply not hold up anymore, yet the economic, social, and political tensions that fed instability and helped create Marxist revolution remained constant. The transition to civilian rule would thus be an intricate balancing act as the United States faced the task of responding to the democratic surge with moral and financial support while at the same time assisting in the process of lessening the influence of an institution that it had worked closely with for so many years.[25]

When the military "house of cards" began to crumble in the late 1970s the United States was eager to help develop a democratic environment in Latin America. President Jimmy Carter had already set the stage for the decline of military rule with his highly visible human-rights policy and its attendant discontinuation of military assistance to those regimes that were gross offenders of common democratic practice. Argentina, Brazil, Chile, Guatemala, Paraguay, Haiti, and Uruguay were singled out as examples of military governments whose harsh actions against their own citizens necessitated the visible steps by the United States of public condemnation and a cutoff of military aid. The Carter administration received significant support from Congress with the passage of legislation such as the Foreign Military Assistance Act of 1976, which linked military credits to respect for human rights.[26]

During the Carter presidency the transition from military rule to civilian democracy had only limited success. Carter was able to usher in democratic rule in the Dominican Republic despite the theft of the ballot boxes by President Joaquín Balaguer's military.[27] In Ecuador and Peru, however, where the process of civilianization began earlier than in the Southern Cone nations, the Carter administration had little impact on the transition to democracy. In both Ecuador and Peru the military faced increasing opposition from a wide range of societal groups and left power more out of self-interest than because of international pressure over human-rights abuse or failure to advance democratic governance.

The most visible example of Carter's antiauthoritarian posture was in Nicaragua, where Anastasio Somoza was forced out of power by the Sandinista revolution and the unwillingness of Washington to prop up a dictator who had served the interests of the United States. President Carter's policy toward Somoza revealed the internal contradictions in the antimilitary policy of the United States as the administration vacillated over whether replacing an authoritarian leader was more important than handing over power to revolutionary leftists who publicly castigated the United States while proclaiming their ties to Cuba and the Soviet Union.[28]

Although the campaign of the Carter administration to translate its ideals about human rights and democratization into concrete changes in government met with limited success, the approach of the United States toward authoritarianism during this period had a more subtle effect. Military leaders in Latin America were taken aback by the swift and vigorous arms-assistance cutbacks of the Carter administration. The generals in power were faced with an uncertain relationship from a country that had courted them through three presidencies. The stubbornness with which President Carter pursued his antimilitary policy served to isolate authoritarian leaders and strengthen those in Latin America who were fighting for a change. In many respects the Carter policy toward military regimes in Latin America was a mix of high ideals and raw emotion—two ingredients often not found in the policy process but in this case effective catalysts for initiating steps toward civilian rule.[29]

The transfer of power from Carter to Reagan in 1981 did little to advance the antimilitary wave that was forming in Latin America. Military regimes in the Southern Cone, in Paraguay and Bolivia, and in Central America reinforced the image of the region as solidly in the authoritarian tradition. Once in office President Reagan did little at first to encourage democratic forces in their struggle against the generals. The Reagan approach was to accent so-called quiet diplomacy with authoritarian governments and encourage them to modify their policies toward political opponents and gradually move the country toward democratization.[30]

The primary attention of the first Reagan administration was with the revolutionary left. Secretary of State Alexander Haig and later Assistant Secretary for Inter-American Affairs Elliott Abrams made bold threats against the Sandinistas and the Cubans and set the stage for the development of the destabilization of the Ortega regime. In order to advance these objectives Latin American policy-makers moved to formulate alliances with military governments for the purposes of advancing the war against the Marxists. Military leaders and military governments were viewed as allies in the war against the Marxist threat in the hemisphere.[31]

This was the time when Panama's Manuel Noriega was put on the CIA payroll because of his willingness to provide vital intelligence, training, and if necessary, clandestine operations against the Sandinistas. The Reagan administration also developed close ties with the Argentine generals and enlisted their support in developing the contra army. The United States valued the expertise of the Argentine military in handling leftist opposition and seemed to be unconcerned with its reputation as brutal oppressors of human rights.[32] Moreover, despite the Reagan administration's support of Britain in the Falklands/Malvinas dispute in 1982, the United States quickly moved to patch up its differences with the Argentine generals after the war. Washington pushed for renewed arms sales to Argentina and quietly showed its support for the military despite the emerging democratic movement in the country.[33]

Not only did the Reagan administration turn to military regimes to fight the Sandinistas but it quickly sought to turn around the antiauthoritarian policies of the Carter administration. Ties with Chile, which had cooled under Carter, were resumed almost immediately along with pledges of support for vital international loans; military assistance to Argentina, Brazil, Guatemala, Haiti, Paraguay, and Uruguay was resumed and public support for military leaders again became the norm.[34] In 1982, for example, President Reagan praised Guatemalan president General Efrain Ríos Montt as getting a "bum rap" from human-rights critics despite extensive evidence to the contrary. The Reagan administration was clearly sending a signal to the military governments in the region that the United States valued their contributions to stability and anticommunism and was willing to back up that view with a renewal of assistance and support.

The alliance between the Reagan administration and Latin American military leaders was short-lived as the United States was again overtaken by events and forced to reevaluate its commitment to authoritarian stability. By the end of President Reagan's first term Latin America was on the verge of a democratic revolution of historic proportions and U.S. officials were scrambling for ways to deal with this transition. As military governments fell from power the United States got on the democratic bandwagon and began not only supporting the call for elections but criticizing those military governments that remained intransigent and wedded to their old practices. This was the time when Vice President George Bush traveled to El Salvador and lectured the military leaders of that country on the importance of constitutional democracy and presented them with a list of human-rights abusers in their ranks.[35] President Reagan began publicly to show dissatisfaction with the human-rights record of the Pinochet regime and U.S. officials began leveling uncharacteristically sharp criticism at the corrupt practices of the military charged with the war on drugs in countries like Bolivia, Peru, Colombia, and Mexico.[36]

The new antimilitary posture of the Reagan administration also came at a time when domestic budgetary restraints required that the United States either cut back on its foreign military assistance or target its assistance to the war on drugs, which meant that sophisticated weapons were replaced by walkie-talkies, small arms, radar devices, and other equipment designed to compete effectively with the armies of the drug empire. Although military assistance programs continued to provide monies to modernize aging equipment, the trend was clearly down and the emphasis was away from supporting aid for big-ticket items.[37] This redeployment of U.S. assistance forced the military to define its mission anew and concentrate on fighting the drug wars rather than the political wars. Also, as military assistance dried up the military hierarchy had to look elsewhere for assistance or, as was the case in most countries, concentrate on more efficient means of allocating resources.

Although traditional "hard" military assistance decreased, the United States during the Reagan years stepped up its commitment to military training. The Reagan administration placed heavy emphasis on increasing IMET (International Military Education and Training Program) funding to Latin American countries in an effort not only to enhance the training of military officers but to provide them with an exposure to a professional military establishment committed to civilian rule and democratic practice. Although such training programs have come under increased criticism for their lack of emphasis on democratic values, the United States continued to bring thousands of Latin American officers to Fort Gulick in the Canal Zone for intensive management training and a sprinkling of U.S. government.[38]

One of the more significant developments within the Reagan administration regarding the Latin American military was the tying of assistance to the attitude and behavior patterns of the officer corps. During the presidency of Raúl Alfonsín in Argentina the Reagan administration began a modest military assistance program designed to "reorient the military from politics toward professional concerns." Organized specifically through the civilian-run Ministry of Defense, the program's first phase was designed to strengthen the democratic commitment of the military; the second stage offered the military help in refurbishing U.S.-made transport helicopters and armored personnel carriers. This kind of carrot and stick philosophy is an example of how the Reagan administration sought to further the concept of officers as professional managers rather than professional politicians.[39]

But although the Reagan administration was more vigorous than before in its opposition to military governments and more willing to work for reform within the officer corps, it still had to deal with regimes in countries where the armed forces were either visibly in control or used their power of intimidation to ensure that civilian leaders did not change the rules of politics. The biggest challenge for the Reagan administration was the quasicivilian government in El Salvador. Despite playing a significant role in bringing free elections to El Salvador for the first time in its history, the United States was faced with a military establishment that clearly was operating without civilian control and had little patience for the principles of institutional accountability, constitutionalism, and negotiated settlement of disputes.[40]

Although many in the Salvadoran military hierarchy were trained by the United States and were dependent on the hundreds of millions in assistance they received, the military leaders (often appointed directly from graduating classes, or *tandas*, from the national military academy) held firmly to their traditional beliefs in the necessity of destroying the revolutionary left even if that meant compromising the rule of law, the human rights of innocent civilians, and the fragile democracy that had developed within the country.[41] The Reagan administration was able to achieve some limited success in lessening the incidents of political violence from right-wing death squads and in convincing military leaders to publicly embrace democratic governance. These advances, however, were mostly cosmetic; it became clear that Christian Democratic president José Napoleón Duarte had little room to maneuver and could not initiate programs that threatened the power base of the military or its allies.

Because the Reagan administration feared the implications of a defeat at the hands of the Marxist FMLN rebels, it ignored the obvious signs of military dominance and democratic weakness in El Salvador and concentrated on the very small steps the generals had made toward reform. In return for supporting the appearance of democracy and for its stern resolve to defeat the FMLN (Farabundo Marti Liberación National), the Salvadoran military was provided with over $1 billion in military assistance during its two terms in office. This assistance allowed the military to bring the guerrilla war to a standstill and provided the Reagan administration with the right to say that Communist expansionism had been effectively contained.[42]

The policy positions of the Reagan administration in El Salvador underscore the dilemma faced by officials in this country who must link the twin objectives of establishing civilian democratic rule and military involvement in the containment of Marxist revolution. The Reagan solution was to work diligently for democratization while at the same time accepting the reality of military dominance. Democracy was important, but so was stopping the revolutionaries, and if the military overstepped the bounds of democratic propriety or ignored the entreaties of the civilian president, then those infractions of proper democratic behavior would be protested but little would be done to correct that behavior. As President Reagan stated in his address to Congress on April 27, 1983, "We will support democracy, reform and human freedom. This means using our assistance, our powers of persuasion and our legitimate leverage to bolster humane democratic systems."[43]

It is important to state, though, that the compromises supported by the Reagan administration in El Salvador were not applied to situations in countries where Marxist revolution was insignificant. In Haiti, for example, the Reagan administration came out harshly against the military leaders for their brutal intervention to stop the 1987 presidential elections that the United States had pushed for and for which it had provided extensive technical support. Military assistance was cut quickly and President Reagan criticized the Haitian military for its refusal to allow the democratic process to run its course. With little in the way of an organized Communist movement in Haiti and no evidence of a revolutionary guerrilla movement, the Reagan administration was the model of support for democratic rule and military retreat. Unfortunately, its actions against the Haitian military did little to change the political configuration in that country or spur the generals toward internal reform.

Comparing the military policy of the Reagan administration toward El Salvador and Haiti, one is struck by the fact that U.S. policymakers have had more success in developing the framework of democratic governance than in attaining real reforms within the military establishment. Although on the surface of politics in Latin America there was a great deal of change during the Reagan years and the hopes of democratic leaders were advanced, there is too much evidence to support the view that the military paid only lip service to democratic reform. Public declarations of commitment to elections and peaceful transfer of power were what the United States was able to get from the generals, not substantive changes that transformed them into ordinary players in the political process. At the end of the Reagan presidency the Latin American military leaders remained shrewd power contenders because they knew that the United States retained a latent fear of leftist revolution and could use that fear to hold off U.S. presidential pressure for meaningful reform.

GEORGE BUSH AND THE LATIN AMERICAN MILITARY IN THE 1990s

The 1990s are certain to provide a test of democratic government in Latin America, not only in terms of the ability of civilian leaders to address pressing social and economic issues but also in terms of the willingness of the military hierarchy to remain out of the political arena and continue to concentrate on institutional development. The United States will certainly be an important factor in directing the course that Latin American politics will take in the coming years. Democratic heads of state will look to the United States for support as they deal with the continuing debt crisis and the social upheaval that is spawned by the inability to meet the increasing demands of a growing population. But although the struggles of civilian leaders will most likely gain the headlines, the heads of the various branches of the armed forces in Latin American countries will also be interested in how the United States views the role of the military and how tolerant we will be if faced with heightened instability and political paralysis.

The administration of George Bush could easily be torn between its commitment to democratization and its fear that internal upheaval in Latin America will feed the fires of Marxism and eventually revolution. Although President Bush does not have to approach the Latin American political scene with the same anti-Communist fervor as his predecessor, he nevertheless is aware that social conflict and economic uncertainty create a climate where U.S. interests are threatened. It is difficult for a U.S. president to espouse the benefits of authoritarian rule, but that reluctance can be assuaged when business opportunities, trade patterns, loan obligations, and corporate holdings are placed in jeopardy by governments incapable of maintaining order.

Early in his administration, President Bush strengthened his image as a champion of democracy and an opponent of authoritarian rule when he initiated the invasion of Panama to capture General Manuel Noriega and install the rightfully elected government of Guillermo Endara. With Panamanians embracing U.S. soldiers who freed them from Noriega's grip and civilian leaders thanking the Bush administration for defeating the hated Panamanian Defense Forces, President Bush basked in the glory of public adulation. Although the decision to invade Panama was difficult in terms of its implications for international law, relations with Latin America, and the prosecution of other drug kingpins, the flagrant lawlessness and brutality of the Noriega regime made it easy for the Bush administration to strike out at an authoritarian leader and begin the dismantling of his personal army.[44]

The real test for President Bush in Panama is not Noriega but the Noriega legacy in the military. Since the fall of the Panamanian dictator the United States has been working feverishly to build a scaled-down, depoliticized police force and to embue that police force with democratic values. Although these are noble objectives, the reality of the task before the United States in Panama is that the police force, in the words of one observer, is a "demoralized force, having lost most of its top officers, most of its perks to efficiency drives and most of its weapons to American troops."[45] Panamanian police chief Ebrahim Azbat has been working with U.S. officials to strengthen the judicial system and transform the police force into a respected institution, but he admits, "There's a Latin tradition of a god or a patriarch or a caudillo who comes to unite everyone and make everything better. But nobody's talking hard work, discipline and sweat. . . . This country is still sick, after 21 years of dictatorship, you can't suddenly become a believer in democratic institutions."[46]

Chief Azbat's analysis was a cogent one considering the failed coup attempt of former police chief Col. Eduardo Herrera Hassan in October 1990. Colonel Herrera's dramatic escape from an island prison touched off speculation that the government of Guillermo Endara would fall. These fears were put to rest when U.S. troops left their Canal Zone headquarters and put an end to the coup. President Endara's decision to call in U.S. troops not only created enormous controversy in Panama but forced the questions of whether the authoritarian tradition will ever be laid to rest in the country and whether the efforts of the United States to reform the Panamanian military will meet with intense opposition and eventual failure.

The capture of Manuel Noriega and the democratization of the Panamanian military and police were not the only problems of authoritarian rule faced by the Bush administration. The execution of six Jesuit priests along with two others during the rebel offensive in San Salvador in 1989 was viewed by many observers as the work of the right-wing military officers. The worldwide outrage over the murders was directed not only at the government of President Alfredo Cristiani, which seemed uncapable of conducting an independent investigation, but at the United States, which was unwilling to lay blame on the Salvadoran armed forces despite eyewitness accounts of military involvement.[47]

It was clear that the Bush administration was caught in a familiar bind—how to achieve a measure of legality and respect for human rights in the armed forces while at the same time not alienating the officers conducting the war against the leftist guerrillas. Despite pressure from Congress to cut off military aid, Bush relied on personal phone calls to President Cristiani, urging him to act against those responsible for the murders. Apparently the pressure had some effect, as Cristiani did bring charges against six members of the Salvadoran military including one high-ranking general. Publicly Bush continued his policy of not condemning the Salvadoran military or threatening an aid cutoff, but at the same time he resorted to the quiet diplomacy route in order to silence his domestic critics. This mode of operation worked to achieve the short-term goal of charging soldiers with the murder of the Jesuits (two high-ranking officers were found guilty in a historic trial before a civilian tribunal), but it left open the question of whether the Salvadoran military would abide by the dictates of a civilian leader or be intimidated by the words of a U.S. president. In the view of many critics of U.S. policy in El Salvador, the decision by the U.S. Congress to cut Salvadoran military aid by 50 percent in 1990 was the only weapon that could bring about a reform of the rightist officer corps.[48]

As the presidency of George Bush entered its third year the president continued to gain the support of the U.S. people and received praise for his Panama invasion and the democratization of Nicaragua. But despite U.S. citizens' favorable opinion of Bush, the administration was continuing to put off action on those problems in Latin America that could easily weaken civilian governments and tempt ambitious military leaders to reenter politics. As a study by the prestigious Inter-American Dialogue pointed out, failure by the United States to ease the debt burden facing the Latin American countries will enhance the possibility that civilian governments will collapse and be replaced by the military. The Inter-American Dialogue study reinforced what many experts in the region have been saying for a number of years—civilian democracy, although successful and more secure than in the past, is especially vulnerable to the uneven growth and uncertain pace of development present in the region.[49]

Although many civilian governments in the region have already weathered the storm of social upheaval, they have done so at a time when the Latin American military was in a period of decline and consolidation. Should these same upheavals occur on a continuing basis into the 1990s, some ten to fifteen years after the military left power, it is not unreasonable to assume that the people in the region will begin to tire of civilian rule and look for alternative leadership to address escalating economic crises. In any society, time is not only the great healer, it has the magical effect of helping people to forget the past. Praising the vibrancy of civilian democratic rule a mere five or ten years after the generals have left is premature; it is only after a generation has passed and people's memories have begun to fade that the real test of government popularity and stability occurs.

The real test for the United States and the Bush administration may come if one of the major civilian democracies in Latin America is overthrown in a military coup. Because such a military overthrow would most likely come as a result of lingering social upheaval or economic crisis, Bush would be forced to evaluate not only this country's commitment to democracy in the region but our long-standing desire to ensure that stability is maintained. Although predicting such an event or the response of the Bush administration is foolhardy, it is safe to say that there will come a time in Latin America when the solidarity of the democratic era will be challenged and military governments will be tempted to emerge from their political hiatus. It is at this time that the United States will once again be faced with the conflict over the moral imperative of democratic government and the practical constraints of national interest. How we respond will say much about whether the public commitment to democratic governance in the region was mere window dressing or a conscious decision to support a form of politics that enhanced and strengthened our relationship.

The prospect of a return to military rule in Latin America serves to remind us of the long-held view that although the United States is usually unable to control the process of internal change, it can have an enormous impact on the social, economic, and political forces that bring about change. A key concern today in U.S.-Latin American relations should not merely be the effectiveness and resiliency of civilian leadership but the depoliticization and professionalization of the military. Much of the emphasis of our policy in Latin America is on voting and elections, peaceful transfers of power, democratic institution-building, and efficient public policy administration. No one should question the appropriateness of accenting these aspects of democratization. But at the same time that the United States is building democracies, it is paying only peripheral attention to reforming the antidemocratic elements in the region that have the capability with one swift strike to destroy the fragile institutional frameworks developed in the past ten years.

In our relations with the military hierarchy in Latin America this country continues to send mixed signals by endorsing democratic government and then bemoaning the instability that accompanies social change. Such inability to deal with the "messiness" of change lends encouragement to conservative military elites who are also appalled by the lack of discipline and order in many civilian-run regimes. More important, however, the United States has been negligent in its programs for reforming the Latin American military. The military training programs initiated by the United States in Latin America have failed to adequately stress democratic values and professionalization of the officer corps. U.S. military trainers and embassy attachés have come under increased criticism for their unwillingness to impress upon Latin American officers the importance of supporting civilian rule and abiding by established constitutional principles. As Martin Andersen states:

> U.S. military personnel also need to be reminded that democratization and human rights are not mere window-dressing but reflect American moral standards. . . . Actions and statements to the contrary should be hit with sanctions. U.S. ambassadors should play a key role in overseeing the activities of their military attaches. Each embassy ought to designate a political officer . . . to monitor U.S. military compliance with American political goals.[50]

But although ensuring that U.S. trainers are sending the right message to the Latin American officer corps is an essential component of this country's policy of military reform, the most effective tool of democratization and professionalization remains the assistance that we provide. The temptation of reformers is to use military assistance as a kind of veiled threat designed to force compliance, but such a position ignores the realities of Latin American politics and the traditional objectives of U.S. policy in the region. The Latin American military will remain a vital power contender in politics as will the national security interests of the United States. It is in the interest of the United States to help modernize, train, and support the military institutions throughout Latin America as a means of en-hancing our own security and ensuring that the hemisphere has the capability of defending itself from external threats. It is, however, also in the interest of the United States to work with governments that have values similar to ours, that represent the will of the people, and that do not advance policy initiatives in ways that contradict established norms of law.

Therefore, working closely with military elites, providing needed assistance and training, and recognizing the importance of the military in Latin American politics should remain as the core of U.S. relations with the armed forces of the region. At the same time, though, the United States must work more diligently in the future to move the Latin American military away from its traditional behavior patterns and prejudices, which endanger leadership and governing frameworks that will not only strengthen the political process but enhance our image and position in the hemisphere. Quite simply, it is smart politics for the United States to pursue the objectives of internal and regional stability in Latin America by convincing the military leaders that we support them as professional defenders of the nation but not as political interlopers who threaten democracy and civilian rule.

NOTES

1. Richard Gott, "Twilight of the Generals," *World Press Review* (July 1989): 26–36.

2. The concept of antipolitics has been developed in Brian Loveman and Thomas M. Davies Jr., ed., *The Politics of Anti-Politics: The Military in Latin America*, 2d ed. (Lincoln: University of Nebraska Press, 1989).

3. James M. Malloy and Mitchell Seligson, *Authoritarians and Dem-ocrats: Regime Transition in Latin America* (Pittsburgh, PA: University of Pittsburgh Press, 1987), p. 247.

4. *New York Times*, January 30, 1988, p. 2, in a wire-service article describes the changing nature of U.S. support for Latin American militarism.

5. See Gino Germani and Kalman Silvert, "Politics, Social Structure and Military Intervention in Latin America," *European Journal of Sociology* 2 (1961): 62–81, and John J. Johnson, *The Military and Society in Latin America* (Stanford, CA: Stanford University Press, 1964).

6. As quoted in Loveman and Davies, *The Politics of Anti-Politics,* p. 4.

7. Edwin Lieuwen, *Generals vs. Presidents: Neo-Militarism in Latin America* (New York: Praeger, 1964), pp. 136–141.

8. See David Collier, ed., *The New Authoritarianism in Latin America* (Princeton, NJ: Princeton University Press, 1979). See also Guillermo O'Donnell, *Modernization and Bureaucratic-Authoritarianism: Studies in South American Politics,* Politics of Modernization Series, no. 9 (Berkeley: Institute of International Studies, University of California, Berkeley, 1973).

9. Some of the more recent works on the Latin American military are David Pion-Berlin, *The Ideology of Terror: Economic Doctrine and Political Repression in Argentina and Peru* (Boulder, CO: Lynne Rienner Publishers, 1989); Karen Remmer, *Military Rule in Latin America* (Boston: Unwin, Hyman, 1989) and William C. Smith, *Authoritarianism and the Crisis of the Argentine Economy* (Stanford, CA: Stanford University Press, 1989).

10. Gary Wynia, *The Politics of Latin American Development,* 2d ed. (New York: Oxford University Press, 1984), p. 241.

11. Aaron Segal, "Latin Armed Forces Facing Difficult Days," *Times of the Americas,* November 11, 1989, p. 16.

12. See, for example, an interview with Argentine newspaper publisher Jorge Lanata in which he expresses concerns over the so-called new democratic military in Argentina. *Times of the Americas,* October 18, 1989, p. 10.

13. See Ariel Dorfman, "Adios General; Saying Goodbye to Pinochet," *Harper's* (December 1989): 72–76.

14. Elaine Shannon in her exposé of U.S. drug operations in Latin America points clearly to corruption by high-level military officials as a critical ingredient in the failure of the war on drugs. Elaine Shannon, *Desperados—Latin Drug Lords, U.S. Lawmen, and the War America Can't Win* (New York: Viking, 1988), pp. 359–360.

15. Segal, "Latin Armed Forces," p. 16.

16. For a discussion of these events from a Marxist perspective, see James Petras and Morris Morley, *US Hegemony Under Seige, Class, Politics and Development in Latin America* (London: Verso, 1990), pp. 3–23.

17. Ibid., p. 24.

18. George Grayson, "Mexico: A New Political Reality," *Current History* (December 1988): 433.

19. See Charles Lane, "Death's Democracy," *Atlantic* (February 1989): 18–25.

20. Chris Kline, "Argentina: Security Concerns Surface Again," *Times of the Americas,* February 7, 1990, p. 8.

21. Dorfman, "Adios General," pp. 72–76.

22. Alfred Stepan, *Rethinking Military Politics: Brazil and the Southern Cone* (Princeton, NJ: Princeton University Press, 1988), pp. 139–145.

23. Interview with Virgilio Barco in Paul Boeker, *Lost Illusions, Latin America's Struggle for Democracy as Recounted By Its Leaders* (La Jolla, CA: Institute of the Americas, Merkes Weiner Publishing, 1990), p. 203.

24. See David P. Werlich, "Peru: Garcia Loses His Charm," *Current History* (January 1988): 15.

25. Alain Roque, *The Military and the State in Latin America* (Berkeley: The University of California Press, 1987), p. 404.

26. See David Carleton and Michael Stohl, "U.S. Foreign Assistance Policy and the Redemocratization of Latin America," in George Lopez and Michael Stohl, eds., *Liberalization and Redemocratization in Latin America* (Westport, CT: Greenwood Press, 1987), pp. 231–262.

27. See Abraham F. Lowenthal, "Jimmy Carter and Latin America," in Kenneth A. Oye, et al., *Eagle Entangled: U.S. Foreign Policy in a Complex World* (New York: Longman, 1979), pp. 290–301.

28. Michael J. Kryzanek, "The 1978 Election in the Dominican Republc: Opposition Politics, Intervention and the Carter Administration," *Caribbean Studies*, 19, nos. 1, 2 (April–July 1979): 51–73.

29. Anthony Lake, *Somoza Falling, The Nicaraguan Dilemma: A Portrait of Washington at Work* (Boston: Houghton Mifflin, 1989), pp. 176–180.

30. An assessment of the Carter policy toward military regimes in Latin America can be found in Lars Schoultz, *Human Rights and United States Policy Toward Latin America* (Princeton, NJ: Princeton University Press, 1981), pp. 211–266. See also Roberta Cohen, "Human Rights Diplomacy: The Carter Administration and the Southern Cone," *Human Rights Quarterly* 4, no. 2, (1982): 212–242.

31. Margaret Daly Hayes, "Not What I Say, But What I Do: Latin American Policy in the Reagan Administration," in John D. Martz, ed., *United States Policy in Latin America: A Quarter Century of Crisis and Challenge, 1961–1986* (Lincoln: University of Nebraska Press, 1988), pp. 98–131.

32. Martin Andersen, "Kissinger and the Dirty War," *Nation* (October 31, 1987): 477–480.

33. Martin Andersen, "The Military Obstacles to Latin American Democracy," *Foreign Policy* 73 (Winter 1988/1989): 103–109.

34. Abraham Lowenthal, "Ronald Reagan and Latin America: Coping with Hegemony in Decline," in Kenneth Oye, et al., *Eagle Defiant: U.S. Foreign Policy in the 1980's* (Boston: Little Brown, 1983), p. 329.

35. The rationale for this turnaround can be found in Jeane J. Kirkpatrick, "U.S. Security and Latin America," *Commentary* 71 (January 1981): 29–40.

36. From a dinner speech of Vice President George Bush as reported in the U.S. Department of State, Bureau of Public Affairs, Current Policy, no. 533.

37. For a discussion of the frustrations faced by the Reagan administration in the drug war see Bruce Bagley, "Dateline Drug Wars: Colombia: The Wrong Strategy," *Foreign Policy* 77 (Winter 1989–1990): 163.

38. Shirley Christian, "Congress Asked For $54 Million to Aid Latin Anti-Terrorist Efforts," *New York Times*, November 6, 1985, p. I-4.

39. A critique of U.S. military education programs can be found in Richard Halloran, "U.S.-Latin American Military Contact Withers," *New York Times*, April 3, 1988, p. I-16.

40. United States Department of State Bulletin, October 1988, p. 4.

41. See, for example, the dilemma faced by the United States over the killing of six Jesuit priests in El Salvador in December 1989. Douglas Farah, "Officers Reportedly Met Before Priests' Slaying," *Boston Globe*, February 4, 1990, p. 3. The *Globe* speculates on the possible scenarios for Salvadoran military involvement in the slayings.

42. Lane, "Death's Democracy," p. 22.

43. Compiled from U.S. Department of State Bulletins for the years 1980–1989.

44. President Ronald Reagan, address to a Joint Session of Congress, April 27, 1983.

45. Lee Hockstader, "Is it Democracy Yet?" *Washington Post National Weekly Edition*, December 24–30, 1990, p. 15.

46. Ibid.

47. The *Boston Globe* reported that the United States trained nine of the alleged killers of the Jesuit priests at its training facility at Fort Bragg, North Carolina, and at Fort Benning, Georgia. See Michael K. Frisby, "U.S. Reportedly Trained 9 Salvadorans Linked to Priest Killings," *Boston Globe*, April 24, 1990, p. 24.

48. William Catto, "U.S. Military Aid to El Salvador to be Cut," *Times of the Americas*, October 31, 1990, p. 3.

49. Elaine Sciolino, "Latin Debt Crisis Seen as Threat to Continent's New Democracies," *New York Times*, January 17, 1989, p. 3.

50. Martin Andersen, "The Military Obstacles to Democracy," pp. 111–112.

4

THE POLITICS OF
CIVILIAN LEADERSHIP

I am a politician, not a magician.

—Vinicio Cerezo,
former president of Guatemala

The civilian leaders that head most of the governments of Latin America have an enormous responsibility. They not only have been entrusted with guiding their country through a minefield of economic, political, and social challenges but, more important, have become the symbols of a new spirit of democracy in the region.[1] If they are successful at meeting these challenges, and fortifying popular rule, they will strengthen the claim that national development is best achieved in an open and competitive political environment. If they fail, and the countries of the region fall further into decline and instability, it is certain to renew the debate over whether an authoritarian approach is the only solution to the seemingly endless list of problems facing the Latin American republics.[2]

Unlike the transition to democratic civilian government that occurred in the Alliance for Progress era, there is today a less romantic view of democracy and the ability of democratic politicians to make dramatic changes in the governing systems they head. The fall of the old-line dictators and the heady reform movements that spread throughout Latin America in the 1960s helped to elevate leaders like Rómulo Betancourt, Pepe Figueres, Juan Bosch, Galo Plaza, and Eduardo Frei to prominent positions in the region. In many respects the focus of democratic reform was viewed through them and the way they formed their presidencies.[3]

89

In the 1980s and 1990s the transition to democracy is approached from a much different perspective. The new era of democracy has arrived without the fanfare of a major U.S. policy initiative and at a time when much of the romanticism of politics has been destroyed by the ravages of financial indebtedness, social decay, and dirty wars. The anger and desperation of the Latin American people have taken the gleam off the arrival of a new wave of civilian democratic leadership. Although the overwhelming majority of Latin Americans have welcomed the return of popular rule, they are not convinced that the civilian leaders who rose to power through the ballot box can free them from military influence or deal with the policy dilemmas that were left over from previous authoritarian regimes.[4] The joy that filled the streets of the capitals of Latin America when the generals left were more like outbreaks of democratic enthusiasm, not signs of confidence that the power arrangements and rules of the game had been permanently adjusted.

As symbols of yet another experiment in democracy, contemporary Latin American presidents are at a unique disadvantage. Although they represent a new era of popular rule, they perform their leadership functions in a political climate that has the uncanny tendency to maintain traditional power relations. Although much has happened on the surface of Latin American politics, little has changed in the existing framework of politics. The military still wields considerable influence, economic elites are ever wary of economic restructuring, and the critical middle sectors continue to exhibit support for popular rule that has its limits and can be compromised. To further complicate their problems, Latin American civilian leaders not only must deal with the powerful vestiges of the past but also with the explosion of new social pressures and political alignments that have accompanied the transition from military rule. Mass-based groups such as labor unions and peasant organizations retain a vast reservoir of anger over lost opportunities. This powerful mix of heightened democratic responsibility, latent authoritarianism, and apprehensive, if not hostile, power contenders creates a dangerous challenge for civilian leadership. The civilian presidents of Latin America may very well have risen to positions of political power at a time when the prevailing internal and external conditions in the region allow for a very narrow margin of success.

The challenges faced by Latin America's civilian presidents raise a number of important issues that touch on the direction and prospects of democratization in this region. Throughout this chapter we will address these issues and elaborate on the strategies available to Latin American leaders as they attempt to solidify their position and that of democracy. Of primary concern is whether democratically elected leaders will be able to survive the pressure generated by the environment they work in. Latin American presidents must not only deal on a day-to-day basis with a wide range of policy crises but must also develop the skills necessary to ward off the threats to their office. As will be shown, political survival in the new Latin American political environment is not merely a matter of effectively addressing critical economic and social problems but also of honing one's abilities at balancing competing interests.[5] One of the current staples of Latin American political analysis is to celebrate the attainment of near complete democratization in the region. But as has often been the case when Latin America is examined, the eye-catching events in the region mask the more subtle changes in the structures, processes, and personal relationships that drive the political systems. As a result, the new era of democracy and civilian rule in Latin America has been viewed primarily in terms of campaigns, elections, inaugurations, and transfers of power.[6] These very visible signs of democratization, however, are only part of the story of Latin America's attempt to construct a complete and durable framework of democratic governance. At the core of this democratic construction project are the efforts by civilian presidents to respond to the realities of politics and the pressures for more open societies by fashioning new models of leadership and developing more modern management styles that will assist them in meeting the challenges of governing.

It becomes evident in examining the civilian presidents of Latin America that democratic politicians in the region function from within three basic models of executive leadership. These leadership models reflect the responses civilian presidents have made in the 1980s and now in the 1990s to the tasks of running countries alive with democratic promise but also steeped in a seemingly endless sea of crises. In many respects these are not new leadership models; rather they are redesigned formulas for dealing with the endless stream of problems that have beset this region. Contemporary Latin American presidents, in the face of mounting crises, have been required to embrace these leadership models not only as a means of responding to governing challenges but quite simply to survive.

DEMOCRATIC POWER-SHARING

In those Latin American states with a strong authoritarian tradition, newly established civilian presidents have quickly come to recognize that political power and control over the policy process do not rest solely in the executive branch. Governing democracies where there is a strong residue of military influence requires that political leaders accept their limitations or face futile, if not foolhardy, attempts at challenging the existing power relations. Civilian leaders who function in a power-sharing environment often carve out areas where they know policymaking power exists and then utilize that power to attain their stated objectives.[7] Conversely, power-sharing democrats realize that there are certain policy areas where change or reform are unlikely and therefore resort to cosmetic initiatives or public relations ploys as a means of covering up their weakness.

There has always been the temptation to describe what here is called democratic power-sharing as puppet presidencies. The common image is of a weak civilian politician controlled from behind the scenes by a powerful figure or by a group of elites. The puppet presidencies erected by the Somozas in the 1960s and Noriega's sham presidencies in recent years are examples of this type of democratic facade. But it is important to stress that in this new democratic era in Latin America the concept of puppet presidencies does not adequately explain the internal dynamics of civilian leadership.

The powerful political forces that may lurk behind the elected president are usually focused on a particular objective or source of concern. Those political forces then use their power to ensure that the civilian leader does not make policy decisions that would jeopardize the attainment of the objective or compromise their commitment to the concern. Civilian presidents often have a wide latitude of policymaking power as long as that power does not infringe upon or limit those carefully defined areas of nonpresidential power. Furthermore, civilian presidents have come to recognize that by allowing their adversaries to focus on a particular objective or reap the benefits from a particular public policy initiative, their ability to act more independently and to push for change is enhanced.[8]

In Latin American countries like El Salvador, Chile, and Argentina, where presidents clearly are forced to share power, civilian leaders are not helpless pawns of the military establishment or the conservative elites. They have been able to advance their own policy agenda, especially when economic and social crises have required bold action. It is in areas such as leftist activity, amnesty for human-rights abuser, and the handling of protest tied to shortages, income inequality, and structural reforms related to agricultural lands that civilian leaders have been forced to realize that presidential power has its limitations.

Although President Alfredo Cristiani of El Salvador has had some success in making the government a more visible agent of change and in rebuilding a country shattered by war, he has had difficulty reigning in the death squads and convincing the military that negotiating with the leftist rebels is just as effective in ending the war as counterguerrilla tactics.[9] Cristiani's failure to speed the trial of those responsible for the execution of the six Jesuit priets further reinforces the image of a president at the mercy of the military. In Chile, President Patricio Alywin, despite his popularity and the consensus that he will be a better leader than Augusto Pinochet, must share political power with his predecessor, who has stated publicly that he intends to remain a participant in the determination of Chile's future.[10] Alywin has on occasion brought Pinochet into his office and dressed the former military leader down for his anti-democratic statements, but the new president has been unable to contain the open hostility and periodic shows of force that emanate from the barracks. Alywin has had an especially difficult time pushing for the prosecution of military officers responsible for human-rights offenses in the aftermath of the coup against Salvador Allende. And in Argentina, Carlos Menem has taken some imaginative and aggressive steps to respond to his country's economic malaise, but he must constantly face recalcitrant elements in the armed forces who refuse to accept limitations on their power or threats to their security.[11] Menem's decision in late 1990 to grant pardons to former military presidents connected to the so-called Dirty War era pointed clearly to the precarious nature of his relationship with the armed forces.

The power-sharing model of democratic leadership need not always be linked with a strong military. Former President Virgilio Barco of Colombia faced the power realities of his country's drug cartels, which not only have their own armies but their own base of popular support. Mixing ruthless violence with shrewd use of showcase building projects for the poor, the drug empire emerged during his presidency as a quasigovernment that could not be ignored and on occasion seemed as powerful as the national government. Barco's highly acclaimed assault on the drug lords in 1989 was at once a response to the assassination of a leading presidential hopeful, Luis Galán, and a desperate attempt to regain control of the country. Barco was seeking to reestablish his authority and move Colombia away from a political system where governing power was compartmentalized and national leadership was viewed as a captive of the narco-traffickers.[12] Barco's successor, Cesar Gaviria, has emerged as even more of a power-sharer; he opposed extradition to the United States of key drug kingpins and worked quietly to develop amnesty agreements with the cartels. Gaviria was clearly anxious to end the rein of terror that has gripped Colombia, but his methods reveal a willingness to share power rather than destroy a powerful challenger to government authority.

The power-sharing model of leadership is currently the most common formula for exercising executive power in Latin America. Because civilian leaders throughout the region must face the prospect of working with and being limited by powerful individuals or groups within the political system, many presidents have come to recognize the necessity of sharpening their leadership skills and developing styles of decisionmaking that strengthen their ability to cope with the realities of democratic power-sharing. Democratic leaders in Latin America have become adroit balancers and cautious reformers. They have learned early on in their tenure that survival is directly related to their talent for knowing when to push forward and when to hold back, when to take action against an adversary and when to remain silent, when to favor one interest and when to seek consensus.[13]

Civilian leadership in Latin America is expressed through fine-tuning the political system rather than through grand reform initiatives. Because these leaders share power, change comes in increments and compromised decisions; promises are made but fulfilled only if expedient; reform policies are started, but always with a careful eye to the reaction of key elites. Not surprisingly, this careful leadership balancing act and cautious reformism is prone to criticism and protest from those who expect their president to be unrelenting in the pursuit of death squad killers, upper-class tax evaders, intransigent landowners, and conservative advocates of the status quo. Civilian leaders are accused of weakness and dishonesty and increasingly dismissed as mere democratic window dressing hiding the real power of the military and its allies.[14]

Although one cannot ignore the severe restraint that democratic power-sharing places on many Latin American civilian leaders, the adroit balancers and cautious reformers who occupy the presidencies in the region must be admired for the progressive steps they have made, no matter how small or how limited in scope. Bringing military oppressors to justice in Argentina, challenging the drug lords in Colombia, and standing up to the military establishment in Chile are important developments that have changed the character of politics and national life in these countries. Moreover, the campaign of Mexico's Carlos Salinas to root out corruption in unions and among the police and the efforts by Bolivia's Jaime Paz Zamora to restructure the tax codes to address the pervasive evasion problem suggest that some Latin American presidents are not content to merely share power or refrain from controversial policies. To say that these developments are insignificant gestures or partial answers to deep-seated problems is not only unfair but misses the point. Most of the countries of Latin America are but in the infancy of democratic governance, and the civilian leaders that lead these democracies are unsure of themselves and the resiliency of the systems they head. The fact that power-sharing requires compromise and an occasional bow to the traditional forces that want to remain in control should not detract from the accomplishments of leaders who are still feeling their way through some extremely dangerous waters.

DEMOCRATIC POPULISM

Latin American leaders are no strangers to image-making or the use of *personalismo* as a means of engendering popular support and ensuring that their enemies are placed at a disadvantage. Just as their caudillo predecessors employed the strategies and tactics that have come to be called populism, so too have the modern-day democrats developed their own populist model for dealing with the ever-threatening political environment. Contemporary Latin American presidents have become proficient at strengthening their hold on office and advancing their policy agenda through effective use of populist themes and modern public opinion techniques. Although the realities of power-sharing have limited their field of operation and the prospects of widescale reform, the fashioning of a leadership model designed to gain greater popular support has allowed many civilian democrats to survive the frequent threats to their office and preserve constitutional rule.

One of the more visible examples of contemporary Latin American populism is the emphasis being placed on marshaling support for debt relief from foreign, in particular U.S., banks. Unlike populists such as Peron and Vargas, who in the 1950s sought to solidify their position by building labor union and lower-class organizations, the civilian leaders of the 1980s and 1990s are aggressively promoting themselves as nationalistic protectors of the economy and outspoken challengers of North American financial power. Peru's Alan García permitted only 10 percent of that country's export income to be channeled back to foreign banks, and Venezuela's Andrés Pérez called for a policy of debt forgiveness. These policy positions reflect the attitude of many Latin American leaders who believe they must protect their economies and their political future by portraying themselves as champions of independence from foreign control. As President Pérez has stated, the foreign debt, "is the greatest challenge to our national sovereignty in modern times."[15]

Civilian presidents are becoming increasingly aware of the social and political dangers inherent in the continuing debt crisis in the region and see foreign banks, multilateral lending institutions like the International Monetary Fund, and of course the United States as ready targets for their populist attacks. Placing the blame for trade imbalances, diminishing foreign exchange, and budget deficits on external sources is viewed by Latin American leaders not only as a correct assessment of reality but as one means of deflecting the anger of the public away from the executive branch. These leaders do not want to be seen as unwilling to speak out against foreign financial power or to take measures that protect domestic interests.

But although taking on foreign financial interests has become one of the basic principles of the new Latin American populism, civilian presidents have also looked for ways to generate support from domestic sources. In moves that are filled with grave political risks, Latin American leaders are attempting to create a new economic environment built on the foundation of privatization and the market economy. Although the actions of democratic leaders to dismantle state enterprises have caused enormous outcries of opposition from public employees who face the loss of secure jobs, urban and rural poor who must endure price increases, and business sectors that benefit from government subsidies, the push to move Latin America away from its statist mode is clearly underway. The presidents of Latin America who have embraced privatization are seeking to present themselves and their administrations as on the cutting edge of significant social and economic transformation. They believe that despite the opposition and the dislocation that accompanies privatization, in the long run the complete overhaul of the Latin American statist approach will bring not only greater prosperity to the region but a broadening of support for civilian leadership.[16]

The fact that most leaders in Latin America have jumped on the privatization bandwagon attests not only to the seriousness of the economic malaise in the region but to the desire of civilian presidents to present themselves as more than "fine-tuners" of public policy. By leading the push for a complete overhaul of the domestic economy, Latin American leaders want to be perceived as democratic revolutionaries willing to bring about radical change in order to revitalize economies that are severely depressed. This willingness to take political risks and endure economic dislocation and social protest may at first appear to be anything but a populist strategy. Yet it is important to remember that the populists of the 1950s were not shy "fine-tuners" but bold architects of societal transformation who created a bond between public policy and public opinion. Today the privatization strategies of Menem of Argentina, Salinas of Mexico, and Collor of Brazil are not designed to attract the support of one group such as Peron's "shirtless ones" or Vargas's unions but rather to convince a cross-section of citizens that an economic overhaul will benefit all sectors of society and move their country out of the debt-induced doldrums.[17]

For many who are critical of the move to embrace a market economy in Latin America and see privatization as a boon to the entrepreneurial class, this new-age populism is viewed as sowing the seeds of democratic destruction and as destined to disengage popular support for civilian rule. The efforts to place the critical components of the nation's infrastructure such as natural resources, electricity, communication, and heavy industry in the hands of the private sector may indeed provide a boost to ailing economies, but the process of transforming a statist economy is certain to create a host of new problems in the areas of unemployment, retraining, and social welfare. More important, the move toward privatization is also certain to foster what can only be termed "psychosocial" problems as generations of Latin Americans raised in a statist environment are then thrust into the harsher realities of a market economy. The combination of traditional public policy problems and the radical change in the social-economic environment could easily lead to social upheaval and unrelenting opposition to the civilian leaders who introduced the changes.[18]

Convincing wary citizens that privatization and the market economy will indeed enhance their lives and strengthen the nation is certain to be the greatest challenge faced by Latin American leaders. If civilian presidents want to convince the public that a period of austerity is necessary as the country engages in this radical restructuring, they will be forced to ensure that the needs of those who face dislocation and a harsher life are addressed. If civilian leaders recognize that an economic overhaul can only be achieved if it is accomplished without losing popular support, then the move toward privatization and the market economy may not only transform Latin America but preserve democratic governance.

One of the more effective strategies that Latin American political leaders are using today to enhance their image and strengthen their ties to a wary public is the sharpening of their media skills. Gone are the days when Ecuador's president José María Velasco Ibarra stood on a balcony and mesmerized a crowd. The contemporary Latin American leader has become a populist by employing the wide array of populist techniques. Presidents and presidential aspirants have become experts at media politics. Policy programs are skillfully packaged to present to the legislature and to the people; television is used extensively to show the hardworking and concerned chief executive; and political advertising has advanced from the rudimentary handbill to the slick newspaper, magazine, billboard, and media blitz. Brazil's Fernando Collor, for example, used his family's involvement in television and connections to the powerful TV Globo network to launch and sustain his candidacy; in Peru, radio personality Carlos

Palenque used the power of the airwaves to help him win the mayorality of Lima.

What is even more obvious in Latin American politics is the recognition that the age, appearance, style, and sex appeal of the president or presidential aspirant are important ingredients to success. Most presidential candidates now hire U.S. media consultants to help them promote the proper image to the voters. Both the Acción Democrática and COPEI (Cómmittee for Independent Political and Electoral Institutions) parties in Venezuela have for years used New York- and Washington-based political consulting firms to advise them on techniques of media campaigning. Once in office some Latin American presidents who may be tainted by scandal (such as President Linden Pindling of the Bahamas) have relied on consultants to salvage their image and ensure that their relationship with the United States will not be jeopardized.[19]

The new breed of media-driven presidents in Latin America is a reflection not only of the realities of electoral politics in a world dominated by television but also of the realization that the region's population makeup is overwhelmingly young and attracted to candidates who appear to be like them and share their values. Most of the civilian presidents now increasingly play to the youth-oriented, image-conscious populations that have grown up on television and slick advertising. In Peru, Alberto Fujimori traveled around the country in his "Fujimobile" to attract the attention of the voters and utilized his Japanese heritage to convince disheartened Peruvians that he could do for Peru what the Japanese have done in their homeland. In El Salvador, the election campaign for president provided a revealing example of the impact that proper packaging of a candidate can have on the final result. The ARENA party of Alfredo Cristiani employed slick campaign techniques that mixed loud rock music, sexy cheerleaders, and flashy rallies designed to excite the youthful Salvadorans. The campaign strategy, largely designed by ARENA leader Roberto D'Aubisson, was weak on issues such as human-rights abuse and a formula for ending the war; he instead sought to distract voters by presenting the governing Christian Democrats as weak and stodgy.[20] Even Nicaragua's Daniel Ortega borrowed a page from the slick campaign handbook with his song-and-dance routines in tight jeans and flowery shirts. Unlike Fujimori and Cristiani, Ortega's new campaign tactic did not erase the memory of ten years of Sandinista rule.

The emphasis that Latin American leaders are placing on shaping the political images of the voting public has changed the character of politics in this region. Although these stylistic strategies can certainly be termed a new form of *personalismo*, they are a different form of contact with the people in the sense that the Latin American presidency has become a less formalistic office and the individual presidents are now convinced that *personalismo* must be linked with technology if leadership is to be successful. The relationship with the electorate in the 1990s is less and less a matter of the patron handing out favors or solving personal problems in staged encounters with the public. It has become commonplace, for example, to see leaders such as Oscar Arias of Costa Rica walk the beach or jog with citizens, Carlos Menem play soccer with a local team, or Fernando Collor dance on the beaches of Rio—all in front of the television cameras and documented by the press.[21]

Argentina's Menem, in particular, is gaining extensive media coverage for his flamboyant style of leadership. The reputation of the sixty-one-year-old Peronist leader has been damaged by marital problems, corruption charges, and relentless womanizing, yet his approval rate after two years in office is higher than for any president since Peron. The Argentine people appear to identify with his open, no-holds-barred style, which has brought the presidency down to a more human level. The fact that Menem's administration has been viewed as tough and competent despite the fast cars, face-lifts, and late-night frolicking is a credit to the changing character of political culture in Argentina, a culture that is concentrating on the considerable economic successes of the government and tolerating the foibles of its president.[22]

The most recent addition to the ranks of the personalist leaders is Haiti's Reverend Jean Bertrand Aristide. Aristide won the election in 1990 on a wave of popular support that bordered on the fanatical. Using symbolic gestures such as having a peasant woman place the presidential sash over him to bolder moves like jailing his predecessor for plotting a coup, Aristide quickly transformed Haitian politics. By building on his reputation as a spokesman of the poor, Aristide promised to reallocate Haiti's meager resources and stand firm against the obstructionist Duvalier faction in the country. But after a brief six months in office, Aristide was removed from power by the military. Upset over signs that the Haitian president was seeking to develop an elite military force and encouraging the poor to retaliate against those in the armed forces responsible for past repression, the high command of the armed forces led by General Raoul Cedras brought the brief experiment in civilian leadership to a grinding halt.

The ouster of Aristide, who escaped to Venezuela, brought worldwide condemnation along with trade and diplomatic sanctions from the OAS and European nations such as France. Aristide could do little but wait and see whether the military and its supporters in the business community would allow his return. Many in and out of Haiti were skeptical that Aristide would ever regain power primarily because the deposed president continued to be viewed by the conservative elite as a radical bent on weakening the hold of the rich and sponsoring antimilitary policies. The wave of populism and charismatic appeal that swept Aristide into office could not match the raw power of those who feared change. Aristide may have had the talent to win the hearts of the masses, but his burning desire to right the wrongs of the past was based more on emotion and principle than on realism and practicality.

Although Latin American presidents use modern techniques to enhance their image and strengthen their power base, they recognize that democratic populism will be a successful strategy only if it reaches out to the people with programs that face up to the social and economic crises that grip this region. Populism remains a political approach whose foundation is built on empowerment and redistribution. Flashy campaigns and television presidencies may help for a time to create the impression of empowerment and redistribution but if the reality of change does not filter down to those who are the targets of the image-making, then the populist strategies will ultimately fail.

DEMOCRATIC CAUDILLOISM

Amidst all the democratization in Latin America it is essential to remember that old ways die hard in this region. Although government leadership, in particular, has changed dramatically with the transition to civilian rule and the increased emphasis on openness, competition, accountability, and consensus-building, the onset of new leadership models and values has not completely replaced the traditional formulas for managing the social order, administering public policy, and responding to political challenges. Latin America retains its essentially cautious mode of operation and concern that past practices continue to be followed. In a manner that is typically Latin American, leaders have incorporated modern democracy and modern leadership techniques while being careful not to dismantle some of the central components of a unique system of politics.[23]

Nowhere is this attempt at blending more in evidence than in the way democratic leadership has evolved. Latin American civilian presidents today reveal a style of leadership that can best be called democratic caudilloism. Though the linking of these two terms may seem contradictory, the term *democratic caudilloism* captures the attempt by Latin American leaders to embrace modern democratic values and administrative principles while holding on to proven traditional practices that allowed the caudillos of old to retain power and maintain order.

The presence of democratic caudilloism in contemporary Latin America is a kind of additional transition mechanism within the larger democratic transition process.[24] Civilian presidents, unsure of themselves and of the staying power of democratic governance, have decided to construct a model of political leadership that will not be perceived as a radical departure from the ways in which leaders operated in the past. As a result, many of the political leaders in Latin America are continuing their careful balancing act, only this time it is not balancing power contenders but styles of leadership and the public perceptions that those styles engender. Democratic caudilloism as currently practiced is designed to blend traditional modes of operation that are familiar and popular with more modern techniques that are deemed essential in order to ensure the effective functioning of democracy.

Civilian presidents who practice democratic caudilloism can be seen touting the importance of developing modern government. One example is that democratic leaders have sought to convince the public and world of their modernism by forming ever larger advisory systems. More and more the accent is being placed on appointing a team of highly respected technocrats to address the myriad economic and financial problems facing the country. Government by U.S.-trained economic and financial experts, or, as they are affectionately called, "techno-yuppies," has become an important component of democratic leadership in the region.[25] Presidents regularly can be seen trying to convince the public not only of the benefits of a particular public policy but that the team of advisers chosen to implement the policy and achieve the stated objective is eminently qualified and worthy of support. Despite the fact that countries in severe economic straits like Argentina, Bolivia, and Brazil routinely replace their technocrats for failure to deal with key social and economic problems, presidents in those countries continue to seek the restoration of public confidence by appointing a new team that is presented as competent to deal with the crisis. This kind of European-style cabinet shuffling takes some of the pressure off of the president and at the same time sends the message to the people that government remains in the hands of individuals who are capable of solving the issues of the day.

The penchant of many Latin American presidents for promoting a democratic technocracy must be balanced by the fact that at below-cabinet levels there is often a struggle over patronage in a manner not unlike that which occurred in the paternalism of the caudillo period. A president comes into office not only as the leader of the country but as the leader of a party whose supporters see the victory as a means of gaining employment or enhancing their employment opportunities. The world may be looking at how the president and his team of experts are dealing with their policy agenda; the party faithful are looking to their president for patronage jobs.[26] In Mexico, President Salinas has had an especially difficult time shedding his traditional role of patronage dispenser for the PRI. Although he publicly plays the role of reformer bent on changing the image of the PRI as a bastion of corrupt cronyism, he cannot easily ignore the power of union, peasant, and middle-class sectors that for decades have served as the electoral foundation of the governing party.

The patronage pressures faced by a civilian president often are a mixed blessing. On the one hand, the president may relish his ability to secure his political base in the governing party by handing out government sinecures. Serving as the generous patron who takes care of his own is practical politics, especially in a political environment where allies are so vital to remaining in office. On the other hand, however, providing employment to the party faithful can be fraught with danger. With heightened demands to trim bloated public budgets by dismissing employees, presidents may find that patronage politics is a distinct liability. Furthermore, the patronage process often creates friction and factionalism within the party organization as one ideological, regional, social group receives favorable treatment at the expense of another.[27]

Civilian leaders can easily be tempted to use jobs and other financial rewards as powerful weapons to intimidate political adversaries and actually breed party dissension as a means of ridding the organization of unwanted challengers. As Mark Rosenberg describes the presidency of Roberto Suazo Cordoba of Honduras,

> During his four years in office, President Suazo used an array of resources to promote factionalism in the dominant political parties and in labor oragnizations which were perceived as unfriendly. In his own party, Suazo's unpredictable decision-making, often contrary to Liberal customs and rules, resulted in the gradual marginalization of leading Liberal insiders and in the further factionalization of the party.[28]

Suazo's treatment of party faithful and his reliance on the reward system for dealing with his friends and enemies prompted one Honduran source to describe the president as "having been raised in the rancid political tradition where caudillismo, compradrazgo and bribery were the main elements of action."[29]

Latin American presidents also reveal the conflict between modernism and traditional practices in the way they deal with governing institutions outside the office of the executive. The transition to democracy has not only strengthened the electoral process and the stature of civilian leadership, it has also permitted the legislative branch, the courts, and the local governing units to play a larger role in public policy formation. The legislatures, in particular, have become more aggressive in their relations with their presidents and more anxious to be perceived as effective competitors who must be taken seriously if the executive branch is to successfully negotiate its agenda. John Peeler in his study of three Latin American democracies (Colombia, Costa Rica, and Venezuela) points to the heightened bargaining power of the legislature and its ability to counteract the power of civilian executives. As Peeler states, "While certainly not equal to the president's power, the legislative branch in each of the three countries does have and use the capability to force the president to bargain, and can on occasion defeat him outright."[30]

The legislative branch with its growing power is a far cry from what it was in the democracies of the 1960s, when executive-legislative relations were mere window dressing and presidents fashioned laws and ran the government from within a closed environment. Today, the accent is on developing institutional autonomy and enhancing the reputation of government officials outside the office of the presidency. This wave of confidence is not restricted just to the legislative branch. Members of the judiciary have been especially aggressive in asserting their claim to autonomy and respect. Judges in many countries have gone on strike for higher salaries, for greater protection from drug dealers and revolutionaries, and for support for their efforts on behalf of constitutionalism, human rights, and government restraint. In many respects, it is the judges and their often bold moves to gain attention that have shown the extent to which the process of governing has advanced beyond simple executive power.[31]

The growing institutionalization in many Latin American countries, however, must be weighed against the continued reliance of civilian presidents on tried and true centralism. Whether it is the kind of benevolent centralism practiced by a Joaquín Balaguer of the Dominican Republic or the party-controlled centralism of Salinas in Mexico, Latin American presidents refuse to become captives of the checks-and-balances system. By their often shrewd control of the party organization in the legislature, presidents have been able to manage the policy agenda, ensure that legislation mirrors the views of the executive branch, and guarantee that legislative adversaries do not become equal partners in the governing of the nation. Despite the advances made by the legislatures and the courts, the process of governing in this region remains one of presidential decrees and pronouncements, private meetings among cabinet members and influential bureaucrats, and perfunctory votes by legislators loyal to the executive and fearful of creating a policy logjam.

Added to the numerous examples of centralist techniques and procedures used to counteract the rising assertiveness of the legislature and the courts are the stylistic methods employed by civilian leaders to reinforce the image of control within the executive branch. The practice of presidents taking personal credit for infrastructure projects or policy initiatives remains common in Latin America. Hurricane or earthquake relief efforts and social welfare programs targeted for the poor often bear the name of the president, his wife, or an organization founded by the government.[32] What is usually missing from the public policy arena in Latin America is the photo opportunity in which the president calls together legislators from both parties to publicly reinforce the bipartisan nature of governing. Unlike in the United States, bill-signing ceremonies are not an occasion to celebrate cooperation but to show the political and administrative skill of the chief executive.

The centralist style of many Latin American presidents suggests that these modern leaders, much like their caudillo predecessors, are susceptible to the temptations of governing power. Even though they may exude modernism and accept the political and administrative limits that democratic governance requires, the vestiges of prior leadership models remain. Latin American presidents may reject the abuses and excesses of *caudillismo*, but their administrations have not been able to conquer many of the fundamental components of centralist rule. Public corruption below the office of the president continues unabated, examples of nepotism and familial greed are commonplace, and the penchant for garnering attention and support through costly and usually unnecesssary public works projects remains a staple of the policy process. Yet although these are bothersome aspects of civilian rule in Latin America, they simply point up the difficulty of moving beyond elections to a more thorough transformation of the executive branch.

But although the old may linger, it is important to stress that much has changed within the framework of civilian leadership in Latin America. Unlike the caudillos, today's presidents are no practitioners of *continuismo*. Rather they relish the concept of limited tenure in office and proudly leave the presidency not only to another individual but often to another party. Today's Latin American civilian leaders are intelligent, hardworking, dedicated politicians who rarely take on the image of the cruel, sex-crazed buffoon that served as the stereotype for North American readers. If anything the civilian presidents of the contemporary period are astute balancers who recognize the importance of mixing the old with the new, the democratic with the centralist, the modern with the traditional.[33]

U.S. POLICY AND CIVILIAN PRESIDENTS

For U.S. policymakers the transition from authoritarian to civilian rule in Latin America has been a mixed blessing. The ascension to power of democratically elected presidents has offered the United States an opportunity to work with leaders who share our values and function within a common governing framework. U.S. presidents are no longer reluctant to develop an open association with Latin American heads of state. With most of the generals unwilling to assume power, or for that matter to take a visible role in national politics, the fear of being perceived as supporting authoritarian regimes and working with repressive dictators has diminished.

The democratization of Latin American politics, however, has also provided the United States with a number of challenges. The return to civilian rule in the region has forced this country to formulate new strategies for dealing with open and competitive political environments. More important, U.S. policymakers now must expend additional energy, resources, and political capital in order to ensure that democratically elected leaders are able to weather the regular waves of crises that are endemic to the Latin American governing situation. For years the United States talked about the importance of Latin America embracing democratic governance and civilian rule. Now that those goals have been accomplished, the expectation both in Latin America and in this country is that Washington will match its rhetoric with more than lofty words of support.[34]

Although there is an undeniable spirit of confidence among U.S. policymakers concerning the benefits of democratic governance and civilian rule in Latin America, there nevertheless are a number of political problems and systemic deficiencies that must be addressed if democratic leadership is to be more than a temporary respite from authoritarianism. The United States is aware that its role in helping new democracies and new leaders is critical and that it must work to strengthen and stabilize governments threatened by antidemocratic elites. The attainment of these goals is therefore dependent on whether our leaders can help their counterparts in the hemisphere deal with a range of leadership challenges. If these challenges are unmet or dealt with in a haphazard manner, the prospects for vibrant and resilient civilian democracies will certainly be reduced. The task ahead is thus as critical for the United States as it is for the Latin Americans. If democracy means as much to us as we say it does, then how we work to meet these challenges will say much about our commitment to new leadership in Latin America.

Friends or Foes?

Perhaps the most delicate challenge facing the United States as it attempts to strengthen and stabilize civilian democracies in Latin America is the ability to work with a wide array of leaders who often do not hold similar views on regional issues or are unsympathetic to our position. One of the more salient characteristics of the new democratic movement in Latin America is the outspoken nature of national leadership. Today's Latin American leaders see themselves as symbols of political independence and regional self-determination. Taking stands in opposition to U.S. policy and U.S. interests is looked upon by civilian leaders as essential to the maintenance of popular support. The outspoken positions on trade, aid, diplomacy, and debt taken by leaders such as Salinas of Mexico, Arias of Costa Rica, Andrés Pérez of Venezuela and García of Peru not only play well in their individual countries but mark them as hemispheric leaders who are willing to take on the Colossus of the North.[35]

The assertiveness and aggressive pursuit of national interest by today's Latin American leader has posed a problem for U.S. policymakers. Although the United States has praised the civilian presidents for their ability to lead nations in crisis, at the same time it has been displeased and surprised with their often aggressive pursuit of national interests. The civilian presidents of Latin America regularly reinforce the changing character of U.S.–Latin American relations and the fact that Washington will not be permitted to conduct foreign policy from a one-dimensional perspective.

The emphasis placed on asserting independence and demanding respect has not gone unnoticed in the United States. Presidents have come to realize that Latin American leaders will not tolerate being ignored or taken for granted. President Jimmy Carter set the tone for this more equitable relationship with his pursuit of the Panama Canal Treaty but was reminded of the ease with which U.S. presidents fall back on old ways when he sought unsuccessfully to convince the Organization of American States (OAS) to support a peacekeeping operation during the fall of Somoza.[36] The Latin American leaders would not tolerate a return to the use of the OAS as a means of propping up a Latin American dictator.

President Ronald Reagan, after years of stepping over Latin American sensibilities with his contra policy, was forced to acknowledge the reality of the Arias peace plan and the willingness of the Central American presidents to conduct the foreign policy of the region without the consent or participation of the United States. The peace initiative was an enormously significant event for Latin America and for Latin American leaders in that it validated the process of independence and regional leadership that had been evolving since the transition to democratic rule.[37] George Bush continued the tradition of telling the Latin Americans what was good for them with the invasion of Panama in December 1989 but had to endure a stream of criticism from every corner of the hemisphere. The opposition to the U.S. intervention, though, may have had some positive effect on U.S.-Latin American relations in that the drug summit in early 1990 was conducted in an atmosphere of cooperation and equality. President Bush agreed to many of the proposals of Barco of Colombia, García of Peru, and Paz of Bolivia and accepted the principal contention of the Latin Americans, that the drug problem is not one just of supply but of U.S. demand.[38]

One of the most significant characteristics of the changing relationship between Latin America and the United States is the gradual "evening out" of the leadership balance. Although the United States continues to hold most of the cards in terms of military and economic power, Latin American leaders are going on the offensive and seeking to adjust a leadership balance that was skewed in favor of Washington. Harsh criticism from Latin leaders is now being accompanied by more confident demands for equal treatment and respect for their point of view. Civilian presidents in Latin America are willing to work with the United States to achieve mutually perceived objectives, but their cooperation is now based more on the principle of give-and-take and on an occasional outright concession. Perhaps the clearest manifestation of this evening out process is the forming of the so-called Group of Eight in Latin America. Presidents from the eight major Latin American nations not only meet regularly to discuss issues of mutual importance but see themselves as an emerging diplomatic force in the region to solve problems and avoid crises. For the Latin Americans this is a welcome step toward greater control over their future; for the United States it is another example of a changed relationship.[39]

Training and Supporting Democrats

One of the areas of leadership relations in Latin America in which the United States has maintained a degree of consistency over the years is in the training and support of potential candidates for public office and positions within critical social organizations. From the days of training the Trujillos and Somozas to take over after the marines left to the heady days of the Alliance for Progress when Latin American social democrats flocked to Washington to better prepare themselves for the reform challenges awaiting them, the United States has remained committed to strengthening its political position in the region through programs that target our friends and work to ensure that they have the necessary resources to succeed.[40]

In today's Latin America the United States is involved in a full range of programs to enhance democratic leadership. In large part because of the need to dismantle authoritarian regimes in countries like El Salvador, Honduras, and Guatemala and because of the Kissinger Commission's recommendations on the importance of "supporting democratic processes and institutions by backing . . . technical skills and the development of leadership skills,"[41] the United States during the Reagan presidency relied heavily on the National Endowment for Democracy (NED) as a prime training organization. Established by Congress in 1983, NED, with its four institutional backers—the AFL-CIO, the U.S. Chamber of Commerce, and the Democratic and Republican parties—provided financial assistance and training assistance to a host of Latin American groups from the Conservative party in Nicaragua to a nonpartisan studies center in Guatemala.[42] Although a major portion of the NED funding went to leadership groups that were in opposition to leftist regimes or espoused an anti-Communist ideology, the stated objective of NED was to "contribute to the development of democracy through assistance to counterparts abroad."[43]

The Agency for International Development (AID) also became involved in the training of prodemocratic allies in Latin America.

AID developed the Inter-American Center for Electoral Assistance and Promotion (CAPEL), which provides training and services to countries holding elections. Although the major thrust of the CAPEL programs is in the area of technical assistance—computerized voting lists, election procedures, and seminars on election laws—the State Department viewed the program as, "building a valuable network of individuals and institutions committed to promoting well-administered, free and competitive elections."[44] In conjunction with the CAPEL program, the State Department and AID also has developed a series of programs designed to promote exchanges among legislators from the Caribbean Basin region. The United States sees the exchange as vital in order to ensure that legislators in the region have the skills necessary for effective policymaking. To date, exchange programs have been developed in El Salvador, Honduras, and Guatemala.

Support for leadership training has also been a priority at the United States Information Agency (USIA). USIA developed a pilot program called the Central American Program for Undergraduate Scholarship (CAMPUS), which aims to bring thousands of Central American students to the United States. Taking a cue from Eastern bloc countries and Cuba, which have been providing scholarships to Latin American students for years, the United States now is making a major commitment to educate students from the region in a democratic and capitalistic setting. The CAMPUS program has also been enhanced by an expanded USIA program called Partners of the Americas, which provides student exchanges, and by the ongoing Rotary Club efforts to provide scholarships to needy Latin American students.[45]

The U.S. government's concerted effort to train the Latin American leaders of tomorrow in democracy is by no means the only leadership development. Labor unions and business associations have for years been involved in the training of union and private-sector leaders. The AFL-CIO has been most aggressive in building ties to Latin American labor leaders and in bringing those leaders to the United States for training sessions at its George Meaney Center for Labor Studies in Maryland. The AFL-CIO has also supported financially the campaigns of prodemocratic labor leaders for union leadership posts in Latin America. Joining the AFL-CIO in the support of Latin American labor leaders is the American Institute of Free Labor Development (AIFLD). The AIFLD and its president, William Doherty, have since the 1960s been articulate supporters of labor union organization and democratic politics in Latin America. Although the AIFLD has in the past been the subject of criticism by leftist labor leaders and politicians as an arm of the CIA and a meddler in labor affairs, it continues to wield significant influence with Latin American unions.[46]

Although unions in the United States have a longer record of involvement in democratic training, the business community in this country has moved quickly to make its contribution. In large part due to the promotion of the Caribbean Basin Initiative by the Reagan administration, business groups such as the Caribbean/Latin American Action organization have formed close ties with their counterparts in the region and have fostered numerous programs to not only strengthen commerical ties but emphasize the importance of linking private enterprise with democratic governance. Business leaders in this country are increasingly becoming convinced of the importance of consolidating democratic government in Latin America and there-fore working to convince the business community in the region that a return to authoritarian rule would be disastrous.[47]

The mix of public and private initiatives designed to strengthen democratic values in Latin America and provide leaders with the support and training necessary to survive does not complete the picture of how the United States is working to ensure that the leaders of today and tomorrow are friendly and democratic. One of the most effective, although controversial, strategies for achieving the goal of friendly and democratic leaders is to intervene in the electoral process. Again, the United States has a long history of intervention in Latin American elections in order to guarantee that the victor is "our man." But in recent years presidents have been reluctant to engage in the Wilsonian method for "civilizing" the Latin American electoral process. Jimmy Carter, for example, utilized what can be called passive intervention when he threatened the Dominican president Joaquín Balaguer with an aid cutoff if he did not permit the resumption of the ballot count, which clearly showed the opposition candidate in the lead.[48] Ronald Reagan was not so passive in his efforts to guarantee that Napoleón Duarte would be the first democratically elected president of El Salvador. Fearing the possible victory of death squad leader Roberto D'Aubisson, the Reagan administration approved the funneling of over $300,000 in campaign funds to Duarte and made it clear to Salvadoran elites and the military that it would not accept the victory of the rightist leader.[49]

The invasion of Panama by President Bush in order to install the duly elected government of Guillermo Endara may bring the policy of supporting democratic leaders in Latin America full circle. President Bush proudly stated that one of the objectives of the invasion was to reestablish democratic government in Panama, a statement that could easily have been made by Woodrow Wilson. Although Bush received rave reviews in the United States for the invasion, Latin American leaders were clearly disturbed by the reintroduction of intervention as a tool of democracy.[50] Furthermore, the fact that Endara was sworn into office on a U.S. military base and would have to be propped up with enormous injections of U.S. aid made many in Latin America wonder whether the Panamanian leader would be an independent executive heading a sovereign nation. The coup attempt in 1990 and the U.S. mini-invasion to put down that coup raised new fears that the United States might have to prop up Endara with more than money in the coming years.

The actions of Carter, Reagan, and Bush in dealing with democratic leaders and democratic transition in Latin America reveal the range of options available to U.S. presidents as they seek to support individuals who reflect our values and want to work with us. The United States is certainly correct in establishing programs that lay a democratic foundation and prepare leaders for the rigors of democratic governance. The problem lies in the more aggressive attempts by the United States to ensure compliance with our objectives or to guarantee that an electoral outcome will be to our liking. Policymakers in this country must recognize the dangers of interfering in the leadership selection process and be prepared for the backlash that can occur when voters and elites react to military intervention.

Running Elections and Buying Time with Dollars

Although U.S. support of democratization in Latin America often lends itself to the rhetoric of high principle and good government, policymakers in this country know that civilian rule will be maintained only through the injection of foreign assistance and capital investment. One election or a peaceful transfer of power does not make a democracy, especially if the socioeconomic climate is such that the political leadership is regularly threatened by general strikes, demonstrations, urban violence, and guerrilla warfare. As a result the United States has developed a democratic strategy for the region that is built on providing preelection assistance designed to lay the groundwork for successful popular participation and post-election assistance designed to ensure that democratically elected presidents have the resources available to deal with the never-ending array of policy challenges. In a real sense the United States is buying time for the civilian presidents with dollars, because time to establish a democratic system and deal with economic crises is one of the most precious commodities available to a new Latin American leader.[51]

The preelection assistance of providing computers, ballot paper, training in electoral law, voting list coordination, and educational programs on the meaning and importance of democracy has not received a great deal of attention because it is largely logistical and technical in nature and is not specifically targeted toward the critical issues of candidate selection or transition. But it is important to realize that by providing the preelection assistance the United States contributes to the development of a new popular mind-set within those countries so used to the quiet palace reshuffling of generals or the occasional brutal struggle for power. Voters in countries with little or no experience in electoral politics begin to see that choosing their leaders in an open and fair process is a complex and modern experience that places them in the political arena. Politics becomes more organized and sophisticated; the concepts of regularity and legality are accentuated; and the crucial qualities of faith in government and belief in the democratic process are enhanced.[52]

The preelection institutional and procedural support of the United States is in the main noncontroversial, but that does not mean that providing the assistance is always easy or effective. U.S. election advisers must overcome enormous educational, technical, and cultural obstacles in their task of helping Latin American countries develop a complete election system. In some countries such as El Salvador the United States had to construct a complete electoral system because the country had no experience with popular rule and few resources to develop a system that could be certified as fair and accurate. When the Salvadoran elections were held in 1982, 1984, and 1989 the success of the democratic process and the election of civilian leaders overshadowed the work that had been done jointly by U.S. advisers and Salvadoran officials to ensure that those opposed to the process would not question its validity.[53]

The institutional and procedural support from the United States is usually complemented by the more controversial contributions to the campaigns of candidates with views supportive of our interests. The monies filtered into the campaign of Napoleón Duarte in 1984 mentioned earlier and the financial support from the United States provided to the campaign of Violeta Chamorro in Nicaragaua are not unique examples of aid, yet such assistance continues to anger those in the region who brand the United States as a meddler in the internal affairs of Latin American countries. Both the Reagan and Bush administrations have expressed little concern over the protestations of those who viewed the financial support of pro-U.S. candidates in Central America as a new form of intervention. The response to these criticisms from Washington has been that the Soviet Union or Cuba are also pouring money into the region to influence political outcomes, so it is necessary for the United States to respond in kind.

The reality of public campaign contributions from the coffers of the State Department, the Central Intelligence Agency, or the National Endowment for Democracy point up the seriousness with which the United States approaches the democratization in Central America and its commitment to assure that those who assume national office are friends of this country. Although we are concerned with building democratic institutions and guaranteeing fair elections, it is the end result of this process that interests us the most. Elections may be the watchword of our policy in Latin America, but it is the election of a pro-U.S. leader that occupies our attention and motivates our policymakers to action.

But once civilian democrats assume power in Latin America the United States faces a new challenge—how to ensure that these presidents can survive the political and economic crises that appear with all too frequent regularity. To achieve the objective of stabilizing the power of civilian presidents and addressing the problems that threaten their political base, the United States can employ a wide range of "leadership supports." Statements of praise and cooperation, high-level diplomatic or presidential visits, preferential trade agreements, promises of widening technology transfers, and new initiatives to encourage private capital investment are but some of the more common measures that this country has used to show goodwill and help bolster governments that share our values and interests.[54]

Although the above measures can be effective and are certainly welcomed by Latin American presidents, the critical stabilizing ingredient for civilian leaders remains foreign aid. With most Latin American democracies running dangerously high public deficits and burdened with enormous debt obligations, the presidents in the region are desperate for injections of U.S. economic assistance. Furthermore, countries such as El Salvador, Nicaragua, and Panama, which have experienced various levels of damage to their infrastructure and their economies due to guerrilla warfare, trade boycotts, or invasion, need massive levels of assistance if they hope to rebuild their countries and maintain their struggling democracies.

During the Reagan administration the United States recognized the importance of providing new democracies in Latin America, and particularly Central America, with economic assistance. The introduction of the Caribbean Basin Initiative by President Reagan in 1981 with its commitment to provide the region with $350 million in assistance (along with a twelve-year free-trade arrangement) was the first major aid program for the region since John Kennedy's Alliance for Progress in the early 1960s. The Reagan administration firmly believed that containing communism was not only a matter of military containment but also required capital in order to provide democratic leaders with the financial resources to shore up their economies and meet the growing demands of increasingly restive populations. The words of Henry Kissinger in his report on Central America concerning the need to show our support by the commitment of aid also reinforce the view that the United States recognized the importance of buying time for democratic leaders with dollars. As Mr. Kissinger said, "There might be an argument for doing nothing to help the government in El Salvador, there might be an argument for doing a great deal more. There is, however, no logical argument for giving some aid, but not enough."[55]

From the perspective of the Reagan administration the aid commitment to Central America was designed to thwart the expansion of communism by helping new governments and new leaders offer their people an alternative to Marxism and provide them with a thin cushion of support from the political threats posed by economic decline. The principle of buying time with dollars took a somewhat different turn once President Bush entered the White House. In many respects Mr. Bush had a similar perspective on the need to support democracies and democratic leaders through our aid program, but he was limited in the implementation of his program by budget constraints and new demands elsewhere in the world. The Gramm-Rudman-Hollings budget reduction bill limited the ability of the president to make promises to Central American democratic leaders about continuing the massive aid programs. Moreover, the upheavals in Eastern Europe introduced not only new opportunities but new aid requests from governments anxious to realign their diplomatic and economic ties. But because both Guillermo Endara of Panama and Violeta Chamorro of Nicaragua faced threats from recalcitrant military institutions and headed economies that were near collapse, President Bush felt it essential that the United States pledge to commit substantial monies to each country. In both cases Bush stated that $1 billion was needed to ensure that these two struggling democratic leaders would have the resources necessary to begin rebuilding and dealing with the inevitable threats from a dissatisfied and impatient citizenry. However, once the budget debate ensued over aid to Panama and Nicaragua, both nations received substantially less than they were promised (Panama, for example, as of early 1991 had received only $120 million), prompting anguished calls for more support and disappointment that the Bush administration seemed more interested in the immediate transition to democracy than the long-term development of stable democratic governance.[56]

The precipitous decline of communism worldwide and the continued resiliency of democratic governance in Latin America has certainly strengthened the position of the United States in its traditional sphere of influence. With the Soviets unable to make major commitments to revolutionary Marxism in the hemisphere, Castro weakened at home and in the region, and the Sandinistas now an opposition party, it may appear that the strategy of buying time with dollars is unnecessary. But although some democratic leaders may feel more secure from leftist threats, they continue to face dangerous political and social threats because of the growing gap between the masses and those who have achieved a modicum of prosperity.

The United States may need to rethink its strategy of using foreign assistance as a stabilizing agent and a "leadership support," because there are new threats in the region that have less to do with ideology and more to do with unmet promises and unfulfilled expectations. President Bush's Enterprise for the Americas Initiative announced in 1990 with its accent on free trade, debt reduction, and capital infusion may be the first step in this rethinking process. Although this initiative has been accepted enthusiastically by the Latin Americans as a revolutionary approach to hemispheric relations, many questions remain concerning the commitment of the United States to hemispheric free trade and debt reduction and the ability of the Latin Americans to develop stable and efficient governing regimes that would attract capital and lay the foundation for market-based prosperity.

The U.S. commitment to democratic governance and democatic leadership will be severely tested in the future as the temptation to bring order to unstable societies increases. The military option has only been pushed aside, it has not been laid to rest. If the United States is indeed committed to the continued advancement of democracy in this region, it will have to maintain, if not expand, its foreign assistance programs or accept the prospect of having to deal anew with those military regimes that have the capability of bringing order.

NOTES

1. See Howard J. Wiarda, *The Democratic Revolution in Latin America: History, Politics and U.S. Policy* (New York: Holmes and Meier, 1990).

2. A discussion of civilian leaders contemplating the "military option" as a way out of economic difficulties and social disorder can be found in James Malloy and Mitchell Seligson, *Authoritarians and Democrats: Regime Transition in Latin America* (Pittsburgh, PA: University of Pittsburgh Press, 1987), p. 9.

3. For an analysis of the 1960s generation of Latin American leaders see Robert Wesson, *Democracy in Latin America: Promise and Problems* (Stanford, CA: Hoover Institution Press), p. 20.

4. See Larry Diamond, Seymour Martin Lipset, and Juan Linz, eds., *Democracy in Developing Countries*, 4 vols. (Boulder, CO: Lynne Rienner Publishers, 1988-1989). See also Scott Manwaring, *The Consolidation of Democracy in Latin America* (Notre Dame, IN: Helen Kellogg Institute for International Studies, University of Notre Dame, 1986).

5. See Barry Ames, *Political Survival: Politics and Public Policy in Latin America* (Berkeley, CA; University of California Press, 1987).

6. See, for example, Ronald M. Schneider, "Changing Leaders in Brazil and Mexico," *Harvard International Review* (February/March 1988): 13–17.

7. Gary Wynia provides an excellent analysis of the Latin American "rules of the game" including the relationship between power, leadership, and policymaking. See Gary Wynia, *The Politics of Latin American Development*, 2d ed. (New York: Oxford University Press, 1984), pp. 37–44.

8. Alfred Stepan, "Paths Toward Redemocratization; Theoretical and Comparative Considerations," in Guillermo O'Donnell, Phillippe Schmitter, and Lawrence Whitehead, eds., *Transitions From Authoritarian Rule: Comparative Perspectives* (Baltimore, MD: Johns Hopkins University Press, 1986), pp. 72–78.

9. Douglas Farrah, "El Salvador's Quest to Squelch All Voices of Reason," *Washington Post National Weekly Edition*, March 12–18, 1990, p. 24.

10. *Times of the Americas*, February 21, 1990, p. 22.

11. Retired colonel Mohamed Ali Seineldin, who led the military uprising against President Raul Alfonsin, was sentenced to sixty days confinement in October 1990 for writing a letter to President Menem in which he warned of an army revolt, claiming, "the stage is set for protests within the army." *Times of the Americas*, October 31, 1990, p. 4.

12. See the interview with President Barco in Paul Boeker, *Lost Illusions: Latin America's Struggle for Democracy as Recounted by its Leaders* (La Jolla, CA: Institute for the Americas, Merkes Weiner Publishing, 1990), p. 196.

13. Ames, *Political Survival*, p. 242.

14. Panama's new president Guillermo Endara was profiled by Jonas Bernstein in "Caudillo's Playground Looted and Left to Conciliators," *Annual Editions: Latin America* (Guilford, CT: Duskin, 1990), pp. 164–165.

15. *NACLA Report*, vol. 23, no. 1, pp. 9–10.

16. President Salinas's views on the statist economy of Mexico is discussed by Susan Kaufman Purcell in "Salinas and Team Look to Future, Not Past," *Excelsior* (Mexico City), October 7, 1989.

17. President Menem's remarks before the Council of the Americas reveal his views on what calls the "popular market economy." *Council of the Americas Washington Report* (October/November 1989), pp. 10–11.

18. See Howard J. Wiarda, "Saving Latin America From the 'Black Hole,'" in *Annual Editions: Latin America* (Guilford, CT: Duskin, 1990), pp. 130–133.

19. The role of consultants, public relations agencies, and law firms and their role in improving the image of Latin American leaders is discussed in Lars Schoultz, *Human Rights and United States Policy Toward Latin America* (Princeton, NJ: Princeton University Press, 1981), pp. 44–65.

20. Ken Silverstein, "El Salvador: The Selling of ARENA," *NACLA Report*, vol. 23, no. 2, pp. 15–23.

21. President Bush likened Brazil's President Collor to the dashing movie hero Indiana Jones. See *Boston Globe*, March 15, 1990, p. 3.

22. As reported by the Associated Press in the *Brockton Enterprise* (MA), September 3, 1991, p. 3.

23. Charles Anderson, *Politics and Economic Change in Latin America* (New York: Van Nostrand Reinhold Co., 1967), pp. 104–114.

24. President Salinas is described as a modern-day caudillo figure in Brook Larmer, "Salinas Revives Role of Strong President," *Christian Science Monitor*, November 1, 1989, pp. 1, 2.

25. P. Katel, "The Latin Techno-Yuppies," *Newsweek* (November 12, 1990): 58.

26. Howard J. Wiarda relates a situation in Mexico in which the government, in order to comply with IMF guidelines, laid off thousands of government employees only to rehire them again a few months later. Most of these employees were loyal supporters of the PRI. See Howard J. Wiarda, "The Politics of Third World Debt," *PS: Political Science and Politics* 23, no. 3 (September 1990): 417.

27. See my discussion of the PRD in the Dominican Republic, "Political Party Decline and the Failure of Liberal Democracy: The PRD in Dominican Politics," *Journal of Latin American Studies* (May 1977): 115–143.

28. Mark B. Rosenberg, "Can Democracy Survive the Democrats? From Transition to Consolidation in Honduras," in John A. Booth and Mitchell A. Seligson, eds., *Elections and Democracy in Latin America* (Chapel Hill: University of North Carolina Press, 1989), p. 51–53.

29. Ibid., p 52.

30. John A. Peeler, *Latin American Democracies: Colombia, Costa Rica, and Venezuela* (Chapel Hill: University of North Carolina Press, 1985), p. 113.

31. See, for example, the analysis of the Colombian judges' strike over the need for protective measures to combat drug terrorism, *Times of the Americas*, November 15, 1989, p. 3.

32. The caudillo-like behavior of Joaquín Balaguer continues a line that reaches back to his predecessor, Rafael Trujillo. See Howard J. Wiarda and Michael J. Kryzanek, "Dominican Dictatorship Revisited: The Caudillo Tradition and the Regimes of Trujillo and Balaguer," *Revista/Review Interamericana* 7, no. 3 (Fall 1977): 417–435.

33. For background on the ability of the Latin Americans to balance the traditional with the modern see Claudio Veliz, *The Centralist Tradition in Latin America* (Princeton, NJ: Princeton University Press, 1980).

34. See Robert A. Pastor, ed., *Democracy in the Americas: Stopping the Pendulum* (New York: Holmes and Meier, 1990).

35. See Flora Lewis's editorial in the *New York Times* commenting on the greater cooperation between the Latin American leaders, *New York Times*, February 5, 1989, p. IV-25.

36. Anthony Lake, *Somoza Falling* (Boston: Houghton Mifflin, 1989), pp. 222-225.

37. A good summary of the draft treaty can be found in *Facts on File* 44, no. 229 (October 5, 1984): 722.

38. Andrew Rosenthal, "Andean Leaders and Bush Pledge Drug Cooperation," *New York Times*, February 16, 1990, A-1.

39. *Times of the Americas*, October 31, 1990, p. 6.

40. The role that Latin American leaders played in the formulation of the Alliance for Progress is discussed by Jerome Levinson and Juan de Onis in *The Alliance That Lost Its Way* (Chicago: Quadrangle Books, 1972), pp. 52-58.

41. Department of State Bulletin, April 1987, p. 64.

42. For a critical analysis of the National Endowment for Democracy, see Wiarda, *The Democratic Revolution in Latin America*, pp. 143-168.

43. Ibid.

44. See David Shipler, "Missionaries for Democracy: U.S. Aid for Global Pluralism," *New York Times*, June 1, 1986, pp. 1ff.

45. Gene Maenoff, "New Scholarships Aim to Improve U.S. Standing in Central America," *New York Times*, January 12, 1986, I-1.

46. A critical look at the AIFLD can be found in Penny Lernoux, *Cry of the People* (London: Penguin Books, 1982), pp. 211-213.

47. See, for example, David Rockefeller's speech before the Americas Society chairman's International Advisory Council meeting. *Council of the Americas Washington Report*, March/April 1989, pp. 4-5.

48. Michael J. Kryzanek, "The 1978 Election in the Dominican Republic: Opposition Politics, Intervention and the Carter Administration," *Caribbean Studies* 19, nos. 1 and 2 (April-July 1979): 51-73.

49. *Congressional Quarterly*, May 12, 1984, pp. 73-103.

50. *New York Times*, December 21, 1989, p. I-24.

51. See "Democracy in Latin America and the Caribbean," United States Department of State, Bureau of Public Affairs, Current Policy, no. 605, August 1984, pp. 1-16.

52. These traditional views on the process of democracy in the developing world are discussed in John A. Booth, "Elections and Democracy

in Central America, A Framework for Analysis," in Booth and Seligson, *Elections and Democracy in Central America*, pp. 7–39.

53. See Senator Nancy L. Kassebaum, *Report of the U.S. Official Observer Mission to the El Salvador Constituent Assembly Election of March 28, 1982: A Report to the Committee on Foreign Relations, U.S. Senate* (Washington DC: U.S. Government Printing Office, 1982).

54. See, for example, the quick public response of the Bush administration to the electoral victory of Violeta Chamorro. *New York Times*, March 1, 1990, p. A-1.

55. *The Report of the President's National Bipartisan Commission on Central America* (New York: Macmillan, 1984), p. 121.

56. Robert Pear, "Bush to Seek $300 Million in Funds for Chamorro," *New York Times*, March 13, 1990, p. A-7.

5

THE CHANGING FACE OF
REVOLUTIONARY LEADERSHIP

The leaders in a revolutionary process are not infallible receptacles of what the people think. One must find out how the people think and sometimes combat certain opinions, certain ideas, certain points of view, which, in the judgement of the leaders, are mistaken.

—Fidel Castro

No leaders have caused as much excitement, controversy, anger, and frustration in Latin America as the revolutionaries. Revolutionary leadership has changed the face of politics in this region and forced a rethinking of established models of development, economic policy, and social organization.[1] Moreover, revolutionary leaders have redrawn the strategic map of Latin America and made the superpowers shift resources and priorities to an area that has often been considered secondary.[2] But more than anything else, revolutionary leaders have captured the attention of the Latin American people. Leaders such as Fidel Castro of Cuba, Daniel Ortega of Nicaragua, and the mysterious Abimael Guzmán of the Peruvian Shining Path movement have epitomized the disenchantment among the urban and rural masses with both democratic reform and bureaucratic authoritarianism.

There is little common ground when discussing revolutionary leadership. Some see revolutionaries as godlike heroes of the poor and exploited; others equate the green fatigues and guerrilla demeanor as symbols of a totalitarian movement destined to enslave the region. If there is any agreement on the Latin American revolutionaries it is that they are a product of the years of neglect, inequality, dependency, and uncertainty that are the defining characteristics of everyday life

123

in most Latin American countries. The revolutionaries represent the
failure of past policies and leadership models to address the demands
of those who have remained mired in poverty and injustice.[3]

Like authoritarian and democratic leadership, Latin American
revolutionary leadership has not remained static. Although some of
the vestiges of 1960s-style guerrilla movements remain in terms of
public rhetoric, cadre organization, and dedication of socialist ideals,
revolutionary leaders in the 1990s must deal with a much different
political landscape.[4] Because Latin America has been transformed
into a continent of democracy, revolutionary leaders, just like their
counterparts in the military, have had to respond to the tidal wave
of elected presidents pledged to bring liberal reform and pluralistic
societies to their countries. Furthermore, changes in the internal
dynamics of Latin American societies have caused leftist leaders to
either make important adjustments in their regimes or to dig in
their heels to preserve regimes and revolutions.[5]

These are critical times for revolutionary leadership in Latin
America. Little progress has been made to close the gap between
the haves and have-nots, and leftist leaders are on the defensive.
The center stage that they once occupied has been handed over to
a new generation of leaders who are promising change without the
radical restructuring proposed by leftists. Che is dead, Ortega is out
of power, Fidel is getting old, and the guerrilla leaders of the FMLN
in El Salvador and the M-19 in Colombia are working to become
part of the established political system. Increasing criticism has been
leveled against the Latin American revolutionaries for being out of
touch with the changing character of politics in the region and the
concerns of their constituency. As Michael Radu states:

> The nature of the Latin American revolutionary elites generally is
> characterized by their isolation from the reality of national aspirations,
> their closed ranks at the national and continental level, their self-
> assumed duty to change a society about which they know little other
> than what is filtered through books, all in the name of an abstract
> "people" they ultimately despise for lack of political "consciousness."[6]

Yet the fact that this apparent decline in revolutionary leadership
coincides with growing social and economic disparity and popular
disenchantment with the status quo signals that it is essential to

explore the current role and future direction of revolutionary leadership in Latin America. The lack of popularity of revolution and
the revolutionary leader in contemporary Latin America may mask
the political forces that will once again place leftist movements at
the forefront of events in this region. The remainder of this chapter
is an exploration of the reasons for the decline of revolutionary
leadership in Latin America and a discussion of the prospects for a
renewal of leftist activity in the region. The chapter concludes with
an assessment of U.S. response to revolutionary leadership and of
policy changes this country might have to formulate in the future
to deal with a model of leadership that remains resilient despite its
current problems.

THE LIMITS OF CHARISMA

In analyzing Latin American revolutionaries it is important to
separate the socioeconomic conditions that form the basis for this
style of leadership from the personalism and charismatic appeal that
are the critical ingredients for building a power base and mobilizing
the masses. Revolutionary leaders such as Castro and Ortega are
not only point men in a movement for radical change in their
respective countries but self-made political warriors who have con-
sciously created an image and mystique about themselves designed
to enhance their ability to govern. Unlike military generals with
their penchant for discipline and civilian presidents with their
commitment to structural reform, revolutionaries are more closely
tied to the people and depend upon popular support as the prime
source of legitimacy. Revolutionary leaders thus must become adept
at creating a governing regime that keeps its promise to achieve
radical change while at the same time maintains a kind of political
aura that solidifies the bond between guerrilla hero and the expectant
masses.[7]

The personalistic and charismatic talents of revolutionary leaders
have become the stuff of legends in Latin America. Castro's ten-
hour speechmaking, Che Guevara's bold move to rekindle the
revolution in Bolivia, Daniel Ortega's mixture of glitz and fatherly
concern for his people, and Abimael Guzmán's cultlike control over
the Peruvian Shining Path are some of the more well-known examples

reflecting the style and flair for risktaking that are part of the leadership model for revolutionaries.[8] Although ideological commitment, tactical proficiency, and political savvy are often mentioned as crucial factors common to revolutionary leaders, it is the ability of these leaders to foster an image of themselves that becomes an intangible ingredient crucial to success.

The fact that personality and charisma are part of the leadership makeup of revolutionaries comes in large part from the guerrilla experience. Jungle-based comradery, Robin Hood–like attacks against the often unpopular governing regime, and the exhilaration of national liberation all contribute to the revolutionary leaders' reliance on governing styles that accent emotion, community, and an unmistakable us-versus-them psychology. Because revolutions are by nature highly charged events that reshape society, guerrilla leaders transfer the feelings developed during the war phase of the fighting to the governing phase. The revolution becomes a never-ending experience; the guerrilla war continues in a new manner as leaders fight their enemies not with guns and mortar but with literacy and health campaigns, collectivization, and a purge of the old regime.[9]

Once in power, however, guerrilla leaders must prove themselves as policymakers and managers of the revolution. Sharp rhetoric and personal contact must be joined with visible results. Support for the revolution and the revolutionary leadership cannot be maintained simply on reputation and charismatic attraction. The leader must prove an ability to deliver the change that was promised during the guerrilla campaign. Organizational skill, efficient administration, and good judgment about personnel must be added to the list of governing requisites. Adroit revolutionary leaders like Castro who have mastered the role of political hero and have formed a loyal system of military and party support can still rely on their revolutionary reputation and their charismatic gifts, but others such as Daniel Ortega have found that talk and image-making cannot replace a governing regime that is perceived as incapable of bringing peace and prosperity to the country.[10]

One of the major problems facing revolutionary leadership and indeed revolution today is that there are few if any models to emulate. The revolutionary model has undergone little in the way of innovation and redefinition since the days of the tiny band of guerrillas in the Sierra Madre. Castro is now more feared than loved in Cuba, and his attractiveness outside the island has diminished markedly. Ortega has faded into the background and only occasionally accepts the mantle of official opposition revolutionary. Except for Guzmán of the Shining Path, who has not been seen in public for twenty years, Latin American revolutionary leadership is developing no 1990's pantheon of guerrilla heroes. Instead revolutionary leadership has increasingly become more centered within the guerrilla army and defused among a number of leaders who head smaller leftist groups. In El Salvador, for example, the FMLN, which continues its war against the government, is an umbrella organization of some seven revolutionary organizations.[11] Leftist guerrillas such as Joachín Villalabos and Shafik Handal are well-known revolutionary leaders in the FMLN but they have consistently shunned the spotlight, preferring instead to concentrate on organizing the peasantry and conducting their war of attrition, a task in which they appear to have achieved a high degree of success. As Frank Smyth states:

> At least 90 percent of the FMLN's combatants and civilian supporters are drawn from the ranks of El Salvador's radicalized peasantry. Their participation in a revolutionary movement has been an experiment in empowerment; . . . Unlike their leaders, who are better attuned to geopolitical realities, these radicalized peasants resist equating revolution with elections and negotiations with the "enemy."[12]

The fact that a new Castro-like revolutionary has not emerged in contemporary Latin America points to the limits of charismatic leadership. Fidel Castro's rise to international notoriety and the early popularity of Daniel Ortega filled a need within a Latin America that had not seen a leader of hemispheric proportions since Simon Bolívar. The Latin America of the 1960s and 1970s cried out for a kind of deliverance from dependency and dictatorial rule, but the Latin America of the 1980s and 1990s is less enamored with the bravado of the guerrilla leader and the leftist rhetoric of the revolutionary head of state. The current political climate in Latin America is one that can best be defined not so much as antirevolutionary but as anti–revolutionary leader. Today the talk in countries like Cuba is what the revolution will become without Castro; in Nicaragua the Sandinistas are trying to redefine their movement as an entity separate from the Ortega brothers.[13]

It is important to stress, however, that the current lessening of support for revolutionary leaders and growing criticism of their motives and style should not be viewed as immutable. Deteriorating social and economic conditions have historically led to the rise not only of alternative political movements but of new leaders who can capture the attention of a disgruntled populace. Latin America will continue to look for leaders from the left who speak for those outside the mainstream of their societies. Whether those leaders rely on their personalities and their ability to create a popular image will depend on the extent that the revolution needs to be advanced through the perpetuation of a revolutionary aura.

THE DEMISE OF THE REVOLUTIONARY MODEL

While revolutionary leaders have been less able to rely on personal skills and image-making as a primary means of maintaining their power base and espousing leftist doctrine, they have had to face the more serious problem of promoting a model of national development that has been largely discredited. The era of the "revolutionary alternative" in Latin America is long gone. Despite impressive advances in countries like Cuba and Nicaragua in the areas of literacy and health care, the countries in the region have become more impressed with the failure of revolutionary regimes to expand their economic growth, diversify their industrial base, attract capital investment, and provide their citizens with adequate supplies of consumer goods.[14]

Besides the generally negative data concerning the ability of revolutionary regimes to affect comprehensive social and economic change, revolutionary-led countries have had to contend with the harsh reality that radical restructuring has fostered a consumer economy characterized by long lines, food shortages, drab surroundings, and a constant din of complaints from an agitated populace. Although financial support from the Soviet Union and Eastern Europe along with preferential trade agreements has allowed Cuba to experience periods of moderate growth, particularly in the early and mid-1980s, the general economic pattern for revolutionary regimes has been dismal. As Tad Szulc comments about Cuba and Castro, "The Cuban economy has been in poor shape for decades, and living standards have been low, largely because of mismanagement of the island's considerable natural resources and the waste of the generous Communist aid from the USSR and Eastern Europe. . . . Undoubtedly the principal culprit has been the increasingly dogmatic Fidel Castro himself, who still insists on total control of all decision-making in the country."[15]

Revolutionary leaders are therefore saddled with the dilemma of supporting a developmental model that may be able to address certain social needs but has been shown to be inept at managing and advancing the general economy. Promising the masses programs in education, health, and housing can be an attractive means of gaining support, particularly in the current Latin American social climate where inequalities in these areas are endemic. Yet revolutionary leaders have been reminded with increasing regularity that providing consumer goods, controlling inflation, and modernizing the country's economic base are equally important. One need only look at Daniel Ortega's stunning loss to Violeta Chamorro in Nicaragua, where the voters expressed their disillusionment with the severely depressed economy (inflation rates of 30,000 percent) and the heavy emphasis placed on military rather than consumer needs (resulting in empty stores and long lines) by removing the Sandinistas from power. As one Sandinista activist stated after the election defeat: "There was arrogance here, people said the Front promised them rice and beans and dignity and for the last six years they have been eating dignity."[16]

Faced with promoting a developmental model that has not lived up to its expectations, leftist leaders such as Castro and Ortega have bolstered their position and sought to revive revolutionary fervor by emphasizing external threats. Castro and Ortega became nationalist protectors of the revolution rather than revolutionary leaders intent on continuing the transformation of their respective countries. The United States contributed to this transformation by its isolation and intimidation of the Castro regime and its contra war against the Sandinistas, but the precipitous collapse of communism in the Soviet Union and Eastern Europe also created an environment in Cuba and Nicaragua that forced the revolutionary leadership to shift the rhetoric from class struggle to protecting their revolution from external threats.[17]

By becoming revolutionary nationalists and rallying their nations against the United States, Castro and Ortega were buying time while they sought ways to shore up their crumbling economies. Castro, of course, has been more successful than Ortega in his new role as revolutionary nationalist because of the deep-seated respect that the Cuban people have for him and because of his stranglehold on the key institutions within the country.[18] Ortega's attempts to buy time by stressing external threats and rallying the population were nullified by the presence of strong opposition groups in the country and the fact that he never commanded the kind of blind loyalty from his people that Castro was able to engender.[19] Both leaders, however, went to great lengths to criticize the failures of the revolution and the inability of revolutionary institutions to meet economic goals.

Castro, in particular, was the most aggressive (and doctrinaire) in his attempt to place the revolution back on track. On numerous occasions Castro grumbled about Cuba's "mistakes" and the need to engage in a campaign of "rectification of errors . . . and negative tendencies."[20] But instead of opening up the economy and allowing greater personal control and local autonomy, Castro kicked off the rectification campaign in 1986 by shutting down private farmers' markets, outlawing cottage industries and a popular program of private homeownership, and cutting back on workers' incentives in favor of so-called spiritual incentives and self-sacrifice.[21]

As long as revolutionary heads of state like Castro face the difficulty of trying to adjust the leftist model to the realities of economic development and a changing world, guerrilla leaders who are fighting to gain political power can still rely on slogans, promises, and dreams of class struggle as they work to organize the masses and bring down governments. Perhaps no current revolutionary group epitomizes this commitment to Marxist orthodoxy more than the Shining Path guerrillas of Peru. Shining Path's ideology is a mix of Marxism, Leninism, Maoism, and the indigenous proclamations of Abimael Guzmán, who is known by his supporters as President Gonzalo.[22] Gonzalo Thought has emerged as the 1990s version of Mao's little red book, with revolutionary statements such as "War is the most conscious act of man. On a mountain of cadavers a new society is built. The masses learn by means of repeated revolutionary and belligerent acts that are hammered into their heads."[23] Despite the fact that Guzmán has remained a shadowy revolutionary figure, the depth of the commitment to his ideas and his vision of a Maoist state is phenomenal. As one supporter jailed by the Peruvian government stated, "We are part of a collective. We form ourselves in the image of President Gonzalo, in his image and spirit. Our work is to impose the third and new stage of Maoism."[24]

The fanatical allegiance of Guzmán's following has prompted the government of Alberto Fujimori to link the military campaign against the Shining Path with a propaganda campaign designed to tarnish the myths surrounding the rebel leader. The government achieved a breakthrough of sorts in 1991 when it televised a videotape of the elusive Guzmán dancing at a party. The tape caused a major uproar in Peru because it showed the Shining Path leader for the first time and also presented him in an "unrevolutionary" situation. The Fujimori government continued to flash the pictures of Guzmán to the Peruvian people in hopes of not only effecting his capture but diminishing his stature as a spartan revolutionary leader.

The growing success of the Shining Path along with the tenacity of Marxist guerrilla groups in Colombia and Guatemala and the resurgence of urban leftist organizations in Argentina and Chile suggests that revolutionary leadership may still possess some residual popularity even though Ortega has fallen and Castro's future is at best uncertain. It is important to remember, however, that espousing lofty rhetoric, controlling portions of the countryside, and engaging in periodic attacks are not necessarily the signs of a new revolutionary era. There are now quiet but perceptible changes in the political culture of many Latin American countries that mitigate the advancement of revolutionary doctrine and leadership. Tied to the spread of democracy and the opposition to constant conflict and violence, the mood in the region is at least in the short run clearly against a new round of hemispheric revolution.

The reluctance to embrace revolution can be seen, for example, by the failure of the FMLN's "final offensive" in December 1989. It is one thing to claim, as Joaquín Villalabos did, that El Salvador was on the brink of a "social explosion" and that the guerrillas would deliver a "strategic blow" to the government of Alfredo Cristiani and another to enlist the involvement of the urban poor, who refused to cooperate with the infiltrating leftist army. One cannot deny that many urban poor were intimidated by the presence of Salvadoran army troops and unwilling to engage in the FMLN's call for a "general uprising," but at the same time the FMLN leadership was dismayed that its "final offensive" was not embraced by those with the most to gain from a rebel victory. Many of the citizens who were pressed into service by the guerrillas showed little interest in bringing down their democratic government and engaging in a wider revolutionary war.[25]

If the FMLN's experience in 1989 means anything, it is that democratic governance and societal stability have at least as much support as revolution and that the violence and destruction that accompany revolution severely limit the prospects for broadening support. Unlike in the 1950s and 1960s when harsh dictatorships were discredited and democratic reform governments were in their early stages of development, in the 1980s and 1990s the revolutionary alternative faces not only a viable and increasingly legitimate governing system that can hold its own but a population more interested in building on the past than in destroying it.

The growing legitimacy of Salvadoran democracy coupled with declining revolutionary fervor has contributed to the first real break-through in the long civil war. In 1991 the Cristiani government and the FMLN, under the auspices of the United Nations, signed a historic peace agreement. Both sides praised the agreement and promised that they would move quickly to the next stage of negotiations, in which issues such as reform of the military, reintegration of the rebels into national life, and a political role for the FMLN would be addressed. The euphoria over the peace agreement, however, would have to be balanced with the realities of Salvadoran military intransigence. The FMLN, for their part, appeared willing to engage in a cease-fire, but the Salvadoran armed forces continued to view the peace process as an opportunity for the rebels to consolidate their positions and garner favorable world opinion. In order for the peace process to be successful, the rebels and the generals must break through years of mistrust and hatred while the civilian leadership of President Alfredo Cristiani is forced to act as part cheerleader and part referee trying to guide the two camps toward a lasting agreement.

THE SUBTLE EFFECTS OF TIME

The success and failure of leaders is often thought to be connected to factors such as effective administration, shrewd balancing of political interests, an ability to sense the critical policy issues that need to be addressed, and a talent for communicating governing objectives. Although leaders survive and prosper largely because of their governing skills, it is important not to ignore the role of factors such as age, length of service, and the inevitable gaps that occur between the head of state and those youthful generations that arrive on the scene long after power has been attained. The influence of time on revolutionary leadership is especially critical for analyzing its current state of decline and disarray. Because revolutionary leadership has evolved as a result of protracted warfare and years of organizing the masses, those who rise to power in order to advance a radical program tend to have spent much of their adult lives as guerrillas or leftist agitators. Revolutionary leadership is thus a kind of career track where time in service becomes an accepted part of the job description and where issues such as age and generational compatibility become crucial elements of the leader's overall popularity and longevity.[26]

Contemporary Latin American revolutionaries such as Fidel Castro and Daniel Ortega have experienced time-related problems and have seen their position threatened by those who question the necessity of their becoming permanent leaders. Castro, in particular, has come under increased criticism for building a governing system that is so dependent on him that there is little opportunity to develop future leaders or formulate an effective mechanism for the transfer of power. As Castro moves beyond the age of sixty and begins to show the gray in his beard more and more, Cubans wonder about life after their leader and lament the fact that the revolution might benefit from the injection of new ideas and new methods of governance.[27]

Articles about the so-called "graying" of the revolution are now commonplace as observers of Castro suggest that the limits of political effectiveness have been reached, if not passed, by the Cuban leader. Such articles cite examples such as the growing distance between Castro and Cuban youth, his growing reluctance to admit that the Communist world has changed since 1959, and his stubborn adherence to policy initiatives that have been shown to be ineffective as signs that the Cuban leader is out of touch with his own revolution.[28] To counteract these criticisms about his age and his ability to invigorate the revolution, Castro continues to maintain a herculean schedule of personal appearances, engages in impromptu streetcorner discussions with his people over the future of the revolution, and forever keeps up the image that he is trying new policies (even if they are part of the old Marxist repertoire) to enhance the life of his people.

As Cuban expert Jorge Dominguez correctly describes Castro,

> Castro's style of leadership has caused great problems for managing public policy. But it is also an important part of his public appeal. . . . A world-class orator, able to express ideas thoughtfully and at great length, he can address sophisticated audiences on esoteric subjects and can speak simply, with affection and humor, to little children. A man of extraordinary energy, a renowned night owl, he projects an image of omniscience and hides the reality of his near omnipotence in Cuban politics.[29]

Castro can be expected to continue to rely on his enormous personal qualities to reinvigorate his leadership and to develop the image of a revolutionary not limited by age or the changes in the Communist world. Yet perceptions about how time has affected Castro and the revolution persist and will undoubtedly increase in the future. It is enormously difficult to quash the prevailing views that a revolution has reached its nadir and its leader no longer possesses the magic than can propel the revolution forward.

Many of Castro's leadership problems stem from the perception that he has remained in power too long and no longer is able to meet the expectations of a new generation of Cubans. One source of Daniel Ortega's defeat in Nicaragua was also related to the role that time can play in directing the fortunes of leftist revolutionaries. The decline in support for the Sandinistas and the eventual electoral victory of Violeta Chamorro was tied in large part to the feelings of many Nicaraguans that Daniel Ortega had been given enough time to create the revolutionary change that he promised and that he and his Sandinista brethren had failed to meet the needs of the people after holding power for over ten years. As Dionisio Marenco, Ortega's deputy campaign manager, reflected on the Sandinista loss, he stated, "In ten years the Front adopted the psychology of a party in power. . . . We lost our capacity to converse, to listen, to criticize ourselves, the capacity to measure."[30]

Because the revolution in Nicaragua pledged itself to a major overhaul of the economic, social, and political structures put in place by the Somoza dynasty, revolutionary leaders such as the Ortega brothers, Interior Minister Tomás Borge, and Foreign Minister Miguel D'Escoto faced not only an enormous task of reordering national priorities but the inevitable problems related to delivering results in a timely manner and avoiding the dangers of complacency and arrogance. All political leaders must endure the prospect that they may not have sufficient time to implement their agenda and as a result may be criticized for their inability to produce change, but revolutionary leaders are more vulnerable to the charges of inefficiency, delay, and unwillingness to reject failed ideas.

The fact that revolutionaries promise too much and envision a drastically reformed nation free of the past evils places a burden on them that is difficult to lift. In the case of the Sandinistas and in particular Daniel Ortega, the U.S. trade embargo, the contra war, and the downturn in Eastern bloc aid contributed significantly to the economic crisis and the electoral victory of the National Opposition Union (UNO) movement. But besides these obstacles, Nicaraguans simply sent a message with their ballots that they had had enough and that it was time for a change. The people may have been grateful for the Sandinista victory over Somoza and the renewed sense of national pride that filled the country, but it was clear from postelection comments that Daniel Ortega, and all that he stood for, had lost the race with time.[31] Revolutionary leaders gain power and lose power for a wide range of reasons; there is no common denominator that details the core factor for longevity in office or resiliency to political challenge. But if the recent difficulties of Fidel Castro and Daniel Ortega can be used to better understand the manner in which revolutionary leadership evolves and responds to crisis, they would show that charisma and ideology are not sufficient anchors of the revolution. Revolutionary leaders, despite their penchant for creating closed political systems, are not immune to the everyday realities of age and time. Revolutionaries like Castro and Ortega mastered the charismatic and ideological facets of leadership, but they were not able to avoid the inevitable challenges presented by their view that a revolution is a lifetime experience. In the case of Ortega, the Nicaraguan people could not wait a lifetime; in the case of Castro, the Cuban people are wondering whether their leader will have the strength to maintain the revolution for a lifetime.

COPING WITH COUNTERREVOLUTION
AND DESTABILIZATION

The ability of revolutionary leaders to maintain their popularity and power base is not only a factor of personal skills but also the result of dealing with the intense counterrevolutionary pressure that has been directed at them and their regimes. Revolutionary leaders have had to endure relentless attacks from opponents dedicated to the removal of Marxist ideology, socialistic programs, and radical formulas for change from the Latin American scene. Fidel Castro facing the seemingly endless U.S. attempts to dislodge him from power, Daniel Ortega fighting the contra rebels and a U.S. boycott, Che Guevarra running from the Bolivian army, and guerrilla leaders such as Antonio Navarro in Colombia and Abimael Guzmán in Peru battling the superior firepower and sheer numbers of government troops reflect the fundamental paradox of leftist leadership in Latin America—political survival requires constant military preparedness and national vigilance, which, although necessary, create the prospect of economic collapse and popular disenchantment.

Revolutionary leaders in contemporary Latin America must possess governing skills far and above what their counterparts in the democratic or military setting are required to develop. Besides addressing internal needs tied to the leftist program, revolutionaries are forced to construct an effective defense of the country from outside threats and pressure. A leader like Fidel Castro or Daniel Ortega must assume a number of roles beyond that of revolutionary manager. Castro became the permanent commander in chief of an enormous military machine, the organizer of the civilian militia and domestic support groups, and a tireless "cheerleader" taking on the United States and defending the nation from all external challenges. Castro seems to relish this role of standing up to the United States and protecting his revolution from contamination, but it does force him to split his attention and concentrate on both defensive strategies and the essentials of revolutionary management.[32]

Because revolutionaries, whether in power or in the jungles, must respond to the counterrevolutionary attacks of government forces and the destabilizing programs of the United States, they are at a distinct disadvantage in terms of presenting an agenda for change and justifying the need for social and economic restructuring. Democratic leaders may face powerful opposition groups that criticize the government and offer alternative programs; revolutionary leaders are challenged almost immediately from external sources that are committed to the dismantling of the revolution and the replacing of the leadership elite. It is one thing to lead a country of divergent voices and competing centers of power and quite another to lead a revolutionary process bent on radical change in an environment characterized by armed opposition, covert maneuverings, and economic restrictions. As Daniel Ortega lamented about the external threats early in the revolutionary process: "We have decided to defend our revolution by force of arms, even if we are crushed, and to take the war to the whole of Central America if that is the consequence. . . . We have an historical prejudice towards the United States, because of that country's . . . attitudes which make us fear attack from it, and look for all possible means of defense."[33]

In response to the constant barrage of sabotage, trade embargoes, freedom fighters, propaganda ploys, and international campaigns of diplomatic isolation, revolutionary leaders are almost inextricably drawn toward centralized political control, repression of their domestic adversaries, and massive campaigns to unify the people against the external challenges to the revolution. But although these authoritarian and public relations moves may allow the revolutionary leaders some breathing space, they ultimately weaken legitimacy and sow the seeds of dissension. The revolutionary leader is transformed from popular hero to a kind of unscrupulous political boss whose primary concern seems to be controlling the political process in the name of national defense. Gary Wynia describes this transformation to authoritarianism in the face of external opposition:

> Revolutions always create enemies, both foreign and national, who resent being deprived of their property and privileges. Unlike constitutional democrats who take their chances with the rules of competitive politics, revolutionaries want to control their own fate totally, if possible. Consequently, internal and external security absorbs much of their attention and, when threatened, they may decide to turn their society into a fortress dedicated to the revolution's defense.[34]

Although they may hold out the promise of a new social and economic order, revolutionary leaders are also increasingly viewed as catalysts of an inevitable struggle with the United States. The overarching threat of a U.S. response plus the heightened probability that revolutionary leaders will employ authoritarian means internally in order to combat the external challenges has created a major dilemma for leftists in Latin America. Revolutions have traditionally been popular uprisings led by charismatic leaders who promised a better society free of repression and foreign influence. Revolutions in today's Latin America are uprisings against unpopular governments, that, if successful, lead to years of hardship, a restrictive political process, continued dependency, and the prospect of facing opposition from the United States or its proxies. When faced with the reality of what revolutions will very likely become and how revolutionary leaders will behave, the Latin American people are faced with a less-attractive option and a less-appealing leadership elite.

DEALING WITH REVOLUTIONARIES: THE U.S. APPROACH

Since the fall of Cuban dictator Fulgencio Batista and the rise to power of Fidel Castro, the United States has had a near obsession with ridding the hemisphere of leftist leaders and the Marxist doctrine they promote. Castro's victory and his subsequent embrace of communism triggered a litany of counterrevolutionary responses from Washington designed to remove the Cuban revolutionary from power and return our Caribbean sphere of influence back to its original geopolitical configuration. Since those early days of anti-Castro fever, the United States has formulated and implemented a series of strategies aimed at either pushing leftist leaders from power or severely weakening their ability to advance the revolution. Mixing diplomatic and economic isolation with regular doses of intimidation, destabilization, and intervention, the United States sought to prove to revolutionary leaders that the price of power would be too high and only result in ravaged economies, clandestine attacks, and well-financed counterrevolutionary armies of liberation.[35]

Although this mix of antirevolutionary strategies has not undergone any significant revision since Castro's victory in 1959, the recent collapse of communism in the Soviet Union and Eastern Europe and the impact of that collapse on client states in the Western

Hemisphere requires that we explore the changing nature of U.S. relations with revolutionary leaders and revolutionary movements. As the influence of Marxist doctrine decreases and the romantic allure of guerrilla warfare wanes, the United States has seen its long and frustrating contest for the hearts and minds of the Latin American masses reach an important juncture. U.S. policymakers must now deal with a revolutionary environment that is disintegrating in some countries, poised for compromise in others, and ready for battle in still others. Because the state of revolution is in such great flux and revolutionary leaders are breaking out of the established mold, the response from the United States cannot be wedded to the past. The United States must recognize the changing nature of revolutionary leadership and the new challenges that face this country from leftists bent on dismantling existing political systems and replacing them with another vision.

Because revolutionary leadership appears to have evolved to a new level of description and performance, the United States should begin evaluating its traditional approach to leftist leaders and leftist regimes. Revolutionary movements may be severely weakened, but the counterrevolutionary strategies employed in the post-Batista era may not be appropriate in the post-Ortega era when revolutionary leaders are either seeking compromises or are preparing for their next opportunity to challenge the government. U.S. officials would be wise to reflect on two fundamental questions that need to be addressed in this new era of revolutionary leadership. The old questions about expansionism, the domino theory, and Soviet influence need to be replaced by a more relevant set of concerns that capture the current mood and reality of Latin America.

Is the United States Willing to Negotiate with Leftist Rebels?

During the Reagan presidency one of the most criticized options available to the United States in its approach to the Salvadoran rebels was negotiations with the prospect of some kind of power-sharing formula emerging from the discussions. To sit down with the rebel leaders and agree to a diplomatic settlement of the guerrilla war that would allow the leftists a guaranteed place in the political system was viewed by U.S. policymakers as "negotiating away" democracy and forfeiting all previous efforts to stop the revolutionaries through military means.[36] To Ronald Reagan, negotiations and the acceptance of a power-sharing solution was an admission of defeat and an easy way for the rebels to achieve legitimacy. As a result, the Reagan administration paid only lip service to the calls for negotiations from liberals in Congress and from its Latin American allies. State Department diplomatic missions were sent out to give the semblance of interest in a negotiated settlement, and public statements of support for the Contadora peace process were issued regularly, but there were always conditions attached to U.S. involvement and harsh words for those who pressed the Reagan administration on its reluctance to talk and work out a power-sharing solution.[37]

Much has changed in Central America since the days of Reagan anticommunism, in particular the support for negotiations and a diplomatic settlement to end hostilities. The Central American Peace Initiative signed by the five presidents in the region was a bold rejection of the Reagan doctrine and a clear signal to the United States that the political leaders in this area were willing to take major risks to ensure that the guerrilla war did not escalate. Although the United States was shocked by the independence of the Central American leaders and dismayed that it had been effectively shut out of the negotiations, there was little Washington could do but watch as civilian democrats and Daniel Ortega signed agreements and showed their willingness to move beyond ideological differences toward a diplomatic solution of the contra war.[38]

The Bush administration entered office with the United States on the diplomatic defensive. President Bush showed a greater willingness to support negotiations in Central America and wind down the contra war, but his position was more the result of the political realities in the region than a commitment to avoid military solutions. The invasion of Panama to capture Manuel Noriega, the continued isolation of Castro's Cuba, and the reluctance to press the Cristiani government to end its war with the FMLN revealed that the Bush approach toward negotiating solutions to regional problems was not a major departure from that of his predecessor. President Bush continued to formulate U.S. policy in Central America from the perspective that the mix of military aid and a hovering presence were the most effective means of containing and weakening the leftist threat.[39]

The electoral victory of Violeta Chamorro in Nicaragua and the collapse of communism in the Soviet Union and Eastern Europe have helped foster a new sense of urgency on the part of revolutionary leaders in the region about facing the prospect of declining financial assistance and a weakened base of popular support. In this new climate the Salvadoran rebel leadership has shown a greater interest in negotiating an end to its stalemate war with the Cristiani government, the Colombian M-19 guerrilla army has worked out an amnesty agreement with the government, and the Nicaraguan Sandinistas, now in opposition, appear to have accepted their fate. Only Castro in Cuba and Guzmán's Shining Path guerrillas seem willing to carry on the battle in order to perpetuate the Marxist vision.

With revolutionary leaders facing a crisis of confidence, the Bush administration may be easily tempted to ignore the leftist threat. U.S. policymakers would be wise to remember that one of the key strengths of leftist guerrillas is resiliency. The concepts of protracted war and revolutionary determinism remain central to the mind-set of leftist leaders. Defeat is only temporary and victory is defined in terms of a willingness to maintain the struggle. Failing to convince government leaders like President Cristiani to implement the negotiated peace agreement that brings the rebels into the political system could create the conditions for a kind of endless war.[40] Continuing to provide the Salvadoran military with assistance, even with cutbacks and restrictions, can only send the signal that the United States supports the stalemate approach to fighting revolution and is willing to accept the prospect of an endless war with its endless costs, both human and financial. In this time of scarce domestic resources, the Bush administration must ask itself to what extent it is willing to support military policies in El Salvador at a time when peace with the rebels seems to be in sight.

A somewhat similar question awaits the Bush administration in its relations with the Castro regime. Again, President Bush has avoided the strident Castro-bashing of Reagan, but he has not accepted the view that this country should normalize ties with its archenemy. In fact, the moves by the Bush administration to challenge Castro by expanding the Radio Martí program of beaming information to Cuba to include a television component called TV Martí has intensified the resolve of the Cuban leader and heightened the tensions between the two countries to a level of that found in the Reagan presidency.[41]

Presidents Ford and Carter held the view that relations with the Castro government could be normalized; the Bush administration has sought to create conditions forcing the Cuban leader to carry on a running communications battle with the United States. If there was a time early on in the Bush presidency when a window of opportunity for renewing negotiations with Castro existed (Cardinal Bernard Law of Boston, a close friend of Bush, visited Castro and apparently reported back on the prospects for closer ties), that window was closed by the administration's desire to keep up the heat. There is no doubt that TV Martí was designed to keep up the pressure on Castro, but the decision to use such a strategy also resuscitated a nationalistic climate in Cuba and gave the Cuban leader a new issue to solidify his revolution.

The aggressive approach of the Bush administration toward Castro is but one indication that the United States is intent on continuing its policy of avoiding diplomatic solutions and relying on military or destabilizing initiatives. What some observers feel is a new sign of the Bush administration's continuation of the Reagan approach is its decision to supply aid and advisers to the Peruvian military in its fight against the Shining Path revolutionaries. Although the agreement between Peru and the United States to introduce U.S. military advisers into the country is part of the overall drug strategy of the Bush administration and is a direct result of the drug summit held in Cartagena, Colombia, in 1989, the introduction of U.S. troops into Peru with the clear intent of training the armed forces in counterrevolutionary tactics is certain to intensify the resolve of the Shining Path rebels and create a new level of anti-Americanism. The Peruvian armed forces are in desperate need of equipment and training to deal with the drug war, but the arrival of U.S. troops may cast the Shining Path rebels in a new light as a nationalist alternative to the pro-U.S. government.[42]

Despite the risks involved in allowing U.S. military advisers to train Peruvian troops in antiguerrilla and antidrug tactics, the government of President Alberto Fujimori placed high priority on convincing the Bush administration that the threat to its government was serious. In 1991 the Peruvian president traveled to Washington to meet with President Bush and ask that $94 million in economic and military assistance be released. The administration and the Congress were leery about releasing the funds in light of the regular reports from human-rights organizations categorizing Peru as having the worst record of political repression in Latin America. Fortunately, the Peruvian president made a favorable impression on President Bush and left with a verbal commitment that the aid monies would be released.

The renewed interest by the Bush administration in supporting friendly governments that are beset with a revolutionary challenge is the result of the increasing link being found between drug trafficking and revolutionary activity. The United States is now portraying leftist revolution less in terms of Communist expansionism and more as a narco-terrorist threat that has to be met in order to win the war on drugs. For example, a recent State Department analysis of the Shining Path movement stated, "Sendero reportedly acts as an intermediary between the peasant growers and the drug traffickers, winning higher prices for the growers, taking a cut of the profits, and providing protection." The State Department analysis further stated that Sendero leaders have organized coca growers to protest the government's antidrug operations, describing the program as "imperialist expansion."[43] Similar descriptions of ties between leftist FARC (Revolutionary Armed Forces of Colombia) rebels and drug lords have been used by the Bush administration to lend support to the Colombian government's war against the Medellín cartel. The objective is clearly to paint the rebels as criminals and terrorists with little interest in government reform.[44]

By linking revolutionary activity to the drug war, challenging Castro with TV Martí, continuing the military support of the Cristiani government, and taking pride in the destabilization campaign that helped weaken the Sandinista movement, the Bush administration seems bent on maintaining the Reagan approach to the leftist threat in Latin America. President Bush is intent on keeping the heat on revolutionary leaders rather than moving toward a working relationship with individuals who have the capability of keeping the region on a war footing. Not surprisingly, the demise of Daniel Ortega and the Sandinistas has convinced conservatives within the

Bush administration that the contra war, for all its deficiencies and limitations, had more to do with the victory of Violeta Chamorro than did Oscar Arias and his Central American Peace Initiative.

This debate over the value of negotiations as opposed to destabilization will likely continue for years to come, but in the meantime the United States appears headed for an extension of the Reagan approach toward revolution in the hemisphere. Although President Bush may be more subtle in his presentation of the approach, his embrace of aggressive containment of the revolutionary left and refusal to deal with leftist leaders reinforces the view of many analysts that U.S. policy rarely departs significantly from the established norms. In the case of dealing with the revolutionary left, the United States has a long tradition of isolation, intimidation, and intervention. That tradition will be difficult to change.

What Role Do Nonmilitary Strategies Play in Counterrevolution?

A related question that follows from the discussion of the U.S. position toward negotiating with revolutionary leaders is What level of importance should this country place on employing nonmilitary strategies in its contest with the Marxist left? It is a well-known liberal axiom that revolution is bred in the hunger, poverty, inequality, and injustice of closed societies and that the only way to effectively deal with the outbreak of revolution is to address the sources of dissatisfaction and anger that lead to guerrilla war. Furthermore, revolutionary leaders rise to prominence and promote the importance of armed struggle against established governments because little has changed for the majority of urban and rural poor in Latin America even though democratic leaders promise reform.

The liberal response to Latin American revolution has been the basis for the Alliance of Progress program and countless other bilateral arrangements with countries facing the threat from the left. The liberal response has also served as the underlying rationale for a number of major reports on the region from the Inter-American Dialogue's publications to the Kissinger Report. And yet despite the preponderance of support for attacking revolution by addressing the sources of the problem and ensuring that revolutionary leaders will never get the opportunity to lead governments in the region, the liberal model has endured a mixed reception in Washington. Budget constraints, presidential opposition, congressional concern over cost-effectiveness, and public skepticism about the value of foreign assistance have led to an uneven history of dealing with revolution through massive injections of aid, transfers of food and technology, and programs that concentrate on the people-to-people approach to counterrevolution.

With the onset of the 1990s the liberal model for dealing with Latin American revolution is perhaps facing its greatest challenge. The Reagan approach of joining the market economy with a staunch containment posture has severely weakened the attractiveness of the liberal model in policymaking circles. Fighting the expansion of revolution in third world countries is increasingly being viewed as a matter of strengthening economies, assisting small businesses, and modernizing militaries rather than attacking the more immediate sources of antigovernment activity—poverty, inequality, and injustice. Moreover, there is a strong movement within U.S. society to concentrate our efforts on domestic reform rather than pour billions of tax dollars on the problems in a faraway country. Not only are foreign aid dollars down sharply from past years but the political consensus that at one time made the United States the largest per capita provider of monies to other countries has broken apart.[45]

With the chances for another public aid program like the Alliance for Progress remote, it is important for public officials and the U.S. people to examine what the ramifications of dismantling the tradition of responding to revolution and revolutionary leaders through foreign aid and social reform will be on our ability to control events and protect our interests in the region closest to our borders. By moving toward the conservative approach of the market economy and military preparedness, both the Reagan and Bush administrations developed counterrevolutionary policy from the premise that fighting guerrillas and stopping the onrush of the Marxist left could best be achieved by a short-term strategy that energized the economy through business incentives and allowed the military to stall the rebels by the use of more sophisticated weapons and techniques. The long view of addressing the sources of revolution and thereby weakening the attractiveness of revolutionary leaders was put aside in favor of a strategy that relied on the "miracle of the marketplace" and the ability of the armed forces to fight the rebels to a stalemate.

As a result, President Bush's Enterprise for the Americas Initiative with its emphasis on free trade as the engine of change has replaced the Alliance for Progress, and military assistance continues to pour into El Salvador to support the containment of the revolutionary left. The calls for a multibillion-dollar Marshall Plan for the Caribbean Basin that were heard from Latin American leaders and some liberals in Congress have receded into the background. Few political leaders in this country are talking about what the emphasis on trickle-down theories of market economy and military containment solutions will mean down the road as poverty, inequality, and injustice expand their grip on Latin America. There is, however, the undeniable fact that new leftist groups can be found throughout Latin America and established guerrilla organizations are withstanding the counterrevolutionary attacks from U.S.-supplied civilian governments.

The temptation to respond to crises with quick fixes is not an unusual tactic for a country anxious to protect its interests. The United States has often dealt with a problem in Latin America by using its economic and military power to overwhelm its opponents. What is different, however, with the demise of the liberal model of counterrevolution and the rise to prominence of the conservative alternative is that U.S. policymakers are now convinced that the "miracle of the marketplace" and the injection of huge amounts of military aid are sufficient to deal with the leftist threat.

Despite the fact that foreign investors and proponents of privatization are being accepted with greater regularity in the region, their presence has had only a marginal impact on closing the gap between the rich and poor. There are some hopeful signs that the rush toward the market economy has dampened the revolutionary fervor in Latin America, but much needs to be done, especially in those countries where entrenched elites refuse to link market practices with social responsibility. Even though there is cause for confidence that Marxist-inspired revolution is in retreat, the proponents of the market system, particularly in the United States, cannot ignore the seeds of popular unrest that always seem ready for planting. The United States would be ill-advised to forsake dealing with the social causes of revolution and concentrate on military and market solutions. Developing policies that meet the housing, nutritional, educational, and employment needs of the vast majority of the people in this region will do much to ensure that Havana 1959 is not repeated in the 1990s.

NOTES

1. See Michael Radu, *Violence and the Latin American Revolutionary* (New Brunswick, NJ: Transaction Books, 1988), pp. 1-11. See also E. Bradford Burns, *Latin America: A Concise Interpretative History* (Englewood Cliffs, NJ: Prentice Hall, 1989), pp. 263-299.

2. Jiri Valenta and Virginia Valenta, "Soviet Strategy and Policies in the Caribbean Basin," in Howard J. Wiarda, ed., *Rift and Revolution: The Central American Imbroglio* (Washington, DC: American Enterprise Institute for Public Policy Research, 1984), pp. 197-252. See also Cole Blasier, "Security: The Extracontinental Dimension," in Kevin J. Middlebrook and Carlos Rico, eds, *The United States and Latin America in the 1980's* (Pittsburgh, PA: University of Pittsburgh Press, 1986), pp. 523-564.

3. For background on the factors responsible for the rise of revolutionary leadership see Mustafa Rejai and Kay Phillips, *Leaders of Revolution* (New York: Praeger, 1988), pp. 64-68. See also Ted Robert Gurr, *Why Men Rebel* (Princeton, NJ: Princeton University Press, 1970).

4. Gary Wynia compares the Mexican, Cuban, and Nicaraguan revolution and revolutionary leadership in Gary Wynia, *The Politics of Latin American Development* (New York: Oxford University Press, 1984), pp. 247-304.

5. See "The Greying of a Revolution," *U.S. News and World Report* (January 9, 1989): 37-41.

6. Radu, *Violence and the Latin American Revolutionary*, p. 2.

7. Edward Gonzalez describes Castro as a kind of socialist caudillo whose "authority derived from the popular masses," but whose charisma gradually slipped away when he could not deliver economic prosperity. Edward Gonzalez, *Cuba Under Castro: The Limits of Charisma* (Boston: Houghton Mifflin, 1974), pp. 168-216.

8. See Richard Gott, *Guerrilla Movements in Latin America* (Garden City, NJ: Doubleday, 1971).

9. A good discussion of this transformation can be found in Richard R. Fagen, *The Transformation of Political Culture in Cuba* (Stanford, CA: Stanford University Press, 1970) and Carlos M. Vilas *The Sandinista Revolution: National Liberation and Social Transformation in Central America* (New York: Monthly Review Press, 1986).

10. A critical review of the Ortega years and the downfall of the Sandinista revolution can be found in Julia Preston, "The Defeat of the Sandinistas," *New York Review of Books* (April 12, 1990): 25–29.

11. A revealing discussion of the FMLN is provided by revolutionary leader Joachim Villalobos. See Joachim Villalobos, "A Democratic Revolution for El Salvador," *Foreign Policy* 74 (Spring 1989): 103–122.

12. Frank Smyth, "Negotiations or Total War," *Nation* (August 7–14, 1989): 152–154.

13. See Larry Rohter, "Stunned Sandinistas Seek to Define Their New Role," *New York Times*, March 1, 1990, p. 20.

14. For a critique of Latin American development models including the Marxist model, see Howard J. Wiarda, *Latin America at the Crossroads: Debt, Development and the Future* (Boulder, CO: Westview Press, 1987).

15. Gillian Gunn, "Will Castro Fall?" *Foreign Policy* 79 (Summer 1990): 132–150.

16. Adam Pertman, "Pondering the Lengthy Struggle: Did Reagan's Policies Really Work?" *Boston Globe*, February 27, 1990, p. 8.

17. For a discussion of some of the new themes of revolutionary leadership see *Fidel Castro: In Defense of Socialism; Four Speeches on the Thirtieth Anniversary of the Cuban Revolution* (New York: Pathfinder Books, 1989).

18. Juan del Aguila, "Development and Revolution in Cuba," in Howard J. Wiarda and Harvey Kline, eds., *Latin American Politics and Development*, 3d ed. (Boulder, CO: Westview Press, 1990), pp. 444–447.

19. See a discussion of peasant opposition and East Coast Indian opposition to Sandinista rule in Janusz Bugajski, *Sandinista Communism and Rural Nicaragua* (New York: Praeger, published with the Center for Strategic and International Studies, Washington, DC, 1990).

20. "The Greying of a Revolution," p. 39.

21. Ibid.

22. See David Scott Palmer, "The Revolutionary Terror of Peru's Shining Path," Paper prepared for the Ford Foundation Sponsored Project, Terrorism in Context, January 1990.

23. As quoted in Charles Bennett, "Middle Ground Elusive in Peru," *Boston Globe*, April 2, 1990, p. 7.

24. Ibid.

25. See Julia Preston, "The Battle for San Salvador," *New York Review of Books*, February 1, 1990, p. 7.

26. Radu, *Violence and the Latin American Revolutionary*, p. 3.

27. *New York Times*, August 19, 1990, IV-2.

28. See, for example, Gabriel Garcia Marquez's suggestion to Castro that he open up talks with the United States, *Miami Herald*, April 9, 1990, p. 1-a.

29. Jorge Dominguez, *To Make A World Safe for Revolution: Cuba's Foreign Policy* (Cambridge, MA: Harvard University Press, 1989), p. 250.

30. As quoted in Preston, "The Defeat of the Sandinistas," p. 28.

31. As quoted in the *New York Times*, February 27, 1990, A-1.

32. See Wayne S. Smith, "Castro, Latin America and the United States," in John Martz, ed., *United States Policy in Latin America: A Quarter Century of Crisis and Challenge, 1961–1986* (Lincoln: University of Nebraska Press, 1988), pp. 288–306.

33. As quoted in Robert Pastor, *Condemned to Repetition: The United States and Nicaragua* (Princeton, NJ: Princeton University Press, 1987), p. 235.

34. Wynia, *The Politics of Latin American Development*, p. 301.

35. See Michael Klare and Peter Kornbluh, eds., *Low-Intensity Warfare: Counterinsurgency, Proinsurgency and Antiterrorism in the Eighties* (New York: Pantheon, 1988).

36. For a critical view of Reagan administration negotiating policy see James D. Cockroft, *Neighbors in Turmoil: Latin America* (New York: Harper and Row, 1989), pp. 139–149.

37. Piero Gleijeses, "The Case for Power-Sharing in El Salvador," *Foreign Affairs*, 61:1048–1063.

38. Richard C. Schroeder, "New Approach to Central America," *Editorial Research Reports* (May 5, 1989): 246–259.

39. See President Bush's remarks concerning the Central American peace accord, State Department Bulletin, June 1989, pp. 55–57.

40. James Chace, *Endless War* (New York: Vintage, 1984).

41. *Times of the Americas*, November 15, 1989, p. 1.

42. *Times of the Americas*, April 4, 1990, p. 4

43. State Department Bulletin, December 1989, pp. 49–51.

44. See W. Tucker, "A Wake for Danny Boy," *National Review* 42 (April 1, 1990): 23–24.

45. See President Bush's proposal to reduce foreign assistance to Central America, *New York Times*, February 1, 1990, A-3.

6

LATIN AMERICAN LEADERS: DEALING WITH DRUGS

What these forces seek is the collapse of the state, the de-stabilization of democracy and the destruction of our way of life.

—Virgilio Barco,
former president of Colombia

Drugs and Latin America are now firmly locked together in an infamous tandem that is used by many in the United States as a simplistic gauge of their knowledge about the hemisphere. From this tandem flow somber images of random killings, public corruption at the highest levels of government, citizens engulfed with fear, and the astronomical profits amassed by the narco-traffickers. The Latin Americans that we in the United States have become familiar with are not the heads of state but rather the cocaine lords, crooked officials, drug-running rebels and Noriega types who run their countries as huge drug enterprises.[1] As we in this country look for answers to mounting drug woes, the Latin Americans have become easy targets for our fury.

Lost amidst this backdrop of illegality and violence is a story North Americans have often failed to appreciate. While the drug lords have garnered much of the attention, the Latin American civilian presidents who must face up to this deadly challenge have been pushed to the edges of the media message.[2] Because the drug wars are a mix of danger, violence, and immense wealth, the civilian leaders pledged to fight that war are at a distinct disadvantage in today's world of television journalism. Latin American presidents who are on the front lines of the drug war like the shy, scholarly Virgilio Barco of Colombia or the quiet technocrat Salinas Gotari

of Mexico or the youthful but bland Jaime Paz Zamora of Bolivia
are no match for the likes of Pablo Escobar, the "powerful drug
lord" of the Medellín cartel, Manuel Noriega, the "shrewd" leader
of Panama's drug dictatorship, or Rafael Caro Quintero, the "popular"
head of Mexico's drug empire.[3]

Despite the fact that the civilian presidents of Latin American
countries are the modern-day symbols of the rule of law and honest
government, they suffer from the false sense of excitement that
accompanies the drug war and the inherent weaknesses of their own
governing institutions. The war on drugs in Latin America may
indeed be about cocaine and money, but it is also about power and
authority. Civilian politicians in this region are not only seeking to
bring the drug lords to justice, they are also attempting to establish
their position as the recognized heads of their nation and the ultimate
controllers of political force. While the drug barons continue to set
themselves apart from government and challenge the authority of
elected political leaders, civilian presidents in countries like Colombia,
Peru, Bolivia, and Mexico are forced to run political systems that
resemble medieval fiefdoms with regional power centers, competing
armies, and numerous individuals claiming leadership and the right
to set the rules of their domain.[4]

The civilian presidents in those countries beset by drug politics
are undergoing a critical test of their ability to establish governing
authority throughout the country by forcing the drug lords and
their allies to succumb to the power of a popularly elected official.
From the Latin American perspective, the major objective of the
drug war is the establishment of government authority and political
power by the central authorities so that elected political leaders can
begin to regain control of governing power from those forces in
their society who operate outside the existing parameters of democratic
politics. If there is going to be a victory in the war on drugs in
Latin America, it will be one in which the civilian leaders become
national leaders and are capable of establishing their authority
throughout the country and with every major sector of society.[5]

So that we can fully understand the challenges that face the
Latin American leaders in the drug war, in this chapter I discuss
the range of pressures that these civilian presidents must deal with
as they seek not only to establish their governing authority but also
to respond to the considerable pressure being placed on them from

the United States. Heading a Latin American country that is engulfed in the drug trade requires exceptional skills of leadership primarily because these presidents must exude boldness and bravery in their campaign against the traffickers and also be able to handle the considerable demands of the United States to implement policies that will put an end to the drug trade and the corruption that allows it to continue.

Although the drug crisis has touched some countries more than others in Latin America, it nevertheless is an issue that reveals the complex challenges of leadership in this region. As we shall see, the mix of fighting the drug lords, expanding governing authority, and responding to U.S. pressure provides democratically elected presidents with a herculean task that often approaches a zero-sum game: few winners, little progress. And yet the civilian leaders in countries such as Colombia, Mexico, Peru, and Bolivia are remaining in the game and attempting to attack the problem on all fronts—criminal, governmental, and diplomatic.

THE PROBLEM OF MONEY

The above discussion emphasized the complexity of the issue and the multiple pressures being placed on civilian heads of state who must deal with the fallout from the illegal exportation of cocaine, marijuana, and heroin. But Latin American leaders are having a difficult time bringing the drug war to a successful conclusion because the spark that caused the conflict and continues to perpetuate it is not ideology, land, principle, or revenge, but cash. This is certainly not a major revelation to anyone familiar with the amounts of money that change hands in drug deals either on the streets or in the money-laundering banks throughout the world, yet it is important to remember when discussing the attempts by Latin American leaders to establish their authority and rein in the drug lords.[6]

There are a number of ways to approach the issue of cash and the drug war, but a few numbers may help to begin understanding the enormity of the influence that money has on Latin American economies and ultimately political systems. It is estimated that the Medellín and Cali drug organizations gross between $2 and $3 billion annually from cocaine sales worldwide. Throughout Latin America the profits of drug traffickers are close to an estimated $5 billion. Although much of the money remains in foreign banks and is moved into legitimate enterprises, upward of $2 billion may return to cocaine-producing countries. The profits from cocaine exportation now make up over two-thirds of Bolivia's foreign exchange; in Colombia drug lords reported $12 billion in assets in the United States.[7] The enormous wealth of the drug lords has led to a spending spree that rivals that of medieval royalty. Pablo Escobar, the head of the Medellín cartel, consistently makes the Forbes list of the richest men in the world; his associate, Jorge Ochoa, is not far behind.[8] Moreover, the economic impact of drugs has the capacity of changing the economy of a region almost overnight. Scott Malcomsen describes Tocache in Peru's drug-growing region of the Upper Huallaga Valley: "There are six banks, six Telex machines, several stereo dealerships, a discotheque and one of the largest Nissan outlets in Peru. Tocache also has no paved streets, no drinking water and no sewage system.[9]

The drug wars fought in Latin America are thus in many respects capitalism's version of the wars of national liberation that spread throughout the less-developed world in the 1960s. Small dedicated bands of drug traffickers seek to export their product for profit while fighting the efforts of the governing authorities who seek to destroy them, their product, and the opportunity to make huge sums of untaxed wealth. The Marxist rebels of the 1960s dealt in ideas and a promise of a better future. These capitalistic rebels deal in a commodity that currently has a high market value. But what is perhaps most significant about the cocaine lords is that they do not carry the intellectual and programmatic baggage of the earlier revolutionaries. Their goals are quite simple—making enormous sums of money and creating a lifestyle that is the envy of their fellow citizens.

Because the drug war is fueled by the possibility of amassing huge amounts of wealth for the smugglers and a decent living for the peasant growers, Latin American leaders who rely on tactics related to the criminality of drugs (arrests, prosecution, punishment) or the production and distribution of the drugs (interdiction, crop destruction, high-profile raids) are following a course of action that will meet with only limited success. The civilian presidents in the region cannot expect that new equipment, better training, and more effective cooperation will offset the lure of untaxed profits or intimidate dedicated capitalists from continuing their pursuit of U.S. dollars. Latin American leaders are not only up against a cartel of ruthless drug lords but, more important, they are now dealing with an attractive economic enterprise that has yet to experience a significant down period. The war footing that the Latin American presidents have put their countries on in order to fight the drug lords will have its victories, but combating drugs without addressing the economic incentives that drive the traffickers is doomed to failure.[10]

In the future, the drug war may need to be fought less in the jungle laboratories or the streets of Medellín than in the banks of the United States, Switzerland, West Germany, Canada, the Cayman Islands, and Panama. Because drugs and cash are the critical ingredients that have created this crisis of power and authority in Latin America, it is essential that the presidents in this region gain the support of the major banking nations so they can hit the traffickers where it is certain to have an impact—in their secret bank accounts. Coordinated efforts by major banking nations to counteract the laundering of billions of dollars in drug profits along with more vigilant monitoring by internal revenue and government tax collection agencies have been in place for years and have recorded a number of important victories. But as Scott MacDonald states in his study of money-laundered drug profits and the cooperation of Caribbean countries with banking interests,

> though the United States put considerable pressure on a number of nations, such as Bermuda and the Cayman Islands, to tighten their rules concerning capital origination, money continues to be laundered in other fashions. Moreover, the heavy pressure used to bring Caribbean nations into a new tax treaty have had considerable political ripples, as many nations, such as the Bahamas, greatly resented United States pressure.[11]

Although money is the critical ingredient in drug trafficking, the United States has been slow to recognize the importance of income-replacement programs to entice coca producers away from planting this lucrative cash crop and of increased aid and trade packages to the Andean countries to build a new economic foundation.[12] The rationale behind the aid and trade initiatives is the view held by some that the best way to attack the drug trade is to provide incentives that stimulate alternative modes of enterprise and profit.[13] Increasingly, those who monitor the antidrug campaigns are becoming convinced that an economic rather than a criminal approach will be the most successful. Jeffrey Sachs, a Harvard economist who has advised the Bolivian government on their finances, states, "A sensible economic strategy looks more realistic than all of the nonsense that has happened so far. For all the posturing, all the brave talk, there has been no serious attempt to come to grips with the coca economy and the human realities it creates."[14]

Along with changing the emphasis of the drug war from one of military containment to one of facing up to the economic realites of the drug trade, Latin American presidents also face another money-related issue that if left unresolved will help to perpetuate the flow of drugs northward. The drug lords have profited handsomely from the cocaine, marijuana, and heroin trade; the peasant growers in Peru, Bolivia, Mexico, and Guatemala have also benefited. With weak world prices for many of the traditional staple crops and local governments increasingly seeking to diversify their economies, peasants have come to see that participating in the drug trade is good business. In some parts of the coca-producing regions the decision to grow the illegal crops has been made for the peasants by leftist guerrillas anxious to make money to continue their fight or by powerful local drug lords anxious to ensure a ready supply of their product. But despite the instances of intimidation, the peasant population has become so attracted to the profits that accompany the drug trade and is so distant from the reach of the governing authorities that the decision to grow coca, marijuana, or heroin comes easy.[15]

It is important to point out that much of the analysis concerning the breakdown in governing authority in those nations beset by drug problems stresses the relationship between the drug traffickers and the civilian leaders; little attention has been placed on how weak the ties of the central government are with the peasant population in places like Peru's Upper Huallaga Valley.[16] If the civilian leaders in countries like Peru are to win the war on drugs, they must meet the economic challenges posed by the peasants who are an important part of the overall drug picture. Countries like Peru have been working with the United States to begin replacing coca as a cash-generating commodity with other staple crops as a way of cutting off the supply of drugs at the source. Here again, however, the emphasis on crop replacement has been weak and is often forced to take a back seat to military campaigns and crop-eradication projects that antagonize the peasants and further jeopardize their financial standing. As Gustavo Gorriti, an expert on the drug trade's impact on Peru, has stated, "the mistake in the drug war has been to try to quell what is fundamentally an economic revolution by means of punitive law enforcement."[17]

Latin American leaders have been trying to convince the United States, with little success to date, that the drug war is really a symptom of a much larger revolution that needs to be fought not only with military and prosecutorial methods but also with the tools used by the United States when it first felt threatened by Castro's revolution. In those days President Kennedy introduced the Alliance for Progress and began pumping millions of dollars in U.S. assistance into those countries that were threatened with guerrilla war, the rationale being that our dollars could solve problems, win friends, and weaken the push for Marxist revolution. In the 1990s the Latin American leaders have been unable to show the United States that sending in DEA agents and US military trainers must be accompanied by substantial amounts of economic assistance in order to deal with the needs of the peasant population. Because the drug war is a capitalist form of a war of national liberation, Latin American presidents need more than weapons and training, they need the means through which they can regain the hearts and minds of peasants who have little contact with the central government and have therefore little faith in its ability to address their problems.

Attacking the money laundering and providing peasants with crop-replacement incentives will not bring an early end to the war on drugs and is no substitute for vigilant criminal and containment policies, but placing greater emphasis on these strategies will give the Latin American leaders the means through which they can fight the real enemy—money and the power it can bring in the hands of the drug capitalist and the prospect of using the cocaine cash crop to bring a better life to the struggling peasant class. Moreover, by balancing police action with economic incentives, Latin American leaders leave themselves less open to criticism that they have become helpless pawns in the U.S. drive to eradicate the drug trade and the drug traffickers. By shifting emphasis from a very visible and violent internal war to an international cooperative effort to close down the cash trail and rebuild the rural economy, Latin American leaders enhance their image as nationalists while at the same time striking at the heart of the drug cartels. If the drug war is indeed a contest of power and authority, there is no better way to win the hearts and minds of the populace and weaken the base of the traffickers than by fostering policies designed to redefine the problem in an international context and redirect international assistance in ways that build support. As Colombia's Gaviria stated on his inauguration day, "We expect more of industrialized nations, not just against consumption, but with tighter controls over money laundering, arms trafficking, distribution networks, precursor chemicals and coca leaf production."[18]

THE PROBLEM OF INSTITUTIONAL WEAKNESS

The failure to make significant headway in the war on drugs is often linked to the inability of governments to marshal sufficient resources in their fight against the traffickers. Helicopters, radar equipment, weapons, and training are listed as the crying needs of governments facing the challenge of the drug lords. As a result Latin American presidents view the acquisition of these resources as a key component in their campaign to regain control of their countries. Not surprisingly, the talks between Latin American leaders and the United States over the drug war quickly move to the issue of military aid and the impact that the aid will have on curbing the flow of drugs and destroying the infrastructure of the drug cartels.

Although the antidrug arsenal of democratic governments in Latin America is indeed small and antiquated, civilian presidents in the region need to look not so much at the weakness of their equipment but rather at the weakness of their institutions. In countries such as Colombia, Peru, and Bolivia the war on drugs is a contest between an increasingly sophisticated and remarkably efficient drug-exportation system and governments that respond with a lack of administrative coordination, high levels of official corruption, and an unfortunate presence of timidity in the legislative and judicial branches. What is left many times is a brave president fighting the drug lords with little institutional support behind him or at best with incomplete institutional support. Bruce Bagley states that in Colombia, for example, "The key to an effective international drug control policy is to support and strengthen Colombia's institutional capacity to maintain public order and meet the needs of its citizens. The virtually complete collapse of the country's judicial system . . . is the most dramatic but by no means the only manifestation of this problem."[19]

Stories of conflicts within governing circles over how best to fight the war, police and military officials receiving payoffs from drug traffickers, and legislators and judges refusing to provide the president with tough laws are now documented regularly in Latin America and reinforce the view in the United States that the war on drugs will not be won with helicopters and radar but with a unified and effective governing system. As Rensselaer W. Lee III states, "Cocaine traffickers can manipulate the key institutions of public life, including the political parties, the press, the police, the military and the judiciary."[20] Colombia's criminal justice system, in the view of Lee, "almost ceased to function," and in Bolivia drug traffickers are described as paying police $20,000–$25,000 for a seventy-two-hour "window of impunity for loading major shipments by air, land or river."[21]

Institutional weakness, if not breakdown, in those countries engaged in the war on drugs creates a situation in which the president must not only pursue the traffickers but construct anew a governing system that is capable of reestablishing authority. This is no easy task given the inherent jealousies in the bureaucratic ranks, the lure of money for police and military officials, and the long-held view that the legislative and judicial branches are to receive their cues from the executive rather than chart an independent course. The problem is compounded by the fact that Latin American political systems have traditionally accented governing values that benefit the drug traffickers—personalistic contact rather than institutional action; tangible rewards for service rather than adherence to a legalistic work ethic; and reliance on a strong central leadership figure rather than forming an alternative basis of decisionmaking. Latin American presidents thus are overwhelmed by the task before them because the war on drugs has also become a war on the centuries of common political practice that uniquely define this region.

The sense of frustration and defeat faced by Latin American leaders was echoed in an editorial written in Bogatá's leading newspaper, El Tiempo. A portion of that editorial sums up best the problems of fighting the drug war with weak institutions and a culture battered by violence:

> We have lowered our guard. Valuable ground has been lost in the relentless war against drug trafficking, and we have begun turning in our weapons. This new attitude has led to a dangerous atmosphere of tolerance and permissiveness. The Mafia chieftains move around freely in broad daylight throughout Colombian cities. If we look closely, we will see how they have steadily returned to their privileged positions . . . and are using their money and the law to undermine the weak morale of the government institutions. The country's legal structure is now enough to counter such a powerful empire. . . . Our fragile judicial system has allowed drug-trafficking organizations to consolidate themselves very well . . . the authorities have been infiltrated; and the country remains indifferent. Thus the drug traffickers are guaranteed a sanctuary without risks.[22]

If there is a ray of hope in this battle to remedy the institutional weaknesses that inhibit the war on drugs, it is that the process of democratization in Latin America and the heightened realization that this region does not want to be left behind in the age of a global economy have made the political leaders in countries like Colombia, Bolivia, Peru, and Mexico recognize the importance of transforming their governing systems. President Gaviria of Colombia has pledged to strengthen the judicial system in his country; President Paz Zamora of Bolivia has made significant strides in developing a coordinated effort to control the growing of coca; and President Salinas of Mexico has made a number of well-publicized attacks on government corruption, particularly in the Federal Police. The actions of these presidents support the view that political leaders in the region are becoming aware that the war on drugs is not only a criminal battle but an institutional one as well.[23]

As the democracies of Latin America mature and respond more effectively to the demands of a global economy, the political leaders in this region will also grow in their confidence to deal with institutional deficiencies. The drug problems of these countries must be seen not only as generated by economic opportunity and enormous foreign demand but also as a consequence of the inevitable lag time that occurs when governments hold elections but fail to build a governing structure to match democratization. It will take time to make that transition from elections to institutionalization and to redefine the political culture in ways that benefit the government rather than the drug cartels. Of course time is a precious commodity for fragile democracies and even more fragile civilian leaders. But if these presidents fight the war on drugs with only equipment and weapons and ignore the vital role that competent bureaucracies, loyal police and military officials, and aggressive legislators and judges play in this fight, then they will achieve only limited success and will continue to face the drug lords alone.

THE PROBLEM OF FEAR

Latin American presidents who head nations that are engulfed in the drug wars face a challenge more difficult to overcome than controlling the transfer of huge amounts of money or strengthening the institutional framework. Because the campaign to bring the drug lords to justice and end their illegal trade is at base a contest for power and authority, violence, or perhaps better stated, narco-terrorism, has become a staple of national life in countries such as Colombia, Peru, and Mexico. Although Latin America is not a stranger to violence or political upheaval, the wave of killings, bombings, tortures, and kidnappings has created a climate of fear in the region and limited the ability of public officials to develop a democratic environment of safety, openness, and normalcy. For example, in Colombia there were 4,000 drug-related deaths in 1988, and 660 police officials were killed between 1985 and 1988. The primary cause of death for males between 15 and 44 in Colombia is murder.

The growing realization that government authorities do not have the capability to protect their citizenry has begun to foster doubts about the effectiveness of democracy as a force against the drug cartels. The fear that permeates the political culture of Colombia, Peru, and Mexico is the most tangible sign that the drug wars are having a serious affect on the vitality of democratic governance.

Narco-terrorism has diminished the ability of governments in these countries to conduct their business and generate popular participation. A justice minister resigns out of fear for her life in Colombia, voter turnout in certain regions of Peru is down because of fear of reprisals from drug lords and their rebel cohorts, and residents in some Mexican barrios show greater respect for the drug traffickers than they do for local or national officials. These are examples of the slow deterioration of democratic practice and democratic support.[24]

Colombia has become a test case for the ability of democratically elected leaders to convince the people that they can return the country to normalcy and guarantee that fear of terrorist attacks will not destroy the tradition of civilian rule that has been the mainstay of politics since the 1950s. But when presidential candidates such as Liberal Luis Carlos Galan and leftist rebel leader Carlos Pizarro are assassinated, the police headquarters in Bogatá is bombed, and Medellín becomes the murder capital of the world, the "culture of fear" begins to envelop the country and transforms people from participants and supporters of democracy to apolitical doubters who question the competence of their leaders and the benefits of a system based on the rule of law.

Colombian political leaders are keenly aware of the the dangers to democracy from the "culture of fear" and see it having a visible effect on the way democracy is structured and practiced. Carlos Lemos, the leader of the Liberal party, made a sad commentary concerning the election campaign of 1990: "Now in Colombia, death is the chief elector, and we count votes with the bullets of machine guns. . . . People are terrified. The campaign will be different, because for the first time we will be forced to rely on television and radio, rather than the traditional mass rallies in the public plaza."[25] The observations of Lemos echo throughout Colombia as citizens begin to wonder whether the country can avoid becoming a nation permanently under seige with leaders so intimidated by the violence that they are removed from the political arena and govern by television rather than in the accepted personalistic manner.

The "culture of fear" that grips the Latin American countries engaged in the war on drugs also has international implications. President Bush was heavily criticized for deciding to stage the drug summit in 1989 in Cartegena, Colombia. Newspaper columnists and members of Congress felt that the president was needlessly placing himself in danger by traveling to Colombia and tantalizing the Medellín cartel with his presence. Amid perhaps the heaviest security ever accorded a U.S. president, the Cartegena summit was held without incident, but the sight of thousands of police, helicopters, patrol boats, and a bullet-proof bunker for the talks further reinforced the role that fear plays in the drug war.[26] The public praised the bravery of the presidents for going to Colombia and sending a message to the traffickers that they were not intimidated, but the fact that the police and military resources necessary to protect the presidents were so enormous underscored the crisis facing countries like Colombia. One brave act of defiance against the drug cartel does not change a climate of fear, especially because the act of bravery required a form of security "overkill" that did not impress Colombians who daily face the threat of violence.

The connection between the "culture of fear" and the continued vitality of democratic governance in countries like Colombia is one that all of Latin America and in particular Latin American leaders must pay close attention to. As the war on drugs escalates with governments taking more aggressive actions against the traffickers, the response is certain to be more violent and aimed at the civilian population. Furthermore, a victory in one region or even one country against the drug lords does not mean a permanent break in the production and exportation chain; rather it means that the traffickers will look elsewhere and bring their business, their violence, and their "culture of fear" to a new site. Already Guatemala is being viewed as a source of heroin for the U.S. market, Paraguay has become a major drug transit point and a key money-laundering center for Latin America; Haiti, Bahamas, Dominican Republic, and Honduras are growing in their involvement with the cocaine trade and Brazil has been described by the State Department as "vital in the cocaine trade as a transit country for Andean traffickers . . . and as an emerging coca cultivator."[27]

Latin American leaders throughout the region must prepare for the governing challenges that the drug wars bring to their countries. As can be seen with the Colombian situation, the "culture of fear" that accompanies the drug traffickers is a real threat to democratic stability. Because the war on drugs has escalated in terms of U.S. determination and Latin American cooperation, the traffickers can be expected to raise the stakes and see whether civilian leaders are willing to jeopardize their safety and their popularity by controversial extradition policies or aggressive military campaigns that endanger the population. Democratic presidents must be prepared for the effects that the war on drugs can have on them and on their political systems. They lead democracies that are young and fragile and that can be easily compromised by drug violence and the intimidation that it produces. Such intimidation is the most sinister force undermining citizen confidence in democracy in Latin America today. The challenges faced by Latin American leaders can perhaps best be summed up by a letter sent to a Colombian judge (and published in a Bogotá newspaper) who was involved in a trial of drug chieftain Pablor Escobar. The friends of Escobar wrote the following:

> We want to remind you that, in addition to perpetrating a judicial infamy, you are making a big error that will blemish your life and will make it cursed until the end of your days. You know perfectly well that we are capable of executing you at any place on this planet. You should also know that in the meantime you will see the fall, one by one, of all of the members of your family. . . . Be absolutely certain that in calling Mr. Escobar to trial you will remain without forebearers or descendants in your genealogical tree.[28]

THE PROBLEM OF THE UNITED STATES

One of the most difficult problems Latin American leaders face in the war on drugs is that they are not fully in command. Because drug smuggling is an international operation with the main target market the United States, the presidents of the region must work in concert with their counterpart to the north. Although as democratically elected chief executives they are natural allies with a common objective of ridding the hemisphere of the drug menace, the Latin American leaders must accept the fact that this is a war with more than one general and with vastly differing views over how to properly define national interest. Latin American leaders cannot escape the reality of the United States peering over their shoulders offering advice, expressing support, venting its frustrations, and of course monitoring the expenditure of its antidrug assistance.

The reality of dual leadership in the war on drugs has created a host of domestic problems for the civilian presidents of Latin America. Because the United States has poured millions of dollars in antinarcotics assistance to the countries beset by drug production and trafficking, there is a natural desire on the part of officials in this country to expect that the host country and, in particular, the president of that host country would respond in a manner that approximates our expectations about efficient management, honest government, aggressive pursuit, and bold leadership. Although these are laudable expectations, they often clash with the equally natural desire on the part of the president of the host country to assume an independent posture and to build on that independence to conduct the antidrug campaign in a way that preserves the sovereignty of the nation and allows the president to fight the traffickers in the way he thinks will best serve the national interest.

The attempt by the United States to inject large amounts of antidrug assistance into Latin America has not been welcomed with open arms by all presidents. Virgilio Barco of Colombia lobbied strongly for the $65 million in U.S. military assistance in 1989, citing the need for more modern equipment to fight the increasingly sophisticated armies of the drug lords, but Peru's outgoing president, Alan García, temporarily blocked the U.S. plan to provide that country with $35 million in military assistance in both 1990 and 1991. The U.S.-aid plan would involve the sending of military advisers and weapons to train Peruvian armed forces and police units who are ill prepared to deal with the drug lords and their leftist rebel supporters in the Shining Path revolutionary movement. In García's view the aid plan failed to include economic aid for crop substitution and debt relief. García's strong stance toward U.S. antidrug aid prompted one Peruvian political leader to state, "We need greenbacks [for economic development] not Green Berets."[29] The United States also came to the assistance of Bolivia and encountered similar opposition. Bolivia's president Jaime Paz Zamora, a leftist democrat with a history of revolutionary politics, faced hostility from his traditional bases of support among unions and the ruling Movement of the Revolutionary Left (MIR) party for his acceptance of $46 million in 1990 and $35 million in 1991 of U.S. antinarcotic assistance. Paz's opponents argued that the money would not only bring U.S. military trainers to Bolivia but would lend legitimacy to the militarization of the drug war instead of moving toward income-replacement programs.

Despite the reservations in Latin America about U.S. antidrug military assistance, Washington continues to press political leaders to cooperate. In 1990 the Bush administration inaugurated a five-year, $2.2 billion counternarcotics program "to augment law en-forcement, military and economic resources in Colombia, Bolivia, and Peru."[30] Called the Andean Strategy, the program has earmarked monies "to disrupt and destroy the growing, processing and trans-portation of coca and coca products within the source countries in order to reduce the supply of cocaine from these countries to the United States." In the presentation of the program the State De-partment was conscious of the fact that the Andean Strategy would be perceived by Latin American presidents as a military one that would ultimately strengthen the role of the armed forces in fragile democracies. As a result, the program did include substantial monies for income replacement and crop diversification efforts.[31]

The pressure being placed on Latin American presidents to accept U.S. assistance and the personnel that accompany that assistance raises a serious dilemma for many of these leaders. Although they recognize the need for more funds to fight the drug lords who are threatening political stability, they fear that too close a relationship with the United States will paint them as dependent puppets willing to do the bidding of the U.S. government. Furthermore, many of the Latin American presidents see the drug problem not so much as criminal activity but as a reflection of their depressed economies. They therefore often share the view of Peru's García that their primary objective in dealing with the United States should be to convince U.S. officials to concentrate on economic solutions rather than on high-profile and controversial military campaigns. From the perspective of the Latin American presidents, there is no better way to weaken their popularity and their legitimacy than to endorse a military solution to the drug problem (especially if that military solution involves the presence of U.S. combat troops) over one that pumps money into the country to help peasants change their farming practices or to pay off the huge debt that is impoverishing the nation.

What to do about U.S. antidrug assistance and the question of independence is not the only sticking point with Latin American leaders. Leaders such as Salinas of Mexico are outraged about the cavalier attitude of the U.S. drug enforcement agents toward Mexican law and Mexico's own campaign to combat the narcotics traffickers. Tensions built to a head between Mexico and the United States over the kidnap, torture, and murder of DEA agent Enrique Camarena in 1985. U.S. officials expressed outrage over what they considered the vast corruption of the Mexican security forces and the unwillingness of the Mexican government to bring those responsible for Camarena's death to justice. President Salinas responded to the U.S. charges by condemning DEA agents for apprehending alleged suspects in the death without proper authorization and other U.S. officials for suggesting that his government was not waging the war on drugs with the same intensity.[32] Salinas has been a vocal critic of the U.S. drug war, particularly with respect to charges by U.S. officials that Mexico is not serious about fighting the traffickers or the corrupt officials who allow them to continue their trade.

Of all the leaders in Latin America, the Colombian presidents—formerly Virgilio Barco and now Cesar Gaviria—must be adept at balancing their domestic interests and personal political survival with the intense pressure from the United States to control the flood of cocaine that leaves their country. Both Barco and Gaviria have enjoyed good relations with the United States and have often agreed on the proper course of action to take against the Medellín cartel. But the issue of extraditing the drug lords, the so-called extraditables, has been a major bone of contention and reveals the conflict between the U.S. view of the solution and the Colombian concern for dealing with the problem in ways that do minimum harm to internal stability. From the U.S. perspective the only way to strike at the heart of the drug cartel is to apprehend the criminals and remove them from the country, thus sending a clear message that trafficking will bring a certain jail sentence without the prospect of corrupt plea bargaining. As President Bush stated in an address on the Latin American drug wars, "Colombia must do more, not just to eradicate crops, but to overcome corruption and intimidation."[33]

The Colombian leaders, however, recognize full well that their political system is not at the stage where forceful action can be taken without jeopardizing the system and the individuals who head that system. As a result Barco wavered on the policy, only to cooperate after extensive pressure from Washington, and Gaviria has stated unequivocally that he will not participate in the extradition of drug leaders. The United States has been successful in bringing a number of the key Colombian "extraditables" to the United States, including Carlos Lehder, who ran perhaps the most lucrative drug-running operation in Latin America. But the United States now views the possibility of bringing other major drug barons to justice in this country as remote. Pablo Escobar's surrender to the Colombian gov- ernment in 1991 and his eventual imprisonment in what Washington described as a "country club jail" near his home chilled relations with President Gaviria and solidified the view that the young chief executive had negotiated an unwritten bargain with the Medellín cartel in which terrorist attacks against the government would decrease in return for a guarantee of no extradition. Tensions between the two countries are bound to escalate in the future over the issue of whose interests are being served in the war, Colombia's or those of the United States.

Despite the range of conflicts between the United States and individual Latin American leaders over how best to fight the war on drugs, the pressure from Washington on the civilian presidents of many countries to vigorously pursue the traffickers and eradicate the raw materials of the narcotics trade will continue. The Bush administration is determined to fight the war on the supply side and seems ready to press the Latin American leaders to intensify their efforts. Although the Latin American presidents scored somewhat of a victory at the Cartegena summit when President Bush agreed to attack the drug problem more aggressively on the domestic scene, the majority of the final agreements signed defined the battleground as centered in Latin America.[34]

It will be difficult for Latin American presidents to ignore the pressure from the United States or to resist the economic and military aid that is dangled before them. But what the United States must remember as it expands its war on drugs outside the border of this country is that the popularity of political leaders and the legitimacy of democratic governance are inextricably connected to our heightened involvement in the drug wars. Our campaign to bring the traffickers to justice and destroy the narcotics trade could become a situation in which we begin winning battles in Colombia, Peru, Bolivia, and Mexico but slowly lose the war to develop friendly, cooperative, and popular democratic allies in the ranks of the Latin American leaders.

NOTES

1. There has been a rash of books on the drug wars in Latin America. Some of the better studies are Paul Eddy, *The Cocaine Wars* (New York: W. W. Norton, 1988); Arnold S. Trebach, *The Great Drug War: And Radical*

Proposals That Could Make America Safe Again (New York: Macmillan, 1987) and Bruce Bagley and Juan G. Tokatlian, *La economia politica de narco-trafico entre Colombia y Estados Unidos* (Bogatá: Universidad de los Andes and CEREC, 1989).

2. This theme of Latin American leaders as heroes was echoed when Colombia's president, Virgilio Barco, received an honorary degree at the Massachusetts Institute of Technology in Boston and stated, "good men and women everywhere will not tolerate the misery and violence by those who push and those who consume illegal drugs." Charles Radin, "Colombia Leader at MIT Assails Drug Threat," *Boston Globe*, June 5, 1990, p. 21.

3. See Alan Riding, "Cocaine Billionaires," *New York Times Magazine*, March 8, 1987, pp. 26–39.

4. See a two-part analysis of the territorial control of the Medellín cartel in the *Miami Herald*, "Brutal Cocaine Bosses Terrorize Colombia," *Miami Herald*, February 8, 1987, p. 1, and "At Its Peak, Drug Cartel Was Untouchable," *Miami Herald*, February 9, 1987, p. 1.

5. See David Scott Palmer, "Drug Trafficking, Political Violence and Democratic Stability in Peru and Colombia," Paper prepared for the Colombia Studies Project of the University of Miami, May 1989.

6. The process of laundering money by Latin American drug dealers is explained in Scott B. MacDonald, *Dancing on a Volcano: The Latin American Drug Trade* (New York: Praeger, 1988), pp. 105–107.

7. "Colombia: The Drug Economy," *Economist* (April 2, 1988): 3.

8. David Henry, "Pablo Escobar Gaviria" and "Ochoa Brothers," in "How to Make $7 Billion in 7 Years," *Forbes* (October 5, 1987): 154.

9. Scott Malcomsen, "Cocaine Republic," *The Village Voice*, August 26, 1986, p. 18.

10. See the editorial on economic incentives and the drug war in the *Washington Post National Weekly Edition*, September 4–10, 1989, p. 26.

11. MacDonald, *Dancing on a Volcano*, p. 106.

12. Bruce Bagley, "Dateline Drug Wars; Colombia: The Wrong Strategy," *Foreign Policy* 77 (Winter 1989/1990): 170.

13. Gustavo A. Goritti, "How to Fight the Drug War," *Atlantic* (July, 1989): 70–76.

14. Ibid., p. 76.

15. Kevin Healy, "The Boom within the Crisis: Some Recent Effects of Foreign Cocaine Markets on Bolivian Rural Society and Economy," in Deborah Paine and Christine Franquemont, eds., *Coca and Cocaine* (Peterborough, NH: Transcript Printing Company, 1986), pp. 101–143.

16. See Rensalear Lee III, "Why the U.S. Cannot Stop South American Cocaine," *Orbis* (Fall 1989): 499–519.

17. Goritti, "How To Fight the Drug War," p. 74.

18. As quoted in Douglas Farah, "Gaviria Installed as Colombia Leader," *Boston Globe*, August 8, 1990, p. 20.

19. Bagley, "Dateline Drug Wars," p. 166.

20. Lee, "Why the U.S. Cannot Stop South American Cocaine," p. 507.

21. Ibid.

22. *El Tiempo*, November 8, 1987.

23. A good background study of the impact of violence on Colombian society can be found in Gary Hoskin, "Colombia's Political Crisis," *Current History* (January 1988): 11–12.

24. The respect, if not awe, with which Rafael Caro Quintero was held in certain sections of Mexico is documented by Elaine Shannon in *Desperados: Latin Drug Lords, U.S. Lawmen and the War American Can't Win* (New York: Viking, 1988), pp. 256–257.

25. Douglas Farah, "Drug Terrorists are Forcing Democracy Underground," *Washington Post National Weekly Edition*, May 7–13, 1990, p. 19.

26. "Drug Bosses Give Up Laboratories on Eve of Bush Visit to Colombia," *New York Times*, February 15, 1990, p. A-1.

27. *Department of State Bulletin*, October 1989, p. 56.

28. *El Espectador* (Bogatá), July 31, 1988.

29. *Times of the Americas*, May 2, 1990, p. 4.

30. See Melvin Levitsky, "The Andean Strategy to Control Cocaine," *Department of State Bulletin*, July/August 1990, pp. 71–74.

31. Ibid.

32. See *Congressional Quarterly*, April 16, 1988, p. 998.

33. As quoted in President Bush's certification statement, March 1, 1989, *Department of State Bulletin*, October 1989, p. 54.

34. Andrew Rosenthal, "Andean Leaders and Bush Pledge Drug Cooperation," *New York Times*, February 16, 1990, p. A-1.

7

LATIN AMERICAN LEADERS: DEALING WITH DEBT AND DEVELOPMENT

My administration will move rapidly to reduce the size of the state so that it will no longer be inefficient, gigantic, and corrupt; instead, it will be a light, austere and efficient state.

—Fernando Collor de Mello,
president of Brazil

In the Latin America of the 1990s the problems of debt and development have entered a new period of definition and policy prescription. The 1980s was the decade when Latin America became the debt center of the world with over $450 billion in outstanding loans and countries like Brazil and Mexico piling up obligations well over $100 billion. Moreover, because these enormous debt requirements often led to painful restructuring programs that then precipitated acts of violence and general instability, Latin America remained even longer under the microscope of international scrutiny as the industrialized world worried over the very survival of nations stretched to their limits by scarce resources, unbalanced budgets, trade deficits, and the twin horrors of inflation and unemployment.[1]

Today the Latin America one reads about is cast in a very different light. Although the enormity of the debt continues to hover around the $400 billion mark, there is talk of debt forgiveness or, at the very least, management of the debt crisis, of privatization schemes for huge parastatal institutions, of investment incentives to foreign corporations, and of free-trade zones and market economies. There are also bold new plans to restructure the role of the government in the formation of economic and financial policymaking.[2] And yet, despite these ever-growing signs of economic revolution in Latin America, the problems of the 1980s have lingered on into the 1990s. The countries of the region continue to be threatened by their inability to meet the needs of an ever-growing population, to attract the necessary capital for modernization, and to reform the institutions of government so as to effectively deal with the constant wave of new demands and challenges. To many Latin Americans, the 1980s may have been the worst of times, but the 1990s pose even greater threats as leaders consider new economic formulas to solve problems that remain the engines of crisis.

At the center of this new period of economic readjustment are the Latin American presidents, who in many instances are responsible for taking their countries away from the statist approach to development that dominated the hemisphere since the pronouncements of Raul Prebisch on import substitution and state capitalism in the 1950s and 1960s.[3] Due in part to U.S. pressure on these leaders to dismantle statist economies and reform restrictive governing practices, democratically elected presidents throughout the region have climbed aboard the market economy bandwagon and are now preaching the benefits of privatizing government-owned enterprises, cutting through the labyrinth of state bureaucracy, and expanding opportunities for foreign investment.

But U.S. pressure alone was not the driving force for the change in direction. Latin American presidents in the late 1980s and early 1990s were beset with economies that had never really been revived after the debt shocks. Hyperinflation, devalued currencies, dwindling reserves, heightened foreign competition and trade barriers, and disruptive labor and business groups coalesced into a dangerous mix that forced many leaders to take bold measures to avert economic paralysis. To counteract these threats, not only to economic stability but to democratic governance, Latin American politics spawned a new generation of leaders who pledged to revitalize their fledgling economies even if that meant instituting drastic measures. In Argentina, President Carlos Menem promised economic "surgery without anesthetic" and called for "private enterprise and free trade, with social justice incorporated."[4] In Mexico, President Carlos Salinas de Gotari slashed tariffs on hundreds of imported goods, privatized over six hundred state-owned businesses, and urged foreign investors to take advantage of "new opportunites in Mexico's development."[5] And in Brazil, President Fernando Collor de Mello introduced a rigid austerity plan that froze all bank-deposit funds for eighteen months, eliminated twenty-four government institutes and enterprises, and imposed a thirty-day wage and price freeze.[6]

Although the actions taken by Menem, Salinas, and Collor received the greatest attention and created enormous controversy within their own countries, these leaders were not alone in their embrace of the market economy and in their response to economic crisis with harsh measures. Fujimori in Peru introduced harsh orthodox economic measures to rein in hyperinflation, Paz Zamora in Bolivia endured numerous labor union strikes as he reduced state subsidies and raised prices on staple goods, and in Venezuela Carlos Andrés Pérez began implementing policies that forced his citizens to accept the realities of a drastically scaled-down government sector. From a crisis of debt that crippled their economies in the 1980s, the Latin Americans entered the 1990s facing a new crisis as their political leaders experimented with the promise of free-market prosperity and the bane of unpopular policies designed to put an end to runaway prices and economic stagnation.

Because the future of the Latin American economies hinges on what the democratically elected leaders do with respect to debt reduction, economic restructuring, and national development, it is essential to explore each of these areas to determine how the presidents in the region have come to grips with these critical challenges. Furthermore, it is also essential to examine the political implications of the economic policies pursued by these leaders. Because dealing with debt, restructuring, and development can weaken the popular base of democratic institutions and practice, the actions of the Latin American presidents must be viewed in terms of system stability and longevity. Finally, as with the previous discussions, the relationship of Latin American leaders to the United States cannot be avoided. The United States plays a crucial role in the areas of debt negotiations, aid appropriations, multilateral loan disbursements, trade policy, and investment initiatives. Latin American leaders cannot easily avoid the advice and the pressure of the United States as they fashion their economic revival programs. In many instances, cooperation between the United States and Latin American countries forms the backbone of economic policy and national development and is a key ingredient in the political survival of democratic leaders.

DEBT FORGIVENESS AND DEBT SURVIVAL

One of the many unfortunate results of the debt crisis in Latin America is the preoccupation with the dollar value of the outstanding obligations at the expense of attention to the social and political impact those obligations have created for the region. Press reports, television specials, and a seemingly endless stream of academic and institutional analyses have regularly stressed the enormity of Latin American indebtedness. Unfortunately, on few occasions has interest in the debt delved beneath the surface of loan obligations to view the effects of such obligations on nations coping with the shortfall of revenue and the repayment requirements, which sapped export earnings and budget surpluses.[7] The debt crisis was often portrayed as a kind of game of high finance and political will with foreign governments, banks, international lending institutions, and Latin American political leaders jockeying for position and advantage in order to recoup their losses or to limit the extent of their obligations. It was only when the economic and financial restrictions caused by the indebtedness led to violent outbursts, as in relatively prosperous Venezuela in 1989, that attention begin to switch from the raw numbers to the impact on society as a whole.[8]

The Latin American debt crisis, however, is more than just a matter of astronomical financial obligations or the interplay of powerful countries and institutions. The struggle of the Latin American political leaders to deal with interest payments owed to external sources while also responding to the internal pressures for fiscal stability and social responsibility posed the greatest challenge to their reputations and their positions. This modern-day "tug-of-war" between external requirements and domestic demands forced Latin American presidents to develop new policy responses and unpopular restructuring programs to assuage the concerns of foreign creditors and control the rising level of economic chaos and social ferment that inevitably accompanies indebtedness.

The leaders of this region quickly came to realize that the debt crisis would require them to take on a wide range of identities. In front of the international lending community, they would have to become protectors of their nation's independence and pride and not appear to be controlled by foreign governments or banks. At home in front of worried businesspeople and angry workers, they would have to be capable administrators and tough decisionmakers in order to handle the crush of demands for steady prices, regular wage increases, stable currencies, and continued economic growth. Faced with all those who were affected by the debt crisis, the Latin American leaders had to be able to instill confidence in government and democratic politics and at the same time respond to the social, economic, and political explosions that were set off by the inability of government to meet its foreign and domestic obligations. At a 1987 summit of eight Latin American presidents, their final communiqué stated clearly the enormity of the challenge they faced: "Recovery of sustained economic growth, improvement in our peoples' standard of living and strengthening of democratic practices in the area require a just and permanent solution to the external debt problem, in addition to unpostponable measures to reduce the burden of servicing the debt."[9]

Although each of the Latin American leaders faced unique circumstances resulting from the debt crisis, most presidents were forced to respond to a similar set of challenges. In many of the wealthier countries such as Mexico, Venezuela, and Brazil, a key issue was the extent of flight capital as the wealthy sectors of society took their money out of the country to escape devaluation and monetary uncertainty.[10] In countries like Chile and Argentina, political leaders had to deal with recalcitrant industrialists and labor unions who depended on state subsidies and wage contracts that were affected by revenue shortfalls and shifts in budget priorities.[11] And in most countries, public employees who worked for the parastatal enterprises protested attempts to trim payrolls or to privatize.[12] In addition to these challenges was the impact of indebtedness on the poor, who often bore the brunt of any new restructuring program, which usually included price increases on staple commodities, gasoline, and housing. They responded to these restructuring efforts by demonstrating, striking, and on occasion by engaging in violent protest, as was the case in countries like Argentina, Venezuela, the Dominican Republic, Jamaica, and Peru.[13]

The economic and social problems that developed in response to foreign indebtedness and in many instances intensified the debt crisis also raised the specter of a return to authoritarian rule and the demise of hard-won democratic rights. As the level of foreign obligations increased and the problems associated with debt mounted, Latin American leaders and their counterparts in the industrialized world worried over the fate of democracy in the region. President Alan García of Peru voiced the concern of his fellow democratically elected heads of state when he warned that the choice in the future could very well be "debt or democracy."[14] The domestic damage created by the debt crisis was viewed by many as certain to affect the legitimacy of elected leaders and call into question the effectiveness of democratic governance in dealing with severe economic dislocation.

Sensing the real dangers to system stability and to their own ability to survive politically, democratically elected leaders in Latin America sought to assure their citizens that a return to authoritarianism would not hold the answer to the debt crisis but would in fact put the country back in the hands of those individuals who initiated the foreign loan agreements and introduced a new level of dependence to the region. Most leaders pleaded for time, patience, and cooperation from social and economic groups apprehensive over the prospect of policies that would weaken their position. Although the public response was often critical and laced with cynicism, many Latin American leaders continued to grope for solutions to the debt-generated crisis while reminding citizens that the alternative was a step back to military rule. As Paul Drake correctly states about the current leaders in Latin America:

> Democrats are trying to forge a consensus that economic dissatisfaction should be expressed through regular changes of government rather than irregular changes of regimes. Elected leaders are trying to persuade citizens that authoritarian systems have proven themselves even less capable of solving economic crisis.[15]

But convincing an angry public would not be enough for the Latin American leaders. It would be necessary to take bold new steps to lessen the debt burden and to respond to the cries for switching resources from external repayment to internal development. Early on in the debt crisis Latin American leaders presented a wide range of approaches to the problems brought on by foreign borrowing. Many of these approaches accented the Latin American leaders' concern that they would be perceived as weak in the face of external dependency and too willing to accept the advice and implement the reform policies demanded by the banks, the multilateral lending institutions, and the aid-disbursing countries. Some, such as Brazil's José Sarney, halted interest payments and told the international lending community that the country was unable to meet its obligations and continue to meet its domestic needs.[16] In Peru, President Alan García received international attention when he proposed that his government would set a limit of 10 percent of the revenue from export earnings to service the foreign debt. García struck a chord among his fellow presidents who saw the revenue from exports channeled directly to the debt service while domestic programs begged for new monies.[17]

Although García did not begin a trend in the region with his "10 percent solution," his anger against the international lending community was voiced by other political leaders. Venezuela's Carlos Andrés Pérez became an outspoken critic of the debt crisis and called for a debt summit for Latin America.[18] Andrés Pérez on numerous occasions lashed out at U.S. banks and the restrictive loan policies of the International Monetary Fund (IMF). In the view of the Venezuelan president, the banks and the IMF were forcing unworkable and potentially destabilizing reform programs on the Latin American countries, all in the name of debt reduction. Pérez's solution was a kind of debtors' cartel in which the Latin American nations remained unified in their response to the debt crisis and the demands of the foreign banks and lending institutions.

In the view of the Latin American leaders, the answer to the debt crisis was a recognition by the banks and the developed countries that removing the obligations was the only real solution to the problem. Despite clear evidence that Latin American indebtedness was having a serious impact on the economic, social, and political life in the region, the industrialized nations and their banks were reluctant to accept the calls for forgiveness from the presidents. As Riorden Roett states, the international lending community was satisfied to either "quarantine" intransigent Latin American debtors or "muddle through" with new loans and rescheduling programs that merely postponed and intensified the problem.[19]

The willingness of the industrialized countries to "quarantine" or "muddle through" is reflected in the halfhearted implementation of the Baker Plan for debt relief during the Reagan administration. Introduced in South Korea in 1985, the Baker Plan (named after then–Secretary of the Treasury James Baker) sought to link greater loan commitments from foreign banks in exchange for major re-structuring programs in Latin America.[20] After a preliminary debt-relief agreement was signed with Mexico, the Baker Plan faded as the remaining Latin American nations saw little benefit in the Reagan administration's approach. It was not until 1987 that private banks such as the Bank of Boston, fearing the negative impact of third world loans on earnings, began the process of debt forgiveness. The action of the Bank of Boston to write off $200 million in debt led other banks to follow suit and prompted the Latin American presidents to press for a new era of dialogue on the debt issue. Although the write-off actions of the U.S. banks made a minimal dent in the Latin American debt, they signaled that the concept of debt forgiveness was gaining acceptance and momentum.[21]

With the arrival of the Bush administration in 1989 the Latin American leaders were given further encouragement as a new debt-relief plan was readied. Called the Brady Plan (after Secretary of the Treasury Nicolas Brady), the new debt initiative carried debt for-giveness further than ever before by tying it to the dismantling of the statist economic systems in Latin America and their replacement with market economies.[22] Because the Brady Plan also recognized the need for new loans to meet the desperate social and economic needs of the Latin American countries, there was initial support from regional political leaders. The Brady Plan, like its predecessor, languished as little progress was made in formulating agreements with Latin American debtor countries. After a brief period of encouragement, Latin American leaders complained that the Bush administration was interested in encouraging banks and multinational corporations to employ so-called debt swaps, which convert out-standing obligations into equity and reduce debt while at the same time swelling money supplies in countries already awash in inflation.[23]

By the summer of 1989 the Bush administration did stimulate negotiations that brought about a debt-relief agreement with Mexico that was viewed as a pathbreaking step to ease Latin American indebtedness.[24] The agreement covered over $48 billion of Mexico's outstanding debt of $104 billion and offered commerical banks the option of reducing owed principal, lowering debt-service payments, or lending new funds. Because most of the banks chose the first two options rather than new loans, Latin American leaders criticized the Mexico plan as encouraging commercial lending institutions to withdraw from the region rather than invest in its development. Despite the criticism, many Latin American presidents were quietly confident that debt relief accenting some form of forgiveness had now been embraced by the commercial banks and by the Bush administration.[25] Since the Mexican agreement, little progress has been made in spreading the Brady Plan to other Latin American countries. Although Costa Rica signed a modest debt-reduction agreement, other countries like Venezuela were unable to reach a resolution of their debt problems with commercial banking institutions.

Yet despite the slow pace and frequent disappointment of the debt-reduction negotiations, Latin American leaders were encouraged by the Bush administration when in July of 1990 the president announced a new initiative. Called The Enterprise for the Americas, Bush's proposal included a comprehensive package of trade, investment, environmental, and debt initiatives that accented a hemispheric free-trade zone, a significant reduction in the $12 billion in concessional loans owed to the United States, and support for so-called debt-for-nature swaps that would create environmental funds from the interest payments on restructured official debts.[26] The Bush proposal received wide support from Latin American leaders. García of Peru called the proposal a "radical change of attitude that re-emphasizes U.S. hemispheric relations with Latin America." President Rodrigo Borja of Ecuador stated, "I think it is a very constructive proposal basically because it is no longer the case of a rich country helping poor countries. The idea is now common interests."[27] President Luis Lacalle of Uruguay perhaps best summed up the views of the Latin American presidents when he stated,

> We believe the U.S. Government announcement has a great symbolic value. First, I would say that it neutralizes the fatalist attitude adopted by many Latin Americans who thought that the developments in Europe would capture the world's attention and leave Latin America neglected. We have a sense of optimism and great hope that the

announcement will encourage domestic changes in all South American countries, and shows that there is still a place for us in the world if we are willing to adjust to it.[28]

The near-unanimous praise for the Bush debt and trade initiative (not surprisingly, on the thirtieth anniversary of the Cuban revolution, Cuba's Castro denounced the program as "old and worn out neoliberal formulas") from the Latin American leaders can be interpreted as opening up a new era in U.S.-Latin American relations and lessening the intensity of the debate over repayment schedules and outstanding obligations. It is essential, however, to point out that even though there has been some movement in the direction of debt forgiveness and a greater sensitivity on the part of the United States toward the trade problems of their Latin American neighbors, the evolution of the conflict between the Latin American nations and the United States over indebtedness, austerity, and externally imposed restructuring has raised some important questions about the role and status of the civilian leaders in this region.

On the positive side, it has become increasingly clear that debt and democracy can coexist in a climate of huge financial obligations and the social disorder that often accompanies such obligations without destroying the foundations of popular rule. Despite the uncertain economic circumstances that coincided with the latest round of democratization, democratic leaders showed themselves to be democratic survivors as they weathered the storm of protest and paralysis without surrendering their office or the legitimacy of elected civilian rule.[29] Not only has democratic governance shown itself to be more resilient in the face of economic upheaval but democratic leaders have been able to convince apprehensive elites and angry workers that failure to bring about quick and comprehensive economic relief should not be dealt with through support for a coup or a rejection of a more open and contentious political process.

To some, the survival of democracy and democratic leaders can best be attributed to the negative views toward authoritarian rule with its uncompromising policy process and its legacy of heavy borrowing that laid the foundation for the crisis. But ample credit for the survival of democracy must also be given to the Latin American civilian leaders who showed strength and determination during the darkest hours of debt and recession. Even though some of the early democratic leaders such as Alfonsín in Argentina and Sarney in Brazil had their limitations and struggled with meager success to control the ravages of indebtedness, they created an image of democratic leadership that was marked by a spirit of national pride, a confidence in the governing institutions, and a toleration of dissent.[30] Alfonsín and Sarney did not bring an end to their country's economic and financial dependency, but they faced up to the crisis in ways that solidified their democratic base and allowed their successors to take more ambitious and risky steps.

Although the debt crisis showed the ability of the Latin American leaders to preserve their positions and their legitimacy, the tug-of-war with the foreign banks, the IMF, and the industrialized countries revealed their weakness as equal players in the international community. For over ten years the Latin American leaders harped at the bankers and the international lending agencies and presented position paper after position paper to highlight their displeasure over the worsening debt crisis. It seemed that the more the Latin American leaders criticized the United States and the IMF, the weaker the prospects for resolution of the crisis became.

Riordan Roett views the reluctance on the part of the industrialized nations to move toward the demands of the Latin American presidents as directly related to the negative impressions of these leaders and their inexperience in dealing with the world powers. As Roett states:

> The debt crisis clearly made the Latin American leaders feel impotent. From their actions, if not their words, the leaders communicated their feelings of futility and marginalization. Although their public documents and speeches rang with fervor, their diplomatic and political actions seemed hollow. Their aggregate irrelevance reflected the superior- inferior relationship that has traditionally characterized links between North and South.[31]

Roett's analysis of the limited impact of Latin American leadership on the debt crisis points up one of the sad realities of heading a debt-ridden government in this region. Because of the frequency with which political leaders enter and leave power and the negative reputation that has often been linked with leaders in Latin America, the Western industrialized nations and the financial institutions of the world have shown little faith or respect for those individuals who assume the mantle of president in Latin America. Unfortunately, the Western nations and the banks have been slow to recognize that this latest wave of democracy has brought into office a new class of leader who deserves more than just the cursory reliance on past stereotypes. The result has been that the debt crisis may have lingered longer than necessary simply because the international banking sector needed more time to assess the capabilities and the survival powers of the new class of democratic politicians. In the meantime the indebtedness deepened in many countries and challenged the leadership abilities of individuals who had few options and precious little time to work out those options.

Although the debt crisis had positive and negative results on Latin American leadership, there is one undeniable consequence of $400 million in outstanding obligations and that is the susceptibility of the civilian presidents to U.S. pressure. Latin American leaders from Andrés Pérez to García to Castro may have sounded the nationalist alarm as they castigated the U.S. banks and the U.S. political establishment, but the resolution of the debt problem has been dictated by the United States. The debt debate has been directed by the words and actions of treasury secretaries, by boardroom decisions of major banks, and by the congressional appropriations process. The Latin American nations and their leaders have found themselves waiting for the United States to act or to recognize the worth of a Latin American proposal. The fact that the United States has finally gotten around to accepting the concept of debt forgiveness is less an accomplishment of Latin American pressure than a recognition in this country that some long-term benefits may accrue from such a policy.[32]

It is, to say the least, disheartening to the Latin American leaders that their entreaties about the profound implications of the debt on social and political order were not as effective as the realization in Washington that debt forgiveness could help stimulate regional economies and broaden U.S.-Latin American trade. Latin American leaders have become used to the fact that policy initiatives are often the result of the United States finally recognizing the danger of inaction or the benefits of embracing an idea that emanates from south of the border. Octavio Paz's image of the United States as a giant Colossus, "a bit simple . . . but whose wrath can destroy us," is an appropriate metaphor for the challenge faced by the Latin American leaders.[33] The heads of governments in Latin America must constantly remind the United States of the proper course of action to benefit the hemisphere, but they must also recognize that suggestions, reminders, calls to action, and demands for change do not easily translate into action. The Latin American leaders are beginning to see some acceptance of their suggestions, evidenced by the slow pace of debt relief championed by the United States, but only after years of squabbling and the belated realization in Washington that forgiving the debt just might be economically beneficial to both Latin America and the United States.

DEFINING DEVELOPMENT IN THE 1990s

Democracy and civilian-run government can be viewed in terms of distinct eras. Latin America has also gone through periods in which the concept of development was central to national existence and the subject of definition and unending debate. The memory of the Alliance for Progress era in Latin America is still sufficiently real; its lofty goals and its even loftier rhetoric remind students of development that there were times in which modernization and reform overshadowed debt and austerity. The Latin America of the 1990s is beginning as a period in which development may once again be redefined and become the stimulus for political debate. But unlike the 1960s when Alliance for Progress development was the product of U.S. anticommunism and deep foreign aid pockets, the development of the 1990s in Latin America is taking shape as the decade in which this region comes to grips with the inefficiencies of its own models and transforms those models to respond to the requirements of a new economic age.

Again, as with the debt crisis, the political leaders of Latin America will be playing a key role in defining the most effective development models for their countries and monitoring the implementation of those models in social-political circumstances that can best be described as tension filled and unpredictable. Just as was the case during the 1960s, the process of development will become a contest over national priorities; those stressing the need for greater efficiencies and expanded economic growth will clash with those who want to make development stand for responding to the human needs neglected during the debt-ridden 1980s.[34]

As was also the case with the debt crisis, the Latin American leaders will be influenced by the positions taken by the United States with respect to national development. Although development will undoubtedly have a Latin American "flavor," it will be designed within guidelines promoted by both governmental authorities in Washington and private investors who are seeking access to new markets and new opportunities. Because Latin American development is so closely tied to aid, investment, and trade decisions made in the United States, any decisions made by regional political leaders to restructure and reform the economic and social systems will of necessity have to be made with an eye to north of the border. The new definition of development will most likely be a joint venture with the United States pointing the way and the Latin Americans redesigning growth models in their own image.

The concept of national development that the Latin American leaders are discussing incessantly and implementing with dizzying speed throughout the region comprises the following components:

1. A commitment to adopt a greater balance between the statist models that have dominated the economic policy scene for the last thirty years and the market models that serve as the backbone of the industrialized world.
2. An acceptance of the need to lessen government intervention in the economy and diminish the extent to which local industries and sectors are supported by costly subsidies.
3. A further intensification of the process of diversifying the basic character of national economic life so as to avoid continued reliance on a few staple commodities or precious natural resources.
4. A willingness to integrate their local economies with the growing trend toward free-trade zones and globalization of enterprise.
5. A recognition that economic adjustments and structural reforms must be carried out in ways that do not lead to social upheaval and political instability.
6. A growing realization that long-standing social needs in the areas of health care, housing, education, and nutrition can

no longer be ignored and need to be addressed as an insurance policy against unrest and revolution.

To achieve these objectives and put a new face on development in the 1990s, Latin American leaders are engaging in what can only be termed a full-scale retreat from the economic modus operandi that was generally accepted as the approach best suited to the region's needs and sociopolitical makeup. As Bolivian finance minister David Blanco stated in an interview describing the new approach of President Jaime Paz Zamora:

> Our emphasis will be toward private participation and foreign investment. Although many countries would like to have an ideological approach it would not be feasible because back in the 70's you increased state participation through your internal savings. But in general, the internal savings are gone . . . unless you want to print money and then enter a hyperinflation process.[35]

The leaders of Latin America today present themselves as realists who see the merits of the statist approach with its penchant for central control and broad employment (and of course patronage) opportunities but who are drawn to the free-market model with its potential for attracting capital and stimulating growth. These leaders, however, are reluctant capitalists and wary practitioners of free enterprise. They have moved slowly to downsize the public sector and are fearful of the inherent dangers in dismantling state enterprises that employ huge sections of the work force. For example, Argentina's Carlos Menem has been locked in a conflict with his Peronist union supporters who oppose his tough austerity measures and his campaign to privatize the state-owned telephone company. On more than one occasion Menem has told his Peronist brothers to support his programs and to tone down their opposition because "it is necessary to be where I am now in order to know the hell of governing."[36]

But as realists and leaders who want to demonstrate their adherence to the prevailing economic dogma of the 1990s, the Latin American presidents are ignoring the claims of those who see the rush to a market system expanding class inequities and worsening the social ills brought on by the debt crisis.[37] Talk of the potential unfairness of a market economy is generally ignored by the Latin

American leaders as they sense the public's realization that the statist system has outlived its usefulness. The presidents of this region have thus accepted the transformation of development from a concept that describes the process of state-induced change to one that stresses the importance of corporate entities and foreign investors as the engines of modernization. It is a leap of faith that causes the presidents great uncertainty as they see themselves promoting a development model that is not only foreign to them but fraught with danger.

The concern that the Latin American presidents have over the impact of the market model on their economies and their social systems is certainly appropriate. As the debt crisis begins to show signs of entering a period of limited relief, the political leaders in this region may be entering a new era of crisis as their societies debate the meaning of development and the proper means to attain that elusive goal. The prevailing view that the path to development is through continued economic growth in an ever-expanding market environment is beginning to clash with the harsh realities of social neglect built up over years of unsuccessful coping with foreign indebtedness. The decline in indices that monitor the human face of underdevelopment are stark reminders that the struggle for change in Latin America is more than equity agreements and joint ventures. The 1989 Inter-American Development Bank (IDB) report on the state of economic and social progress in Latin America pointed out the widening gap between the components of economic development (trade balances, debt obligations, investment capital, agricultural and industrial production, and inflationary conditions) and what can be termed the components of human development (unemployment, education appropriations, housing starts, access to potable water, nutrition levels, and infrastucture development in rural areas).[38] Although the IDB report noted some significant improvements in the economic indices, especially in the areas of exports, private investment, and external debt, along with optimistic projections from certain countries such as Mexico, which has embraced the market economy, there were a number of ominous signs that the move to a new system would be conducted in a deteriorating economic climate. Spending on education was down some 25 percent in the region, the basic infrastructure of Latin America was nearing collapse, and few inroads had been made in the areas of nutrition and potable water; in some countries children were at a heightened risk of illness and death. The IDB study remarked that "Latin America entered the final year of the 1980s with reasons for hope as well as disillusionment."[39]

It is within this very mixed view of the Latin American economic future that the political leadership in the region will have to operate. In a very real sense the presidents who have embarked on the free-market road are taking a calculated risk that rejecting the statist approach will in the short run generate enough growth to offset the dislocation and suffering that will accompany the economic restructuring and reform. But as the IDB study and other data on the virtual collapse of human development in Latin America point out, the decision to move to a market economy may be embroiled in a much larger debate and conflict over the need to ensure that economic development and financial stability do not overshadow the crying needs of those Latin Americans who were part of what has come to be called the lost decade of development.

But although the Latin American leaders are gambling that the market economy will pull them out of the "lost decade" and into a period of sustained development, they are much more confident that development in the 1990s will be shaped by the extent to which they link their respective countries to the global economy. The days of import-substitution programs, subsidies for key industries, and protectionist policies in Latin America are slowly giving way to a recognition that growth can best be achieved by participating in the burgeoning movement to open economies to world markets and by attracting foreign investment as a primary source of development capital. Most Latin American presidents appear to be convinced that policies integrating their economies with the European Community, the Pacific Basin countries, and of course the United States will create the foundation upon which long-term growth can be achieved. As President Carlos Salinas of Mexico stated in a speech to the U.S. Congress, "In order for Mexico's economic modernization to be lasting, we must grow, but growth requires greater and more secure access to the world's largest market, the United States."[40]

The view of President Salinas is increasingly being shared by other Latin American leaders who are taking steps to open up trade with the major industrial powers and take advantage of the new spirit of free trade and greater market access that has taken hold in much of the world. For example, Brazil with over $14 billion in bilateral trade with the United States promulgated a new industrial policy initiated by President José Sarney that stresses competitiveness, export performance, and expanded but less-protected domestic markets. Specifically, the Brazilian industrial policy has eliminated or reduced import tariffs for thousands of products and removed hundreds of products from the list of suspended imports.[41] Mexico has followed suit with a number of initiatives designed to speed integration with global markets. President Salinas has made Mexico a member of the General Agreement on Tariffs and Trade (GATT) and participated in the Uruguay Round of trade talks designed to lower restrictive trade barriers. Salinas also signed a broadranging bilateral trade agreement with the Bush administration in fall 1989 that both presidents agreed started a "new era" of relations.[42]

The next step for Salinas is the signing of the more controversial Free Trade Agreement, which will further open up Mexico's border with the United States and lure U.S. investors anxious to benefit from low wages, a weak regulatory climate, and the prospect of not having to deal with powerful unions. Salinas has pushed for the free-trade pact with the United States because he sees the opportunity to expand access to the North American market and the ability to attract investment capital as the keys to Mexico's development. His critics, however, caution that the agreement will open the floodgates of North American control of the Mexican economy and make Mexicans a new class of exploited workers employed by profit-hungry U.S. multinationals. Salinas will have to walk a fine line between development and nationalism as he pursues talks with the Bush administration. Negotiations between the Salinas administration and Washington began in June 1991 and are expected to conclude in 1992. With the U.S. Congress providing President Bush with so-called fast-track authority to negotiate an agreement, many observers feel that the economic border between Mexico and the United States will quickly disappear.

Allowing a greater influx of foreign investment has also become a common practice of the new global-minded Latin American leaders. Venezuela's Carlos Andrés Pérez decreed a sweeping liberalization of the foreign investment code that, in the words of Development Minister Moises Naim, "has placed Venezuela in a position to compete effectively with nations, like those of the far East, that have attracted large volumes of capital from the industrialized world."[43] Venezuela now has joined countries like Argentina, Bolivia, Chile, Brazil, and Mexico in passing legislation that seeks to entice foreign capital to Latin America. Mexico, in particular, has taken the lead in moving away from the restrictive investment codes developed during the administrations of Luis Echeverria and Miguel de la Madrid. The agreement signed between Presidents Salinas and Bush in 1989 stipulated that both countries would form a joint committee for investment and trade in order to enhance the opportunities for external investment in the Mexican economy.[44]

These cooperative efforts on the part of the United States and Mexico are a prelude to the eventual formation of a free-trade and cooperative investment zone that would incorporate Canada, the United States, and Mexico. Taking a cue from the European Economic Community, the United States and Mexico are quietly pursuing the goal of integrating their economies, an integration that already accounts for nearly $50 billion in trade and over $10 billion in direct investment. Much work needs to be done to bridge the gap between the Mexican concerns over U.S. economic domination and U.S. concerns over loss of jobs and illegal immigration. Nevertheless, in a short period of time the spirit of integration and the pressures of a global economy have moved two wary economic competitors to discuss opening their borders to trade and investment.[45]

But despite the significant liberalization efforts of the Latin American leaders and their desire to integrate their countries with the industrialized world, there has been no rush to expand trade with the region or to make major investment commitments. Although overall export figures for Latin America jumped from 14 percent of GDP in 1987 to 18 percent of GDP in 1989, a U.S. Commerce Department study points out that in 1988 Latin America took 13.5 percent of U.S. exports compared to 17.5 percent in 1981; in 1981 Latin America provided 15 percent of U.S. imports compared to 13 percent in 1988. As the study further points out, trade with the United States has been of increasing importance to the Latin Americans in the 1980s, but trade with Latin America has been of diminishing importance to the United States.[46]

In the area of investment the picture is also increasingly dismal. The Inter-American Development Bank report mentioned earlier documents a dramatic reduction in net capital inflows, making the 1988–1989 period "the worst year in two decades in terms of capital inflows."[47] It is well-known in Latin America that foreign investors are wary of placing their capital in the region at a time of such great internal restructuring and the political uncertainty that accompanies that restructuring. Moreover, U.S. investors continue to be attracted to the Pacific Basin, Canada, and Europe despite the proximity of Latin America. Despite some notable investment successes in Mexico's *maquiladora* zones near the U.S. border and in the Caribbean due to the Caribbean Basin Initiative, the forecast for external investment continues to be murky, even though the Latin American leaders are praising their new initiatives to liberalize investment laws and attract foreign business.

The scorecard of success and failure in the process of trade and investment liberalization casts some doubt on the ability of democratic governments to transform their economies and meet the challenges of a new economic order. As Susan Kaufman Purcell states in an article on the global trading system, "The two countries that have gone furthest in restructuring their economies and increasing nontraditional exports are Mexico and Chile. It is perhaps not irrelevant that during this period Mexico has been governed by a single, dominant political party while Chile has been ruled by a general."[48] Although Kaufman is not suggesting that economic reform is unattainable under democratic auspices, she is stressing the great difficulty of changing the system of trade, investment, and internal development in countries where newfound democratic rights often lead to conflict rather than consensus. The Latin American leaders may have accepted the need to transform the way in which they view the external sector and the impact of the external sector on internal development, but the process of applying their newfound commitment to a sociopolitical system that has solidified in a statist mode for over a generation is an enormous task.

The coming years hold much promise for Latin Americans. There is an unquestioned desire to reap the benefits of a fast-changing world and a global economy, and a sense of urgency to finish the restructuring process as proof of their commitment. The success of the Latin American economies and the ability to begin a new era of development, however, will depend on the effectiveness of the leaders, who must ensure that their countries do not get left behind by the interplay of market forces. This is without question the toughest job the Latin American leaders will face in the coming years. Their success could position Latin America on the threshold of sustained development; their failure could return the region to the dark decade of the 1980s.

NOTES

1. A good introduction to the debt problem and Latin American politics can be found in Carol L. Graham, "The Latin American Debt Quagmire," *Brookings Review* (Spring 1989): 42–47. See also Sarah Bartlett, "A Vicious Circle keeps Latin America in Debt," *New York Times*, January 15, 1989, p. 5.

2. See Eugene Robinson, "Latin America is in the Market for a Turnaround," *Washington Post National Weekly Edition*, February 5–11, 1990, p. 9.

3. See Raul Prebisch, *Toward a Dynamic Development Policy for Latin America, ECLA and the Analysis of Latin American Development* (New York: United Nations Economic Commission for Latin America, 1963).

4. *Times of the Americas*, November 1, 1989, and June 27, 1990.

5. See George Fauriol, "Latin America 1989–1990," *Foreign Affairs*, Special issue, *America and the World, 1989–1990*, pp. 121–122.

6. Paul Craig Roberts, "Collor Plan Raises Brazil to New Heights of Chaos," *Wall Street Journal*, May 11, 1990, p. A-3.

7. Pedro Pablo Kuczynski, in his book *Latin American Debt* (Baltimore, MD: Johns Hopkins University Press, 1988) pays close attention to the negative impact of Latin American debt on a wide range of internal economic indicators. See pp. 176–207.

8. *New York Times* ran a three-part story, "The Latin American Debt Quandary," See *New York Times*, March 1–3, 1989.

9. As quoted in Riordan Roett, "How the 'Haves' Manage the 'Have Nots': Latin America and the Debt Crisis," in Barbara Stallings and Robert Kaufman, eds., *Debt and Democracy in Latin America* (Boulder, CO: Westview Press, 1989), pp. 61–62.

10. Robert A. Pastor and Jorge G. Castaneda, *Limits to Friendship: The United States and Mexico* (New York: Knopf, 1988), pp. 253–263.

11. Chris Kline, "Resistance Mounts to Menem's Programs," *Times of the Americas*, January 24, 1990, p. 1.

12. See Peter Ford, "Argentina's Great Phone Sale Stalls," *Christian Science Monitor*, October 10, 1990, p. 3.

13. Judith Ewell analyzes the impact of debt and urban unrest in Venezuela. See Judith Ewell, "Debt and Politics in Venezuela," *Current History* (March 1989): 121–124, 147–149.

14. For a discussion of García's position on the Latin American debt, see Paul W. Drake, "Debt and Democracy in Latin America, 1920's–1980's," in Stallings and Kaufman, *Debt and Democracy in Latin America*, p. 53.

15. Ibid., p. 55.

16. Sarney explained his views on debt in an interview with Paul Boeker in *Lost Illusions: Latin America's Struggle for Democracy as Recounted by its Leaders* (La Jolla, CA: Institute for the Americas, Merkes Weiner Publishing, 1990), pp. 270–281.

17. Rosemary Thorp, "The APPA Alternative in Peru: Preliminary Evaluation of Garcia's Economic Policies," *Peru Report* 1, no. 6 (1987).

18. *New York Times*, January 9, 1989, IV-8.

19. Robert Wesson, "Wrapping Up the Debt Problem," *PS: Political Science and Politics* 23, no. 3 (September 1990): 419–424.

20. See Riordan Roett, "Democracy and Debt in South America: A Continent's Dilemma," *Foreign Affairs*, Special issue no. 2 (1984): 695–720.

21. The options available to commercial banks are discussed in Howard J. Wiarda, "The Politics of Third World Debt," *PS: Political Science and Politics* 23, no. 3 (September 1990): 415–417.

22. See *New Initiatives on Latin American Debt*, The Second Harvard Conference, May 15–16, 1989, Summary Report (Cambridge, MA: Institute of Politics, John F. Kennedy School of Government, 1989).

23. The *New York Times*, March 1, 1989, p. A-1.

24. The debt agreement is discussed in detail in *Council of the Americas Washington Report* (July/September 1989): 1, 3–4.

25. The United Nations Economic Commission on Latin America (ECLA) issued a statement that commercial banks should bear a greater share of debt relief. The *New York Times*, May 21, 1990, p. D-6.

26. *Foreign Policy Bulletin* (September/October, 1990): 87–89.

27. *Times of the Americas*, July 11, 1990, p. 5.

28. Ibid., p. 5.

29. See Howard J. Wiarda, *The Democratic Revolution in Latin America* (New York, Holmes and Meier, 1990), p. 245.

30. Alfonsín and Duarte were praised by the State Department for their ability to prevail under intense pressure. See *Democracy in Latin America and the Caribbean: The Promise and Challenge*, Washington, DC Bureau of Public Affairs, Department of State Special Report, no. 158, March 1987 (Washington, DC: State Dept. 1987).

31. Roett, "How the 'Haves' Manage the 'Have Nots,'" p. 64.

32. Abraham Lowenthal, *Partners in Conflict, The United States and Latin America* (Baltimore, MD: Johns Hopkins University Press, 1987), pp. 185–186.

33. Octavio Paz, "El espero indiscreto," as quoted in Carlos Rangel, "Mexico and Other Dominoes," *Commentary* (June 1981): 27–35.

34. See William P. Glade, Jr., "Latin America: Debt, Destruction and Development," in Michael Novak and Michael P. Jackson, eds., *Latin America: Dependency or Interdependence?* (Washington DC: American Enterprise Institute for Public Policy Research, 1985) pp. 36–49.

35. *Times of the Americas*, October 18, 1989, p. 11.

36. *Times of the Americas*, April 18–May 2, 1990, p. 4.

37. The drive toward privatization has been aided by the publication of Peruvian economist Hernando De Soto's book praising the market system and urging governments to shift from their traditional reliance on state enterprises and central control. See Hernando De Soto, *The Other Path: The Invisible Revolution in the Third World* (New York: Harper and Row, 1989).

38. See a discussion of the IDB report in *Council of the Americas Washington Report*, October/November 1989, pp. 12–13.

39. As quoted in the *Times of the Americas*, September 20, 1989, p. 16.

40. As quoted in the *Times of the Americas*, October 18, 1989, p. 4.

41. *Council of the Americas Washington Report*, pp. 4–5.

42. *Department of State Bulletin*, December 1989, vol. 89, no. 2153, pp. 1–7.

43. As quoted in "Venezuela: Investment, Industry Tourism," An *Advertising Supplement to the Washington Post National Weekly Edition*, July 2–8, 1990, p. F-1.

44. *Department of State Bulletin*, pp. 1–7.

45. See "Mexico: A New Economic Era," *Business Week* (November 12, 1990): 102–105.

46. "Latin American Trade Review: A U.S. Perspective," U.S. Department of Commerce International Trade Administration, Office of South America, June 1989.

47. As quoted in the *Times of the Americas*, November 20, 1989, p. 16.

48. Susan Kaufman Purcell, *Excelsior* (Mexico City), October 7, 1989.

8

LATIN AMERICAN LEADERS: DEALING WITH INTERVENTION

> *Panamanians who speak of democracy are absolute hypocrites, for they live in luxury waiting for a pat on the back from their [U.S.] masters. Would a Panamanian government that obeyed every order of the U.S., one that consulted with the U.S. before making any move be democratic?*
> —Manuel Noriega,
> ousted Panamanian leader

For many Latin American presidents the ultimate test of their leadership capabilities is the manner in which they respond to outside intervention. Although we often think of intervention in military terms, Latin American leaders are regularly challenged by foreign governments, international lending institutions, multinational corporations, and an ever-broadening range of external entities. To Latin Americans, intervention encompasses more than just the image of marines landing and forcing their will on a specific country. Rather, intervention has been expanded to include the stringent requirements of the International Monetary Fund as it demands reform in return for new loans, the power of foreign businesses and banks whose policies on investment and debt have a critical impact on economic development, or the extent to which the industrialized countries seek to expand their influence in the region. In short, intervention applied to the Latin American setting need not mean control or domination but the results of a changed world and dependent economic relations.[1]

Not suprisingly, Latin Americans abhor the reality of intervention and the susceptibility of their nations to outside interference. The contemporary response of Latin America to external intervention is replete with examples of angry opposition and nationalistic fervor. Leaders as diverse as Augusto Sandino, Lázaro Cardénas, Salvador Allende, Oscar Arias, Manuel Noriega, Carlos Andrés Pérez, and Fidel Castro have castigated those from outside the region whose influence is viewed as jeopardizing national sovereignty or as having a deleterious affect on growth and stability.[2] Unfortunately, the rallying cries of independence and self-determination that are so often heard in Latin America are muffled by the realities of continued reliance on foreign trade, aid, and investment; chronic political unrest; and, most important, proximity to the security-conscious United States. Latin America and its leaders long ago arrived at the sad conclusion that they exist in a political environment heavily influenced by the external sector.[3]

As a result of interventionism, Latin American leaders seem to be caught in a continuous battle with the outside world as they fight to protect their interests and on occasion their national sovereignty. Whether it is resisting pressure from the IMF over austerity measures, criticizing the United States for its contra or drug interdiction policy, demanding that foreign banks recognize the economic disaster brought on by halfhearted debt-relief programs, or insisting that Great Britain give back the Malvinas Islands to the Argentines, the decisionmaking agenda of many Latin American leaders often includes issues that require deft negotiations with countries and institutions that have the ability to control the character of regional politics. Moreover, the linkage between external intervention and internal politics in Latin America creates a double burden for Latin American leaders as they must not only protect their nations from external pressures but respond to the domestic "fallout" that may accompany interaction with the foreign sector. The impact that foreign intervention can exert on domestic politics and development has forced many leaders in Latin America to conduct the affairs of government in ways that avoid the inevitable feedback from social groups and political adversaries upset with the course of foreign relations.

Balancing external realities with domestic pressures has created some of the greatest challenges for Latin American leaders. This chapter is an exploration of the manner in which the heads of governments in this region respond to foreign intervention and the internal fallout that follows. Because the United States has often been the primary source of the intervention in Latin America and the bane of many regional leaders, it is impossible to discuss the connection between foreign interference and domestic politics without showing how elected presidents, generals, and revolutionaries handle the "Collosus of the North" as it seeks to impose its will in the hemisphere. The tension that has developed over the years between the United States and the Latin American leaders on the issue of intervention provides one of the best ways of understanding what leadership has come to mean in this region and what it may become in the future.

CASTRO: THE IRONIES
OF RESISTING INTERVENTION

There is no better Latin American leader to begin this discussion of intervention with than Cuba's Fidel Castro. Castro's name is synonymous with resisting attempts by a powerful foreign country to bring a revolutionary regime to its knees. From the Bay of Pigs invasion to the diplomatic and economic sanctions of the OAS to the CIA destabilizing operations, Castro met the challenges to his Marxist leadership and in the process evolved as a kind of living legend of surviving interventionism.[4] Castro also used his success at fighting the Yanquis to rally his people to make domestic sacrifices and to enhance Cuba's reputation throughout the less-developed world as a champion of anti-imperialism. The threats and sanctions from the United States served to consolidate his regime and allowed him to take his revolutionary message throughout the hemisphere.

In the process of resisting the threats from the United States, Castro exposed the critical component of interventionism in Latin America. After stripping Cuba of any vestiges of reliance on the United States, the Cuban leader invited a new sponsor and potential intervenor to support the faltering economy and buildup the national defense. Castro at first hailed the alignment with the Soviet Union as a victory for communism and a sign that the revolutionary message of Marx and Lenin was spreading to the Western Hemisphere. But as the anti-Castro passion of the United States in the 1960s gave way to a kind of quiet annoyance in the 1970s and 1980s, Cuba was increasingly viewed as a client state of the Soviet Union, dependent on Russian assistance and trade and responsive to Russian calls for representing world communism in the battlefields of Angola and Mozambique. Although Soviet intervention was in no way destabilizing to Cuba or Castro, it nonetheless was viewed as one of the many contradictions of the revolution, namely the ease with which one dependency evolved into a new dependency.[5]

Castro's move from champion of combating U.S. intervention to dependent client of the Soviet Union points out the limits that are placed on Latin American leaders who want to chart their own course free of outside influence. The benefits that accrued to Castro from the lingering threat of U.S. intervention were more than offset by the Soviet control of the Cuban economy (the oil-for-sugar arrangements) and the expectation that Cuba would play the role of proxy freedom fighter in Africa. Castro downplayed the influence of the Soviets and often stated his independence from Kremlin policymakers, but it became clear as the Cuban economy began to falter and the Soviets withdrew from Afghanistan that Moscow had as much to say about the future direction of Cuba as the revolutionary leadership in Havana.[6] Soviet decisions about aid, trade, and investment in Cuba coupled with some $25 billion in outstanding debts were the equivalent of economic intervention because the Castro regime could do little in terms of strategic planning and economic restructuring without first determining the future direction of Moscow's relations with Havana.

The effect of both U.S. policy and Soviet policy toward Cuba did limit Castro's options as a leader and required him to fashion his decisions in ways that took into consideration the power and capabilities of an external force. Castro may have played the role of the triumphant revolutionary leader who stood up to the United States, but he was gradually transformed during his evolving relationship with the Soviets into a more cautious and compliant leader who looked to Moscow for direction and support. As the money began to dry up and Kremlin leaders began to look inward, Castro brought his troops back from Africa, toned down his commitment to the revolution in Central America, and began to look for Western support (including that of the United States) for his faltering regime.

But before we categorize Castro as a captive of intervention, both U.S. and Soviet, the Cuban leader must be credited with his resolve in the past few years to chart a course that is free of both superpowers. Since Mikhail Gorbachev's breakneck push for democratization at home and normalization with his adversaries, Castro has emerged as an independent revolutionary leader. The Cuban leader has criticized Moscow for dismantling socialism and for abdicating its role as leader of the Communist world.[7] Castro has also continued his vituperative attacks against the United States and the Bush administration's policy of developing the TV Martí system of programs designed to bring "alternative viewpoints" to the Cuban people. Many analysts of the Cuban leader see this line of action as a sign that Castro is out of touch with the changing character of regional and world politics. But although this may be true, Castro is also exhibiting a leadership style that was absent after those heady days of the revolution. Castro is once again a Latin American revolutionary leader with a message (albeit out-of-step with the current wisdom) and a desire to make his vision of socialism a reality despite the United States or the Soviets.

Without massive Soviet assistance it will be next to impossible for Castro to achieve his vision of a Cuban socialist state. The decision of the Soviets in 1990 to shift all trade with Cuba to a hard-currency basis and to cut fuel shipments by 20 percent is certain to be another devastating blow to the Cuban economy. Moreover, the decision by Mikhail Gorbachev in 1991 to pull Soviet troops out of Cuba in the wake of the stunning political transformation in Russia sent shockwaves through the Castro regime and heightened speculation in Havana and among those in exile in Miami as to when the revolutionary government and its leader would be forced out of power.

But if the revolutionary regime of Fidel Castro has proven anything over the years it is that the vision of a socialist state is not easily compromised. As Castro said in a speech to a group of Communist youth in 1990, "If they told me that 98 percent of the people did not believe in the revolution, I would carry on fighting. Because a revolutionary must be a man who, even if he is left alone, continues to fight for his ideas."[8]

Political leaders like Fidel Castro may have made their reputation as revolutionary visionaries and fighters against foreign intervention, but at the same time they owe their position to the economic benefits of intervention or the legitimacy that the threat of intervention provides. Take away the economic intervention and diminish the threat and leaders like Castro are forced to build support around revolutionary rhetoric or ensure support by widening the reach of authoritarian rule. Castro has already shown signs that he intends to follow the latter strategy as he imprisons or executes his adversaries and introduces more rigid internal security measures. This is a return to old-style Latin American leadership, but it may be the only option left to a leader who has seen the benefits of intervention disappear.

NORIEGA AND ENDARA:
PAYING THE PRICE OF INTERVENTION

Fidel Castro may have achieved some short-term gains as a result of foreign intervention, but Panama's Manuel Noriega provides an excellent example of a leader who flaunted his ability to ward off the United States only to see his *braggadosio* backfire as his regime crumbled under the weight of a U.S. invasion. General Noriega formed his leadership of the Panamanian Defense Forces (and in effect the Panamanian government) around an image of macho courage in the face of unrelenting U.S. pressure and destabilization programs. The clenched fist, the wild swinging of the machete, and the outrageous challenges to U.S. power were designed to stir up nationalistic sentiment in a country that had a long and troubled relationship with U.S. intervenors. Noriega had a keen understanding of how to use the U.S. presence in the Canal Zone as a means of deflecting criticism away from his corruption, his links to narco-trafficking, and his harsh authoritarian rule.[9]

But like many other leaders who mask their governing deficiencies and their personal failings with the mantle of nationalism, Manuel Noriega was unable to maintain his crusade against the United States or quiet dissident groups within the Panamanian Defense Forces. Despite an obvious talent for controlling his troops and quashing popular criticism of his regime, Noreiga's fatal flaw was his ego-driven misconceptions about the limits of U.S. power. As the head of a country that came to be dominated by the drug lords, Noriega believed that the United States was not willing to engage in the ultimate attack against the narco-traffickers. In Noriega's mind the United States would boycott and scheme and bluster, but it would not intervene to remove him from power. Noriega could meet these "fringe" activities of U.S. intervention with belt-tightening, ruthless management of his power base, and his own skills at marshaling public opinion. As the months went by and Noriega became successful at responding to the economic, covert, and diplomatic challenges from the United States, his confidence level increased along with his desire to intensify his attacks on the Bush administration.[10]

What Manuel Noriega learned in the waning days of 1989 was not only that the United States had the will to intervene but that it benefited from a fortuitous location; its forces could muster an attack from military bases a few miles from the general's headquarters. A country that was born as a result of intervention once again experienced the presence of foreign soldiers reconstituting the political landscape. The difference in this intervention, however, was that Manuel Noriega knowingly created the conditions to arouse the United States. His condoning of violent attacks on U.S. personnel and candidates for political office, his declaration of war against the United States, and his clear role as critical link in the shipment of cocaine from Colombia to the United States provided the Bush administration with what they felt was a clear legal and moral basis for invasion. Noriega simply had gone too far and had embarrassed the Bush administration at a time when public outcry against drug trafficking was at an all-time high. There are only so many occasions when one can successfully ward off the United States and survive. Manuel Noriega's role as U.S. antagonist had run its course.

The invasion of Panama and the eventual capture of Manuel Noriega opened the floodgates of fear that had gripped Panama. As the general was whisked away to Miami, Panama City exploded with jubilation as the Noriega era came to a close. Many Panamanians embraced the invading soldiers and condemned the man who transformed Panama into a pariah state. But with Noriega gone and the U.S. military forces providing a stabilizing presence in the country, the Panamanians began the long and frustrating process of building democracy amid the ruins of an economy near collapse. Within days Guillermo Endara, the duly elected president of the country who was denied his office by Noriega's campaign of fraud and intimidation, took power. Endara and his two vice presidents, Ricardo Arias Calderon and Guillermo "Billy" Ford, immediately encountered a number of serious policy challenges, particularly in the area of reforming the military and the police. But Endara and his government had other problems besides internal security and economic collapse; they faced the prospect of being painted as a leadership team dependent on U.S. aid and advice. In the minds of many Panamanians a new era of intervention had begun.[11]

As Panama moved out of the international headlines and settled into the drudgery of rebuilding the country, it became clear that the Endara government would not be able to fulfill its promises, much less survive, without extensive U.S. asssistance. President Endara made a number of impassioned pleas to the Bush administration to speed the transfer of what began as $1 billion in development aid that was held up in Congress.[12] Although the United States moved immediately to house those left homeless by the invasion, congressional wrangling slowed monies to resettle the refugees. The result is that thousands of Panamanians were crowded into camps that became feeding grounds of opposition against the Endara government.[13] Eventually the reduced aid package did move through Congress and into the Panamanian economy, but President Endara continues to be faced with the devastation caused by U.S. intervention. Noriega is gone, the defense forces are in the painful process of being reconstituted, and the soldiers have returned to their bases in the Canal Zone. Yet despite the return to a degree of normalcy, the signs of invasion remain in Panama to remind the political leaders and the people that the enduring costs of the intervention are born by Panama and not by the United States.

ORTEGA AND CHAMORRO: ROLE-PLAYING AND INTERVENTION

Manuel Noriega experienced the full force of U.S. intervention in a matter of weeks; Daniel Ortega and the Nicaraguan Sandinistas had to endure ten years of covert destabilizing intervention that in the end also achieved its objective. But because Ortega headed a regime vastly different from Noriega's in terms of domestic and international support, ideological commitment, and military preparedness, the Sandinista leader approached the threat from the United States in a far different manner than did the Panamanian strongman. Ortega was required to develop a much wider range of leadership styles in order to respond to U.S. attempts at dislodging him and his government. Ortega's task as head of the Nicaraguan revolution was a complex blend of maintaining popularity with a citizenry strapped by the U.S. embargo, of currying favor with the Western European nations and the Soviet bloc to keep his revolution afloat, and of fighting a draining war with the contra rebels. This external "triple threat" created an enormous challenge to the Nicaraguan leader, whose revolution was not only vulnerable to various forms of intervention but was dependent upon his ability to find the right leadership strategy in order to save the hard-fought gains of the Sandinistas.[14]

The struggle of Ortega to find the right mix of leadership strategies to deal with the external sector was complicated by the commitment of the Sandinistas to Marxist dogma and the goal of forming a socialist state in Central America. Ortega was first and foremost a revolutionary leader heading a group of dedicated Marxists who took immense joy in the fact that they had driven out a U.S.-supported dictator. But Ortega quickly came to realize that revolutionary leadership was only one facet of his job description. The tightening grip of economic decline required him to be an efficient manager of his nation's resources; the contra war required him to be a courageous protector of his country; the dependence on outside assistance required him to be an international spokesman for self-determination, and his long-running conflict with the Reagan administration required him to be a fearless critic of North American hegemony.[15]

Few leaders in Latin America were asked or forced to assume as many diverse roles as Daniel Ortega, and few would be able to balance those roles for as long as Ortega. On occasion, Ortega revealed the complexity of pleasing a number of foreign constituents while at the same time holding his base of support at home. When liberals in the U.S. Congress passed legislation limiting aid to the contra rebels as a prelude toward peace in Nicaragua, Daniel Ortega would fly off to Moscow to deepen his ties to the Soviets or boast about his intention to spread revolution throughout Central America. These actions enraged those in the United States who felt that Ortega was hurting the chances for peace in the region. But to the Sandinista leader, showing solidarity with Moscow and leading the cause of revolution in the hemisphere were also responsibilities that he could not ignore.[16]

Daniel Ortega's complex balancing act began to unravel when he was required to turn away from his revolutionary roots and become a popular democrat. Under pressure from his Central American neighbors and with declining support from his Soviet benefactors, Ortega gradually opened up the political system and eventually agreed to an unrestricted electoral process.[17] But by the time of the elections, the domestic and international conditions that required Ortega to be many things to many people had changed. The Nicaraguan people wanted stability and a sign of prosperity. The contras were weak, Ronald Reagan had left the White House, the Soviets were embroiled in their own quarrels, and Latin America had become a bastion of democracy. Ortega recognized these changes and jumped on the democratic bandwagon as he copied pages from U.S. elections with rallies, media hype, and strained efforts to appear as an ordinary Nicaraguan.

The new image did not work. Ortega's opponent, Violeta Chamorro, dressed in white, and with outstretched hands similar to the Virgin Mary, struck a responsive chord with her charges that Ortega had mismanaged the economy, missed opportunities to bring an end to the contra war, alienated the United States and the other Central American democracies, and used Soviet aid to build a huge and costly army. In effect, Chamorro claimed that Ortega had failed to deal with the challenges and the opportunities presented by foreign intervention and was unworthy of leading the country in the future. Chamorro's promise was that her leadership would be less complex and would not require her to assume a range of roles. Chamorro called for an end of the contra war, a normalization of relations with the United States, a renunciation of regional revolution (and the association with Castro's Cuba), and a reordering of domestic priorities from defense and ideology to economic solvency and democracy.[18]

Chamorro's claim that she would be a leader without many of the complex entanglements of Daniel Ortega was not easily believed by many Nicaraguans because she needed extensive U.S. assistance and support from the industrialized world. After her surprise victory over Daniel Ortega, the Sandinistas pressed the point that she would be a leader with obligations to the United States and a willing advocate of U.S. interests. Chamorro did not deny her alignment with the United States and her need for U.S. assistance but stressed that her leadership was based in a desire to reduce the number of obstacles to development and concentrate on rebuilding the economy. Chamorro seemed intent on avoiding the entanglements of Daniel Ortega and creating a more focused leadership style.[19]

Perhaps the most vivid picture of the postelection period in Nicaragua was the sight of an obviously tired and disappointed Daniel Ortega. Amidst the gloom of the defeat, Ortega privately expressed to reporters his sense of relief that the burden of running the revolution and Nicaragua had come to an end. There were bold promises of continuing the fight and a possible return to office in the future, but the crucial emotion was the relief expressed by the Nicaraguan leader. After years of being pulled and pushed in a number of directions, after dealing with a multiplicity of interventionists, and after changing leadership styles to fit the occasion, Daniel Ortega had had enough and was drained from being all things to all people. If he does return to Nicaraguan politics in the future, it most likely will be as a leader with a simpler agenda and a more limited view of leadership.

As for Chamorro, the new democratic leader of Nicaragua did not enjoy much of a honeymoon period. Almost immediately upon taking office Chamorro was beset with a host of problems from dealing with a severely depressed economy to handling entrenched Sandinista leaders such as Humberto Ortega, the army chief. Chamorro's problems deepened as she also incurred the displeasure of the Bush administration for not moving quickly on returning property expropriated by the Sandinistas and for implementing market approaches for the Nicaraguan economy. Over $300 million in U.S. aid was held up in Congress despite pleas by the Nicaraguan leader. After the euphoria of the electoral victory over Daniel Ortega, Violeta Chamorro settled into the gloom of leading a country in great distress and dependent on U.S. assistance.

ALFREDO CRISTIANI AND COMPANY: COPING WITH INTERVENTION

El Salvador's president Alfredo Cristiani has had the unenviable task as his nation's democratically elected leader of not only fighting a leftist revolution and reigning in an aggressive military establishment but also quieting the fears of the United States, whose financial support affects both the guerrilla war and the military's capability of fighting the war. The triangle of democratic leadership, Marxist revolution, and a politicized military pits against each other the three major political forces in contemporary Latin America. In El Salvador, however, this triangle is anchored in a kind of "suspended animation" by the ever-present economic and diplomatic pressure of the United States. Politics in El Salvador has become a complex struggle for power and support among the democrats, the rebels, and the generals carried on amid the often exasperated eye of Washington policy-makers. Although the United States can threaten, cajole, advise, or pamper the major players in Salvadoran politics, it is unable to change the shape of the political system.

It is within this contentious triangle and "suspended animation" that Alfredo Cristiani is forced to function as his country's governmental leader. As with most leaders in the region, Cristiani must possess excellent bargaining and balancing skills in order to handle the delicate negotiations that are required to keep him and his fragile democracy in place. But Cristiani must be adept at more than honing these skills; he must respond to the constant thrust of external demands that are made on his administration. Calls for peace negotiations, claims of human-rights abuse, and charges of official corruption are made regularly by public and private sources in the United States. Cristiani cannot ignore these demands for fear of alienating his primary source of aid, trade, and investment, and yet as a new democratic leader with very powerful adversaries who can influence his ability to remain in office, the Salvadoran president must avoid appearing as a mere pawn in the hands of the United States.[20] Despite the fact that Cristiani has become the focus of the tension between internal control and external pressure, the ability of the Salvadorans to cope with U.S. initiatives, whether public or private, must not be defined in terms of an individual leader. Cristiani's skill at deflecting pressure from the United States rests on the assumption that he possesses the primary political power in El Salvador. However, if the Salvadoran political system is viewed as the interplay of democrats, rebels, and generals, then Cristiani must be evaluated only in his capacity as the most prominent and visible of many leaders in the country. Granted, the generals often speak through Cristiani and the rebels seek negotiations with the Cristiani government, but the Salvadoran president controls only a portion of the political system and can take credit for only a portion of the resistance to U.S. intervention.

The division of leadership in El Salvador has been the key reason for U.S. frustration in its efforts to influence peace negotiations, military professionalism, government effectiveness, and the rule of law. The Salvadorans are perhaps Latin America's most successful example of coping with pressures from the United States. Democratic leaders like Cristiani appear cooperative and supportive of U.S. objectives but are slow to implement policy and fearful of antagonizing political enemies; leftist rebels resist the calls to end the hostilities and reveal a resiliency that contradicts Washington's claims of a guerrilla collapse; and the military unashamedly plays the Communist card as it stonewalls attempts by successive administrations to control human-rights abuses. Thus when Washington focuses its attention on the Cristiani government and places pressure on the democratic president for change or reform, it is only talking to one-third of the political leadership and, more important, the one-third that may be least equipped to resolve a crisis. Cristiani may not be a pawn of the United States, but he certainly is a prisoner of Salvadoran politics, which requires that he be adept at balancing the forces against him but which does not permit him to control those forces.[21]

Over the years the major players in Salvadoran politics have sharpened their skills of coping with U.S. intervention. Whether it is Cristiani showing a sincere interest in good government or the FMLN's apprehension concerning a peace proposal or the military high command's unwillingness to admit culpability, the Salvadoran leaders have been able to control events in the country on their terms. There have been aid reductions from Congress, stern warnings from presidents, and numerous programs designed to influence the manner in which the Salvadorans make decisions and run government.[22] To say that the United States has had little impact on El Salvador would be incorrect because the process of democratization, the rebuilding of the economy, and the gradual institutionalization of the rule of law have slowly led the country away from its authoritarian traditions. But the United States has never really been able to get the Salvadoran leaders to move as quickly as we wanted or to bring about the changes that we felt were essential for a modern democracy. We always faced leaders who were more adept at coping with the demands of an interventionist power than with seeing that those demands became a reality.

In assessing U.S. involvement in Salvadoran affairs one of the conclusions that is unavoidable is that Washington failed to change the shape of the political system from a triangle with equal sides to the kind of square, or "black box," that often is used to describe the policy process in Western countries. After years of aid appropriations and reform programs, El Salvador remains a nation governed by the tension of three political forces. President Alfredo Cristiani may be viewed in this country as heading the organization chart of government, but in reality he occupies just one side of a governing triangle that does not appear to be changing shape.

BARCO AND GAVIRIA: COOPERATION AND INTERVENTION

One of the hardest tasks of a Latin American political leader is facing the realization that some form of foreign intervention may be necessary in order to address a dangerous, if not regime-threatening, situation. Colombia's recent president, Virgilio Barco, and its current president, Cesar Gaviria, have had to face that reality and work with a foreign nation in order to fight the drug lords whose power and daring threaten the very survival of democratic governance. Throughout the drug war against the Medellín cartel, both Barco and Gaviria have exhibited remarkable courage, not only in resisting the pressures to succumb to an agreement with the cartel but in crafting a drug interdiction program with the United States that minimized the level of outside intervention while preserving Colombian sovereignty. Barco and Gaviria have recognized the importance of U.S. assistance and the futility of resisting Washington, yet they have carefully avoided defining the drug war as a joint venture with Washington policymakers as equal partners.

The United States was effective during the Barco presidency in pressuring Colombia on the issue of extraditing top-level members of the drug cartel and in agreeing to allow the Drug Enforcement Agency (DEA) to play a larger role in domestic drug-enforcement operations, but Washington has come to see that there is a limit to presidential cooperation. The Colombian presidents have made it clear that the drug war is being fought on Colombian territory and that Colombia will not become a forward base for the United States as it seeks to curtail the movement of cocaine to its borders. President Barco, for example, was adamantly opposed to a suggestion that the United States build an advanced radar base in Colombia in order to track the fleet of small drug-smuggling planes that leave the country daily.[23] Barco was also upset over the statements made by President Bush that the United States was contemplating the positioning of a naval armada off the Colombian coast to bolster its interdiction efforts. The Colombian president quickly let it be known that his government did not look with favor at this modern-day example of gunboat diplomacy and forced the Bush administration to reformulate its interdiction strategy.

For his part, current president Cesar Gaviria has chosen a less-aggressive approach to fighting the drug war, stressing the continued commitment of the Colombian government to capture or kill the kingpins of the cocaine cartel while at the same time working behind the scenes to develop a working relationship with the drug cartels that could lead to some form of amnesty and an eventual end to the violence. In terms of the role of the United States, Gaviria has clearly rejected extradition and downplayed the importance of military assistance, the cornerstones of the drug war during the Barco era. Gaviria is firmly committed to a Colombian solution to the drug war.[24]

The concern that Colombian presidents have with appearing to be too cooperative with the United States is based on the fact that domestic public opinion in the country is divided over the issues of blame and sovereignty. Columbian presidents, the recent Barco and now Gaviria, face a citizenry that questions U.S. eagerness to push interdiction in Colombia and yet is unwilling to conduct its own war. Colombian newspapers regularly criticize the United States for its reluctance to mete out harsh punishment for drug dealers or its tolerance of drug use.[25] Moreover, Colombians worry that their country may sacrifice a part of its independence in the name of U.S. national interest. As a result, political leaders in Colombia must be very cautious about how they cooperate with the United States. Accepting helicopters and advanced weapons to fight the cartel are viewed as appropriate measures, but agreeing to steps that transform

Colombia into a kind of forward antidrug base are rejected as unnecessary and a threat to national sovereignty.

Colombia is today a country where a kind of reverse intervention is practiced and even supported by some. Colombian nationalists see the cocaine trafficking as an example that their country has an element of control and power over the United States. The fact that the Medellín cartel has used drug exportation as a means to enhance power and expand wealth is by no means a source of pride to Colombians, yet Colombians feel that drug smuggling is providing the United States with a taste of what foreign intervention means. The helplessness, the frustration, the inability to control events, the anger over lost opportunities are emotions that many Latin Americans have felt when the long arm of the United States has reached their country. To the Colombians drugs are a scourge on their society and a source of death and destruction. At the same time, however, the drug trade is also a reminder to the United States that the act of intervention should not be just one of military might initiated by a superpower. Intervention can take many different forms and be used effectively by a much lesser power.

The reality that drug trafficking can lead to kind of reverse intervention and provide the Colombian people with some degree of satisfaction that the United States has come to know the effects of intervention is perhaps the greatest challenge to President Gaviria. He must sustain the war against the Medellín cartel in order to preserve stability, democracy, and the rule of law; he must cooperate with the United States if he is to possess the means to conduct the war in an effective manner; but he must be careful not to create the image of a president willing to compromise Colombian independence in the face of unrelenting U.S. pressure for results. President Gaviria must walk this fine line because although the drug cartel has lost its mystique and is now seen as just another group of businessmen, the fact that it has been able to intervene so successfully in the domestic affairs of the United States has fostered an undercurrent of silent satisfaction among many Colombians. It is this satisfaction over Colombian intervention as much as the fear of the cartel that stands in the way of ending the drug war and stopping the flow of cocaine into the United States.

CARLOS ANDRÉS PÉREZ:
DEPENDENCY AND INTERVENTION

As we have seen, intervention takes on many different forms, from invading troops to clandestine operations to economic boycotts to political reform. In most instances the image of intervention is usually connected to the United States and its unrelenting drive to protect its interests and ensure its security. In Venezuela, however, the interventionist challenge does not come from the White House or State Department or the Pentagon but from the International Monetary Fund (IMF) and is tied to loan policies that require significant government restructuring and societal sacrifice. Venezuela's president Carlos Andrés Pérez has become the primary focus of attention in the economic and political battle with the IMF over the extent that the IMF can dictate internal changes in that country, changes that have already led to a period of devastating internal violence.[26]

Many countries of Latin America have become dependent on loan arrangements with the IMF in order to stabilize their sagging economies. In oil-rich Venezuela the increased dependency on IMF disbursements (a three-year extended agreement of up to $4.6 billion) sent shockwaves of disbelief through a nation that has one of the highest per capita income rates in Latin America and that is viewed as a shining example of economic prosperity through democratic governance. Unfortunately, level world oil prices have combined with high dependence on imports and what some say is a bloated public sector to create an internal economic climate of low growth, high debt, and chronic unemployment.[27] When President Carlos Andrés Pérez entered office in 1989 he quickly agreed to IMF guidelines that required sharp price increases for gasoline, budget cuts, a sales tax, and the elimination of many subsidies. The immediate result was a week of violence in which over 300 people were killed. Since that time the IMF has praised Andrés Pérez and his government for implementing its reform program and for achieving some moderate successes in strengthening its economic picture.

Praise for Andrés Pérez from the IMF did not translate into praise for Andrés Pérez in Venezuela. The Venezuelan leader was often portrayed by his political adversaries as bending over backward to please the IMF and the long line of foreign creditors. Organized labor, the Catholic church, and his own Acción Democrática party are openly critical of Andrés Pérez's austerity measures and his reliance on guidelines proposed by the IMF.[28] In the face of such opposition, Andrés Pérez attempted to distance himself from the IMF and his dependence on their loan disbursements. After the outbreak of violence, the Venezuelan president harshly critcized the IMF for its disregard of the social ramifications of economic austerity and became a kind of international spokesman for those countries under agreements with the IMF who have suffered because of stringent reform guidelines.

Because of Venezuela's dismal economic climate and its reliance on IMF loan disbursements and accompanying reform guidelines, Carlos Andrés Pérez has become a leader with a split personality. To the IMF, the foreign creditors, and the international investment community, the Venezuelan president must project the image of a willing participant in economic and financial restructuring. To his domestic constituents, though, he must be careful not to appear as a silent captive of external institutions bent on reforming Venezuela from afar. The result is that Andrés Pérez is torn between his foreign allies, who are essential if he is to revitalize the Venezuela economy, and his domestic allies, who control his popularity and his legitimacy. Since taking office Andrés Pérez has opted for building closer ties with the IMF at the expense of domestic political criticism. Except for an occasional swipe at the IMF and transparent attempts to deflect attention away from the troubled economy, the Venezuelan president has made his stand with the IMF while promising his constituents that reform will bring a more promising future.

Andrés Pérez fortunately does benefit somewhat from the fact that he led Venezuela during the boom years and now occupies a position as the unofficial dean of the Latin American presidents. Past history and regional status notwithstanding, Carlos Andrés Pérez is no different from his fellow democratic presidents who also suffer from split personalities. Leaders like Andrés Pérez eventually are forced to make a choice between foreign assistance and expertise and domestic criticism. But by choosing to accept the IMF guidelines, Andrés Pérez not only acknowledged his dependence on external support but his responsibility to bring about an effective reform program despite the prospect of continued domestic strife.

Because the IMF has become a ready target of protest in the less-developed world, there is a natural inclination to blame the economic intervention of this multilateral lending institution. But Andrés Pérez's making the IMF the source of his country's economic and social malaise only prolongs the inevitable crisis that will come from ignoring the results of trade imbalances, growing indebtedness, failed public policies, and overactive government. Latin American leaders like Carlos Andrés Pérez will of necessity continue to run their fledgling democracies with a split personality, turning to the IMF for aid and advice while always looking over their shoulders for the expected opposition that accompanies solutions that arrive from abroad.

FINAL OBSERVATIONS

After examining the ways in which these Latin American leaders have responded to foreign intervention, a few concluding observations can be forwarded. One of the most obvious but critically important conclusions is that despite the end of the Big Stick and Alliance for Progress eras, intervention, whether military, diplomatic, or financial, continues to be one of the most fundamental principles of Latin American politics and development. Latin America remains an area that is vulnerable to the security concerns of the United States and dependent on the assistance and advice of the industrialized powers. The United States still views the region as strategically important and worthy of our attention, if not direct involvement. Furthermore, the economic limitations of the area make it susceptible to recessions and shortfalls that require outside aid, capital, technology, and expertise.

Although the paternalism and arrogance that characterized the region in the view of foreign powers has diminished markedly over the years, there is still the evidence of raw power, financial strangulation, and an insensitivity to the customs, emotions, and interests of the Latin American nations. If one thinks in terms of "progress" in the fight to free Latin America from intervention, the evaluation would have to stress only marginal victories amidst a lingering willingness on the part of the external sector to manage the destiny of this region.

It is within this rather pessimistic framework of intervention that the Latin American leaders have been called upon to represent their nations and deal with the power and the control of external forces. As we have seen, Latin American leaders have developed a number of strategies to respond to intervention, some with a degree of success, others with absolute failure. Those strategies that seem to have worked best involved fighting foreign intervention either by inviting support from another intervening power or by working with the interventionists in ways that limited or delayed their ability to influence internal conditions. Latin American leaders who have employed these strategies have been effective at preserving their regimes and their positions while at the same time frustrating the objectives of the interventionist power. Cristiani of El Salvador, Gaviria of Colombia, and Pérez of Venezuela have each become skilled practitioners of cooperating up to a point with their foreign backers. But those leaders who have treated intervention or the threat of intervention as manageable and a source of enhancing their popularity and prestige have been rudely awakened to the reality of widespread internal opposition and a crumbling political base. Noriega of Panama and Ortega of Nicaragua provide the contemporary examples of Latin American leaders whose overconfident belief in their power and support was shaken and eventually destroyed.

For Latin America and Latin American leaders there is no such thing as defeating the forces of intervention, but there is the prospect of using the intervention as an opportunity to achieve some short-term goals. Intervention may indeed bring invading troops seeking to establish order or international economists seeking austerity, but it may also open the door to internal political reform and consolidation, much-needed governmental restructuring, or a shift in public resources and priorities. Leaders who recognize the opportunities inherent in the presence of foreign troops or institutions can enhance their own legitimacy and strengthen their chances for survival. Castro is perhaps the classic Latin American leader who used U.S. intervention to solidify his rule and deepen his relationship with the Cuban people.

One central lesson of leadership in Latin America is that pursuing the opportunities of intervention can be fraught with danger. Not only do the foreign powers eventually get their way but they also can promote conditions that place the Latin American leader who challenges intervention in jeopardy. Intervention presents a real external threat to the Latin American leader, yet it is the domestic backlash to how he handles the intervention that can control his political future. Latin American leaders faced with the various forms of outside intervention must remain ever vigilant to internal discord and political maneuvering. Fighting external intervention will inevitably have a domestic cost whether it be food shortages, forced conscription, an increasingly closed society, or economic restrictions that hit hard at the key social groups. Leaders who must deal with intervention cannot ignore the enemy within as they fight the enemy from without.

Foreign intervention in Latin America is not a critical ingredient of politics and development that will soon disappear. Keeping the United States, the industrialized powers, and multinational or multilateral institutions from meddling in Latin American affairs in fact will become less possible given the increasing interdependence of the world and the continued desire of major foreign powers to influence events in those regions where they have interests. What may happen, however, is that Latin American leaders will become more adept at handling the threats from abroad so that those threats have less of an impact on their sovereignty and the internal structure of their societies. As with all the leadership tasks before them, the Latin American presidents will be called upon to peform nearly impossible feats of political balance and compromise. In dealing with intervention, however, their skills can mean preserving a nation from external sources of pressure and influence that continue to be unwanted.

NOTES

1. For background analysis of intervention in Latin America see C. Neale Ronning, *Intervention in Latin America* (New York: Knopf, 1970). A critical perspective is provided by Jenny Pearce, *Under the Eagle: U.S. Intervention in Central America and the Caribbean* (Boston: South End Press, 1981).

2. The Latin American view against intervention is expresed cogently in former Guatemalan president Juan José Arevalo's controversial book, *The Shark and the Sardines* (New York, 1961). See also Carlos Rangel, *The Latin Americans and the Love-Hate Relationship with the United States* (New York: Harcourt, Brace, Jovanovich, 1977) and Willard F. Barber and C.

Neale Ronning, *Internal Security and Military Power: CounterInsurgency and Civic Action in Latin America* (Columbus: Ohio State Press, 1966).

3. See Lars Schoultz, *National Security and United States Policy Toward Latin America* (Princeton, NJ: Princeton University Press, 1987).

4. A good overview of Castro's response to U.S. pressure can be found in Jules Benjamin, *The United States and the Cuban Revolution* (Princeton, NJ: Princeton University Press, 1988). See also Philip Brenner, *Confrontation to Negotiation. U.S. Relations With Cuba* (Washington, DC: PACCA, Policy Alternatives for the Caribbean and Central America, 1988).

5. See Wayne Smith, *Castro's Cuba: Soviet Partner or Nonalignment?* (Washington, DC: Woodrow Wilson Center, 1989).

6. See Lee Hockstader, "An Economic Hurricane Is Bearing Down on Cuba," *Washington Post National Weekly Edition*, January 7-13, 1990, pp. 18-19.

7. This theme is expanded in Susan Kaufman Purcell, "Cuba's Cloudy Future," *Foreign Affairs* (Summer 1990): 113-130.

8. Hockstader, "An Economic Hurricane," p. 19.

9. Steve C. Ropp, "Panama's Defiant Noriega," *Current History* (December 1988): 417-420, 431.

10. See "Noriega Speaks Out," *World Press Review* (December 1989): 52.

11. Michael Massing, "New Trouble in Panama," *New York Review of Books* (May 17, 1990): 43-49.

12. At one point President Endara began a fast in order to call attention to the crying need for U.S. assistance. See Larry Rohter, "Panama's New Leader Fasts to Dramatize Need for Aid," *New York Times*, March 12, 1990, A-1.

13. Massing, "New Trouble in Panama," p. 48-49.

14. See Thomas Walker, *Reagan Versus the Sandinistas: The Undeclared War on Nicaragua* (Boulder, CO: Westview Press, 1987).

15. See Rose Spaulding, *The Political Economy of the Revolutionary Nicaragua* (Boston: Allen and Unwin, 1987).

16. See Robert A. Pastor, *Condemned to Repetition: The United States and Nicaragua* (Princeton, NJ: Princeton University Press, 1987), p. 251.

17. For an overview of the Nicaraguan electoral process, the documents of the observer mission of former President Jimmy Carter are valuable. The Council of Freely Elected Heads of Government, *Observing Nicaragua's Elections, 1989-1990*, The Carter Center of Emory University, Special Report no. 1 (Atlanta, GA: The Carter Center, 1990), pp. 13-15.

18. Mark Uhlig, "Nicaraguan Rivals Focus on Contras in Election's Wake," *New York Times*, March 1, 1990, p. 1.

19. See "Excepts from the Inaugural Address of President Dona Violeta de Chamorro," in The Council of Freely Elected Heads of Government, *Observing Nicaragua's Elections, 1989-1990*, p. 117.

20. See José Z. García, "Recent Elections in El Salvador," in John A. Booth and Mitchell A. Seligson, eds., *Elections and Democracy in Central America* (Chapel Hill: University of North Carolina Press, 1989), pp. 83–84.

21. Charles Lane, "Death's Democracy," *Atlantic* (January 1989): 18–24.

22. Terry Karl, "Exporting Democracy: The Unanticipated Effects of U.S. Electoral Policy in El Salvador," in Nora Hamilton, ed., *Crisis in Central America: Regional Dynamics and U.S. Policy in the 1980's* (Boulder, CO: Westview Press, 1987), pp. 173–192.

23. *New York Times*, January 8, 1990, p. B-8.

24. James Brooke, "Strong Drug Foe Wins in Colombia by a Wide Margin," *New York Times*, May 28, 1990, p. 1, and James Brooke, "Colombia on the Spot," *New York Times*, May 29, 1990, p. A-10.

25. See Elaine Shannon's chapter, "Why Are We Bleeding Alone?" in *Desperados; Latin Drug Lords, U.S. Lawmen and the War America Can't Win* (New York: Viking, 1990), pp. 401–417.

26. Joseph A. Mann, "Venezuela Caught in the IMF Crunch," *Times of the Americas*, January 24, 1990, p. 15.

27. Judith Ewell, "Debt and Politics in Venezuela," *Current History* (March 1989): 121–124.

28. Ibid.

9

EVALUATING
LATIN AMERICAN LEADERS:
ACHIEVING SUCCESS,
AVOIDING FAILURE

> *The leaders of the past generation had a different concept of the subjects appropriate for public discussion. Debates were limited to political, ideological, and historic themes; economic and social problems were never discussed.*
>
> —Rodrigo Borja,
> president of Ecuador

There is a natural temptation when writing on a subject such as leaders and leadership to move the discussion toward a vision of the ideal and discuss strategies for achieving success or avoiding failure. But when the subject of leaders and leadership is based in the Latin American setting, where heads of state have over the years gained an unfortunate reputation for venality, incompetence, cruelty, and corruption, developing a model of the "good" leader has posed a number of problems. The modern political leaders of Latin America have had to contend with a resilient image that often portrays them as incapable of performing their job, unable to marshal popular support, and unwilling to take the necessary risks to attain critical objectives.

The previous chapters, however, have shown that the individuals who run the governments in the region do not easily fit the stereotypes and images that have traditionally been linked with Latin American leadership. In fact the leaders of contemporary Latin America are indeed part of a new generation of chief executives who must be viewed as departing significantly from their predecessors in a number of critical performance areas. Perhaps most importantly, the Latin American leaders of the 1990s have begun to recognize the value of mastering the art of power politics. They are more adept at bargaining with their adversaries, more flexible in their approaches to change, more demanding of their supporters, and more confident in their ability to control the process of restructuring and reform. Rather than sitting atop a political system and watching the interplay of the power contenders, the leaders of Latin America have entered the fray and asserted themselves as the first among equals. What those schooled in the leadership practices of the industrialized world might see as hands-on governing, in Latin America is a stunning departure from past practice that has transformed civilian leaders from mere administrative window dressing to the key players in national development.

The emergence of a more political and assertive Latin American leader of course does not automatically guarantee success. Although there has been a shift in temperment and a greater appreciation of public power, the leaders of this region remain without a complete sense of how best to define leadership in the 1990s. The issues of vision, reform, and stability remain important considerations for Latin America in this second decade of civilian democracy. The 1990s may very likely become a decade in which leaders are forced not only to attain major policy objectives but also to establish a brand of leadership that is accepted throughout the region.

If the Latin American leaders that control the reins of power today are indeed to serve as the example of what this region wants from its presidents in terms of politics and performance, then it seems essential to discuss the components of successful political leadership and the pitfalls that could lead to a perpetuation of the traditional models. This chapter presents a series of evaluative standards that can be employed to determine whether presidents or heads of state are following a road that will further strengthen their hold on leadership or whether they will be linked with the images and stereotypes of a past age.

RECOGNIZING THE DANGERS OF REFORM

Latin American leaders will face the closest scrutiny and create the highest expectations in the area of structural reforms. This region is clearly immersed in a struggle to redefine the way in which it conducts the business of government. The 1980s was the decade of political transition; the 1990s will likely be the decade of economic and social changes of immense proportions. Latin American leaders may on occasion give the appearance that they are the architects of these trends, but in reality they are the captives of a restructuring process that has a life of its own and has yet to run its course. The bold reform programs offered by Collor of Brazil, Menem of Argentina, Salinas of Mexico, and Pérez of Venezuela, to name some of the most prominent, were initiated by leaders who recognized that a failure to act on the economic front was not only politically harmful but a rejection of a much larger international movement that was changing the way in which governments operated and responded to problems.

Latin America leaders do not want to be perceived as out-of-step with the current models of public administration and national development. The regularity with which leaders promote privatization, joint ventures, investment incentives, and fiscal responsibility is a sign of how pervasive are the new doctrines of market economics and governmental efficiency that have taken hold in the region. There is, however, a potentially dangerous trap inherent in climbing aboard the capitalist bandwagon. Latin American leaders must realize that the push for change is currently running far ahead of government's capacity to cope with the institutional and cultural ramifications of that change. Latin American societies have had little preparation for either the democratic explosion or the introduction of market economics. It is one thing to bring Latin America into the new world of democratic capitalism, but it is quite another task to be able to contain the effects of democratic capitalism on social, political, economic, intellectual, and cultural systems that may still be mired in a different era.[1]

Leaders in this region thus must be ever careful to bridge the gap between the enormous changes they recognize are essential in this fast-changing new world order and the entrenched and powerful remnants of national life that could easily stymie the changes and cripple their ability to follow the movement forward. Latin American leaders need to be receptive to reform while also watchful for signs that the old ways of authoritarianism, statism, and social rigidity and the numerous cultural obstacles to effective modernization do not become so pronounced as to compromise the trends that have been set in motion. Latin America is a part of the world where traditions die hard, and the security of adhering to established norms is attractive to those buffeted by constant unrest and well-meaning, but disruptive, reforms.

CREATING CONFIDENCE AND NORMALITY

Because the reform process in Latin America is filled with both promise for the future and danger from the past, leaders must know how to respond to the inevitable tensions that will arise. The most effective tool for dealing with these tensions will be the ability to build confidence among populations that may easily be disoriented by the changes they see speed before them. The primary leadership challenge of the 1990s in Latin America may simply be the ability to ensure that the people of this region do not lose faith in the ability of government to solve problems and bring forth change. After over ten years of debt-induced underdevelopment and now systemic changes of revolutionary proportions it is not surprising that the political culture of many Latin American nations are in a state of flux, if not chaos. What was common practice a few years ago is now rejected as unworkable; values and beliefs that seemed to be rock solid are now being questioned with great regularity, and the traditional symbols of power and order that lent stability to an otherwise unstable environment are being replaced. The result is that Latin America suffers as much from economic and political restructuring as from the shock of adjusting to the seemingly unending onslaught of change.

Much has been written about the fragility of the democratic tradition in Latin America and the temptation to return to its authoritarian roots during times of instability and uncertainty. The performance of civilian presidents will certainly be the true test of whether democracy survives, but the skills that the leaders reveal in the areas of communicating with disgruntled populations may also contribute significantly to warding off threats to elections, constitutionalism, and respect for human rights. During periods of transition and transformation people look for normalcy and leaders who exude confidence in the ultimate success of change. Those leaders who can create climates of normalcy and convince the citizenry to make sacrifices and support systematic change will go a long way toward ensuring that democracy does not once again become a transitory stage in Latin American development.[2] Already President Collor of Brazil has seen his popularity rate plummet after the economic restructuring policies proposed by him failed to stimulate growth or assuage social unrest. As the economies of many Latin American democracies like Brazil realize few short-term benefits from structural reforms, intense opposition will undoubtedly follow, creating climates of discord rather than normalcy.

Of course not every Latin American president has the special gift of calming the unease of populations pushed to the brink of personal sacrifice. Nevertheless, because the process of change continues in the region, incumbent presidents and challengers to incumbents would do well to remember that reforming and restructuring a nation is not only a process of setting new priorities and building new institutions but also of handling the distress within a society that accompanies the change. The Latin American leaders in the coming years may be wise to reflect on the value of greater personal contact with the people, the importance of showing that sacrifices are being shared equally across the board, and the necessity of explaining clearly and often the reasons that specific departures from the old ways are being implemented. These are admittedly small suggestions that may have only a peripheral impact on system and leadership stability, but they are suggestions that concentrate on an area that is often neglected in the process of change—the need of the people to be reassured that the path on which their government is taking them is indeed worthy of their support and their sacrifice. Governments and leaders that have failed to take into consideration the confidence level of the people have often seen their noble experiments abandoned in favor of something or someone who offered them normality and reassurance.

MAKING GOVERNMENT WORK

Guarding against the enemies of structural reform and ensuring that change will not destroy the fragile social order will only be achieved in the Latin America of the 1990s if the political leaders of the region become expert public administrators. Efficient management of government operations has never been a characteristic of Latin American leadership. Leaders have been charismatic proponents of various ideologies, ruthless practitioners of authoritarianism, and philsopher kings with little authority, but rarely have leaders been associated with the skills of administering large organizations and directing the performance of government employees. Paradoxically, Latin American leaders have often thought of themselves as personalist heads of government who paid attention to even the smallest detail of local politics. At the same time, those same leaders showed little interest in defining their jobs in terms of fiscal management, personnel evaluation, and organizational efficiency. Leaders paid particular attention to whether a peasant's request for a land title was honored or a relative received an acceptable governmental sinecure, but they regularly ignored the "big picture" of how government was working and how the employees of government were performing their assigned tasks.[3]

In the Latin America of the 1990s political leaders will face increased pressure to cope with the problems that emanate from the vast and cumbersome state machine. Besides dealing with the calls for balanced budgets and fiscal restraint from both the business sector and the international banking community, leaders will have to manage the transition in employment that will occur as Latin America moves from a statist to a market economy. Presidents will have to prove that they are capable of constructing new governing frameworks that match the new economic models being put into place throughout the region. As government begins to pare down both in terms of responsibility and personnel, the leaders of Latin America will be required to make tough decisions that reduce operating budgets, cut long-standing subsidy programs, reorder national priorities, and place the security of government employees in the hands of private entrepreneurs who are committed to the bottom line.

The move by Latin American political leaders to downsize government and make more efficient use of scarce human and financial resources holds the potential for widescale social and political opposition. Although leaders are familiar with the social protest that has often accompanied economic restructuring, they are only now beginning to see the force of opposition that can be generated from disgruntled government employees worried over their jobs. Government employees, in particular, are one of the largest groups in many Latin American nations. Heretofore they have not been viewed as power contenders because they had no need to exert influence on their employer. As the state system in Latin America expanded, state employees gained new jobs, reasonably good pay, and a degree of job security not found in other economic sectors. But as Latin America embraces the market economy and dismantles state enterprises, political leaders will have to deal with an angry power contender that sees its position, influence, and security gradually slipping away. The firestorm of public-worker protest faced by Argentina's Carlos Menem for his privatization of the phone company may be a portent of future conflicts from an increasingly vocal sector of Latin American society.[4]

Making Latin American government work more efficiently by redefining its role in society and trimming its labor force is a task that no leader relishes. Presidents make few friends by becoming tough administrators. Latin American leaders can certainly move with caution as they begin the task of changing the face of governmental operations, but the prospect of opposition and disorder should not dissuade them from the essential requirement of making government work in a new economic environment.

CREATING A FAVORABLE IMAGE

A critical ingredient in the reform process for Latin America is the ability of leaders to meet the challenges of the new international economic age. The leaders of this region know all too well that one of their chief responsibilities as heads of state is to present their countries in a favorable light to the world. Leadership in the contemporary period must include the skills to convince the industrialized powers that Latin America is worthy of attention and investment. Leaders in this region must in effect become better salespeople for their countries because the 1990s is certain to become a highly competitive world arena where success is measured by the ability to attract capital and technology, formulate imaginative trading relationships, and build vibrant economies with talented workers and supportive state agencies.

Because Latin America must now compete in a fast-changing global economy, it cannot afford leaders who are unwilling to make the internal political and governmental adjustments that will be necesssary to convince corporate executives and the industrialized powers that this region has promise as a center for manufacturing, finance, and the service sector. Already there are disturbing signs that the industrialized nations are looking less favorably on Latin America as a growth area and instead continuing their association with the Pacific Rim and a unified Europe.[5] Part of this unwillingness to build an expanded base of operations in Latin America is the perception in the industrialized world that the leaders in this region are not doing enough to make their countries attractive centers of industrialization. Some leaders in Latin America are viewed as dragging their feet on issues such as liberalizing trade barriers and profit ratios, reducing bureaucratic restraints, privatizing state enterprises, and creating dynamic internal economies that serve as the basis for dynamic external economies. In some countries, leaders intimidated by entrenched groups unwilling to embrace reform have simply created a facade of change that hides institutions and processes steeped in tradition.[6]

It is of course unfair to paint the leaders of Latin America with one brush as slow to act on the potential of a dynamic global economy, but because image is very important in the formulation of corporate and governmental decisionmaking, the leaders of this region must do all in their power to prove that they head countries willing to take the steps required in order to reap the benefits of a changing world order. What many corporate executives, bankers, and policymakers in the industrialized world see in Latin America are long drawn-out battles over privatization, social unrest over austerity measures, and recalcitrant interest groups fighting tax-reform initiatives or monetary reform. External sectors would prefer to see political leaders push for investment incentives for foreign businesses, balance public-sector budgets, rein in hyperinflation, and transform the state into an efficient engine of growth. The fact that these changes are slow in coming or are compromised to assuage the concerns of powerful interests only further increases the doubts the industrialized world has concerning the development potential of Latin America.

Latin American leaders' ability and willingness to hone their skills at image-making and sales techniques may prove to be two of the most critical factors in determining whether this region is included in the new global economy or whether it will position itself on the periphery of the dynamic changes occurring throughout the world. Latin America still suffers from the common perception that it is incapable of creating conditions conducive to steady growth. Although Latin American leaders cannot singlehandedly fashion the political and economic circumstances that will convince the industrialized world to turn its attention toward their region, they can certainly use their position and their newfound respect to act as symbols of a Latin America that has indeed been transformed into a region with a strong democratic foundation and a public–private-sector relationship that is both attractive and vibrant.

No chief executive in Latin America has captured the attention and respect of the international business community more than Mexico's Carlos Salinas Gotari. Salinas has become the symbol of the new Latin American leader—fighting corruption, encouraging investment, privatizing state enterprises, and bringing inflation down to respectable levels. The fact that Mexico is perceived as on the move is largely attributable to the image that Salinas has created about himself and his administration. Salinas is now recognized in Washington and throughout the financial capitals of the world as a competent administrator and a visionary statesman determined to take his country into the global economy.

With Latin American leaders like Carlos Salinas of Mexico capturing the attention of the industrialized world, the changes spreading throughout the region over the past few years are not being viewed as a temporary phase. Governments, multinational corporations, banks, and international agencies are looking to the leaders in the region for reassurance that Latin America will not slip back into the era of instability, state capitalism, and uncompromising nationalism. What the international community has seen in recent years are political leaders who are beginning to match Salinas in terms of respect and confidence. It is this growing environment of confidence and respect that may prove to be the critical ingredient in Latin America's development.

THE "GOOD" POLITICAL LEADER

The tasks ahead for Latin America's political leaders are indeed enormous. Managing the transition to democracy and capitalism in the midst of shaky economies and angry citizens will require that leaders quickly develop the strength to ward off what is certain to be a constant wave of criticism and conflict. It is tempting to state that judging the performance of Latin American leaders during this era of change will be reduced to standards such as whether these presidents finished their term in office or whether they were able to keep their societies from fragmenting. Such an approach, however, assumes that this new generation of Latin American leaders is incapable of meeting the challenges of the 1990s and beyond. What we have seen throughout this discussion is that the political leaders of Latin America are different from their predecessors in terms of their commitment to change, their willingness to take risks, and their competence as governmental administrators. In short the contemporary Latin American leader possesses the skills and the vision to rise above survival and stability and direct the process of social, economic, and political change that is sweeping the region.

But possessing the skills and the vision may not be enough. The Latin American leader of the 1990s and beyond could easily become a prisoner of the old regime and turn away from the structural reforms and the tough policy decisions that cause hardship and unrest. The Latin American leaders of the future may choose to follow the popular will and forsake further institutionalization of democracy, wider application of the market approach, and expanded reductions in the size and role of the state. Leading the Latin American republics in this modern era may prove too dangerous and contentious for many civilian presidents. Leaders may simply choose the path of caution, incremental "tinkering," and cosmetic attempts to appear bold and progressive. This approach will certainly create a sense of normalcy that most societies seek, and yet such an approach could easily limit the development options available to Latin America. The region may continue to be perceived as trapped in the past and incapable of the reforms necessary for a modern state. As Marcelo Selowsky, a Chilean economist at the World Bank states, "Unless our leaders have the will to enact serious, sustainable reforms, there is great danger that everything could be lost."[7]

Latin American leaders thus will have a number of critical choices to make in the coming years, choices that go to the core of political leadership. Those leaders who choose the path of least resistance and opt for the cautious approach may be rewarded with completed terms and social order. Those leaders who choose the path of comprehensive structural reform and risktaking may lead their countries in the twin directions of dynamic modernization and debilitating fragmentation. But the "good" leaders will be those not afraid to use their political, electoral, and administrative skills to dismantle the old and inefficient while building for the future. Latin American political leaders who are adept at balancing the traditions and practices of the past with the requirements of the future will not only survive but prosper. This is no guaranteed formula for leadership, because little is certain in the Latin American political arena, but it is a formula that may prove essential if the leaders of Latin America hope to take their countries into a world in which much has changed and in which more change is anticipated.

NOTES

1. See Howard J. Wiarda, "Political Culture and National Development," *Fletcher Forum of World Affairs*, 13, no. 2 (Summer 1989): 193–203.

2. See Enrique Baloyra, *Comparing New Democracies: Transition and Consolidation in Mediterranean Europe and the Southern Cone* (Boulder, CO: Westview Press, 1987).

3. Barry Ames elaborates on this theme when he describes a series of "survival strategies" employed by Latin American leaders. See Barry Ames, *Political Survival: Politicians and Public in Latin America* (Berkeley: University of California Press, 1987), pp. 211–137.

4. Despite the criticism from public-employee unions, Argentina completed the sale of the phone company in a November 8, 1990 sale to French, American, Spanish, and Argentine financial consortiums. See *Times of the Americas* November 14, 1990, p. 9.

5. The failure of The Uruguay Round of trade talks under the General Agreement of Tariffs and Trade (GATT) in fall 1990 proved to many that the Latin Americans would increasingly have to turn to the United States and a regional trading block because the Europeans were showing little interest in recognizing the trade position of the region. See Richard C. Schroeder, "Latin America and the GATT Cave-in," *Times of the Americas*, December 26, 1990, p. 25.

6. One of the major problems faced by Latin America as it attempts to attract foreign investment is its image of corruption and lack of

commitment to change. See Eugene Robinson, "In Latin America, An Honest Day's Work is Hardly Working," *Washington Post National Weekly Edition*, December 10-16, 1990, p. 23.

7. As quoted in Pamela Constable, "Latin America's New Pragmatism," *Boston Globe Magazine*, May 12, 1991, p. 37.

10

LEADERS AND THE FUTURE OF U.S.–LATIN AMERICAN RELATIONS

My advice [to the president of the United States] is that he listen more to those who have been elected by our people to direct the destiny of our countries. Some policies should be formulated jointly, so that different points of view, and different opinions, held by Latin Americans are taken into consideration before a decision is taken.

—Oscar Arias,
former president of Costa Rica

Just as the Latin Americans are assessing the impact that the new generation of leaders has had on their societies and where those leaders may take the region in the coming years, so too will U.S. policymakers attempt to determine the future direction of this critical hemispheric relationship. Despite the fact that security concerns defining the relationship for so many years have diminished, a group of issues that was positioned at the periphery of the policy debate has moved to center stage to challenge anew the ties between these reluctant friends. The economic competition from Europe and the Pacific Basin, the continued flow of illegal immigrants and drugs, the rescheduling of billions of dollars of debt, the prospects for investment opportunities and resource development, and the ever-present worries over democratic stability will test the strength and flexibility of the "special relationship" that both the United States and Latin America claim exists.

In the coming years both the United States and Latin America will be forced to define more precisely what they want from this

231

relationship. As interest in the region competes with events and crises in Eastern Europe, the Middle East, and the Pacific, there will be a temptation to define the relationship in traditional or status quo terms and return to an era of "benign neglect." U.S. policymakers could easily be swayed by the argument that democracy and the miracle of the marketplace have created a spirit of cooperation and an appreciation of consistent policy approaches that will lead to slow but certain resolution of Latin America's most pressing domestic problems. Confidence is building, so the argument goes, in the ability of visionary government leaders and a dynamic institutional framework to work with the United States to address the issue agenda of the 1990s.[1]

Throughout the Bush administration and the business and trade associations involved in Latin American trade there is an infectious spirit of optimism as the prospect of a common market stretching from Canada to Tierra del Fuego gains greater attention and support. Furthermore, the regular stories from Latin American capitals of privatization schemes and financial reform programs have created the impression that the region is finally on the right track after so many years of being captivated by the Marxist model and influenced by leaders who took pride in criticizing capitalism and North American purveyors of the market system.

Yet alongside the euphoria that fills the halls of the Commerce Department and the Council of the Americas, there is another set of emotions that could also rise to the surface in the region. Latin American leaders reeling from the destabilization caused by structural reforms, austerity, recessionary trends, and more aggressive political opposition may head governing regimes that are forced to endure a kind of administrative "gridlock" that not only compromises democracy and stalls the market economy but, more important, mixes with "benign neglect" to form a policy climate where there is scant evidence of constructive change and meager interest from the United States in helping to stimulate change. Latin American leaders thus become weak and discredited victims of a process of political and economic transformation that held out so much hope and was championed by the United States as the solution to the region's age-old battles with instability and dependence.[2]

Also under this scenario, Latin American leaders and Washington policymakers will become preoccupied with damage control and crisis management and find scant interest or opportunity to transform the "special relationship" to a higher level. Rather than force the United States to rewrite the rules, the relationship will be anchored in the assumption that Latin America is again the victim of an unfinished revolution and is returning to the status quo ante. Latin American leaders will see what little leverage they might have enjoyed disappear as they become advocates for old solutions rather than partners in a new order.

Because Latin American leaders are certain to be either the beneficiaries of the new economic and political order that President Bush proudly proclaims or the targets of popular unrest and waning U.S. interest, it is essential that they establish the ground rules for what is likely to be a completely redefined "special relationship." Civilian presidents must prepare themselves and their countries for the opportunities and the dangers that the new economic and political order may bring while also developing policy positions that advance their countries' interests. The 1990s will require new leadership strategies to deal with both the internal challenges and the inevitable shifts in the way the United States views the region. If there is anything that can be stated with a degree of certainty about the coming years in Latin America, it is that political leaders will face new uncertainties as the old system is replaced and long-standing relationships are reevaluated.

The uncertainty of the leadership climate in Latin America offers the civilian presidents an opportunity to rewrite the ground rules of hemispheric relations or at the very least to require the United States to recognize the need for a more expanded and equitable decisionmaking role for regional leaders. Latin American leaders can build upon their democratic base and market economies to convince the United States that they are now within the mainstream and can therefore demand greater respect, trust, and fairer treatment. The possibility of Latin American leaders becoming true partners with the United States in formulating inter-American policy and resolving contentious disputes is no longer an unattainable dream. Already Latin American leaders such as Salinas of Mexico, Pérez of Venezuela, and Collor of Brazil are using their newly acquired status as aggressive reformers to demand that the United States cooperate with them as equals on issues such as trade, drug policy, and debt reduction.[3] Furthermore, Latin American leaders can use this changed political and economic climate to fashion more independent approaches to dealing with the United States. This may be the right time for Latin American leaders to play the "European card" and begin showing U.S. policymakers that greater competition, diversification, and national pride will be the catchwords of the 1990s. For years Latin American leaders have bemoaned the lack of an alternative source of trade, aid, and investment. But with the advent of the European Common Market and the sweeping changes that will arrive in 1992, Latin American leaders are hoping that they can capitalize on the commercial opportunities in Europe to lessen their reliance on U.S. aid, trade, and investment. Caribbean leaders, for example, are already working to ensure that the so-called Lome Convention IV, which provides access for Caribbean-based products to the European market, will be continued beyond 1992.[4] Unfortunately, the excitement over Latin American ties to Europe has waned somewhat. Heavy start-up costs in Europe plus interest by member countries in strengthening the new trading relationship before making external commitments has led to a reevaluation of the impact that the 1992 trade pact will have on Latin America. Leaders in Latin America are now coming to the realization that the "European card" is not as powerful a strategy as once thought and that the key to future development may still lie with trade and investment ties to the United States.

Although it is easy to shift the onus of change onto the United States and state that the new ground rules will require a substantial shift in perception and values on the part of those charged with developing U.S. policy in the hemisphere, the attainment of a truly new relationship must be based on mutual agreement and shared responsibility. If Latin American leaders want the United States to look on them and the countries they represent in a different light, then they too must recognize the concerns uppermost in the minds of North American policymakers. Fortunately, because the formation of this new relationship comes at a time when the Latin American leaders and their Washington counterparts are talking the same language, the prospect for establishing new ground rules is not impossible or unworkable.

At the top of the list of rules that should guide the future of relations between the United States and Latin America is the acceptance of the principle that hemispheric security is best achieved through hemispheric development. This, of course, is not a new idea, but in the post-Marxist world in which the Communist threat has been greatly reduced it is now easier for the United States to embrace a concept that the Latin Americans have been promoting since the days of Castro's march into Havana. Latin American leaders have an opportunity to use the changing nature of geopolitics in the region to convince the United States to see regional security in a new light. They can use the heightened status they enjoy to frame the policy debates over how the United States should expend its limited resources in the region.

An issue such as the drug war can be defined by the Latin American leaders as one of economic transformation rather than military neutralization. U.S. aid can be directed toward introducing and subsidizing new crops for coca growers rather than place prime emphasis on armed struggle and interdiction. Furthermore, leaders in those countries experiencing revolutionary activity can link their acceptance of new economic models and efficient governance to a commitment by the United States to fight the left with investment and aid rather than weapons. The end result of a campaign by the Latin American leaders to define hemispheric security as tied to development could bring about a dramatic shift in attitude and involvement. The Latin American leaders cannot hope to change the United States into an isolationist neighbor, but they can work to convince the United States that the time is right for a more balanced approach to security, one that relies on cooperating with a new kind of leader and employing the tools of the private sector to bring about a more stable political climate.

Latin American leaders can also work to change the way economic opportunity is defined in inter-American relations. Too often negotiations between individual Latin American countries and the United States were hampered by U.S. trade representatives or Commerce Department officials insensitive to the importance their Latin American counterparts placed on natural resources or to their desire to penetrate our markets. Much of this insensitivity could be traced to the view in Washington that Latin American economies are not like ours and that Latin American trade was more of a threat than an opportunity. Now that Latin American leaders are talking the same language as the trade representatives and Commerce Department officials, there is a new chance to drive home the importance of access to our markets. Latin American leaders, as heads of emerging private economies, can more easily demand that they not be treated as second-class statists but rather as partners in democratic capitalism with the same objectives and the same economic rights as the United States. Again, Latin American leaders cannot expect the United States to negotiate with them as equals for the simple reason that there remains an enormous gap between our economies. But Latin American leaders can use their newfound support for the market system to remind the United States that they expect to be treated as partners rather than as adversaries. One sign of this confidence is the formation of new or revitalized trading blocs in Central America, the Caribbean, and the Southern Cone. Latin American leaders are anxious to play by the new rules of the international marketplace and to show the United States that they intend to become active partners as the hemisphere moves toward a global economy.

Finally, Latin American leaders can change the ground rules of inter-American relations by convincing the United States that there is no need to employ intervention and intimidation as a prescription for domestic order. Perhaps the most significant development in terms of contemporary Latin American leadership is the ability of civilian presidents to deal with internal unrest in a manner that does not create the specter of authoritarianism or eradicate the hard-won rights of the citizenry. Latin American leaders can use the success they have achieved in running their countries during periods of severe economic distress to show the United States that democratic governance is not in jeopardy and that a corps of competent political leaders is quite capable of handling crises without the guidance or involvement of the United States. U.S. policymakers have gotten into the habit of not trusting the ability of Latin American political leaders to handle the regular incidents of internal disarray and have too frequently interjected their views and their pressure to "guide" the process of change or "remind" political combatants of official U.S. displeasure. Latin American leaders now have a wonderful opportunity to establish the understanding that they are in control and can survive without the constant doting of Washington policymakers.

Changing the ground rules for inter-American relations is like many aspects of Latin American life—the process of change is made up of fits and starts and the end result may be less than was expected. The suggestions for changing the way the United States deals with Latin America are by no means radical. They are instead suggestions for how Latin American leaders, who will be at the vanguard of changed inter-American relations, can use their new status and their past successes to show the United States that it must match its praise for the new economic and political developments in the region with a willingness to accept a reformulation of the ways in which it defines issues, negotiates agreements, and participates in change. If in the coming years the Latin American leaders can get the United States to move away from its penchant for militarizing security issues, demanding more for less in its negotiations, and meddling in the internal affairs of its neighbors, then they will have made a lasting contribution to transforming the "special relationship" into a "hemispheric partnership."

NOTES

1. Howard Wiarda provides a thoughtful analysis of the new Latin America and the implications for U.S. policy in *The Democratic Revolution in Latin America, History, Politics and U.S. Policy* (New York: Holmes and Meier, 1990), pp. 263–281.

2. See Richard C. Schroeder, "Privatization Trend Spreads in Latin America," *Times of the Americas*, November 1, 1989, p. 14.

3. See, for example, the bold and candid statements of the presidents of Argentina, Bolivia, Mexico, and Paraguay to the Council of the Americas. *Council of the Americas Washington Report* (October/November 1989): 10–11.

4. Ann LaVigne, "Europe/1992 Also Coming Into Play," *Times of the Americas*, December 26, 1990, p. 28.

ABOUT THE BOOK
AND AUTHOR

Because the governing framework in many Latin American countries is weak or unstable, the United States has often resorted to formulating and implementing policy based on its ability to deal with a wide array of national leaders, from military dictators to civilian politicians to Marxist revolutionaries. Leaders and leadership style are therefore important factors in U.S. perception of the region and in the development of policies that affect Latin American countries.

In this book Michael Kryzanek examines the ways in which the critical interaction between individual leaders and the U.S. policy community affects the substance and direction of hemispheric relations. Throughout, the author uses case studies to illustrate how individual heads of state respond to the issues of drugs, debt, trade, and regional security. Such leaders as Salinas of Mexico, Gaviria of Colombia, Chamorro of Nicaragua, Endara of Panama, Cristiani of El Salvador, and Menem of Argentina are examined at close range to analyze their mode of operation and to assess their ability to attain national objectives in a region in which U.S. influence is substantial.

Michael J. Kryzanek is professor of political science at Bridgewater State College.

INDEX